HEROES OF MODERN ADVENTURE

A CHARACTERISTIC INCIDENT OF THE COURT TREATT
EXPEDITION FROM THE CAPE TO CAIRO

Fr.

HEROES OF
MODERN ADVENTURE

BY
THOMAS C. BRIDGES
AND
HUBERT HESSELL TILTMAN

ILLUSTRATED

Essay Index Reprint Series

 BOOKS FOR LIBRARIES PRESS
FREEPORT, NEW YORK

First Published 1927
Reprinted 1971

INTERNATIONAL STANDARD BOOK NUMBER:
0-8369-2216-6

LIBRARY OF CONGRESS CATALOG CARD NUMBER:
76-152160

PRINTED IN THE UNITED STATES OF AMERICA

AUTHORS' NOTE

EVERY boy is an adventurer at heart, and it is not surprising, therefore, that the present generation of explorers and travellers have performed feats of courage and endurance at the ends of the earth as fine as any in the records of the hardy pioneers of former generations. These modern explorers of our own and other lands have, indeed, accomplished journeys which will go down in history among the great stories of exploration. They have penetrated into the great white South to the Pole itself; sailed ships into seas where no ship had ever been before; flown across the world; photographed life in the wild at the risk of their lives; marched thousands of miles across barren lands and braved innumerable dangers and hardships, not for the sake of money but for the unselfish ideal of adding to our knowledge of the world in which we live. In this book we have gathered together the stories of nineteen of the greatest explorers of our day and related the simple narratives of their exploits, which in some cases they are too modest to tell themselves. Every chapter is a record of heroism and endurance as fine as anything in the story of mankind.

H. HESSELL TILTMAN
T. C. BRIDGES

CONTENTS

ILLUSTRATIONS

HEROES OF MODERN ADVENTURE

CHAPTER I

ON the night of June 16, 1903, in torrential rain, a little herring boat of forty-seven tons cast off from the quay of Christiania. There were seven men on board and a little crowd of friends stood on the quay in the pouring rain to wave their good-bye.

It might have been a fishing boat putting out on an every-day trip to the Dogger Bank for all the fuss that was shown when this tiny vessel, called the *Gjoa,* set sail. No excitement. No firing of guns or rockets to wake the echoes of the harbour as the craft slipped out and was swallowed up in the darkness.

Three years later—on August 31, 1906—that same small vessel anchored off Nome, Alaska, and received a welcome in strange contrast to that quiet departure from Christiania. At Nome an electric searchlight from the shore lit up the *Gjoa.* A steam launch filled with American officials greeted the herring boat with whistling, shouting, and cheering. As the gallant little crew stepped on shore, from the launch a roar of welcome issued from a thousand throats, and the whole population of the town, standing bareheaded, facing the sea, sang the Norwegian National Anthem.

Between those two dates the *Gjoa* and her gallant crew had accomplished a voyage which will rank forever among the most glorious annals of the sea.

Facing unknown risks, enduring hardships greater even than those that faced Columbus, that little herring boat had written her name on the scroll of fame by being the first craft ever to navigate the Northwest Passage. For three years, far up within the Arctic Circle, those men with their little herring boat had grappled with ice, storms, and a dozen other perils every explorer with any experience of that region of eternal ice knows too well. The *Gjoa* had survived. She not only had survived, she had won through —succeeded where hardy explorers like Franklin had met only disaster. And that hard-won success may be said to have been due to one man more than any other—the commander of that tiny expedition that faced the massed forces of Nature in Nature's own battle ground. His name, almost unknown in the days when the *Gjoa* set out, is Roald Amundsen.

After his return from that voyage of discovery Roald Amundsen wrote many new and glorious chapters for the story of exploration.   He was the first man to reach the South Pole.   He flew across the North Pole by airship. His name has a place with the names of Nansen, Scott, Shackleton, and Stefansson as those of the greatest explorers of the twentieth century.

But nothing that Amundsen accomplished was finer than that first voyage that proved, for the first time, that it was possible to find a way in and out among the ice-blocked necks of water that lie north of Greenland, far above Hudson Bay—on the edge of the Pole itself.

How perilous that voyage must have seemed to Amundsen and his companions when they sailed from Norway with the perils still ahead. On board was a little thirteen-horse power motor to carry the *Gjoa* forward when there was no wind to fill the sails, and food and equipment sufficient to last for five years.

Every inch of space was filled with packing cases and

supplies. Nothing was left to chance. Roald Amundsen had talked with Nansen before organising the expedition and well knew the importance of preparing for every emergency. It was typical of the thoroughness with which he planned his great adventure that in the summer of 1901 he had taken the *Gjoa* up to the Polar Sea and thus learned from actual experience how to handle her. And the food for both men and dogs was hermetically sealed and had been tested by experts.

It was just as well that these precautions had been taken, for even Amundsen himself did not know whether the voyage, if successful, would take two or four years to complete, and during all that time the seven in their tiny craft would be out of any touch with civilisation and would have to rely entirely upon the supplies they carried with them.

The first stage of the voyage which carried the *Gjoa* to Greenland was uneventful. Heavily laden as she was, the vessel did not show much speed, and it was July 9, 1903, when Amundsen and his companions sighted ice for the first time. It was pack ice in dense masses, and in its wake came the companion of ice—fog. These same two things—ice and fog—were to keep the *Gjoa* company during the greater part of that long-drawn-out voyage.

A month later, the expedition reached Dalrymple Rock, a wild Eskimo outpost in Northern Greenland, where a Scottish whaling vessel had deposited stores for the *Gjoa*. One hundred and five cases of stores were taken aboard as deck cargo, together with six barrels of petroleum.

The *Gjoa* was now more heavily laden than her builders had ever intended. Amundsen's stock of petrol for the motor was 4245 gallons alone, and the weight of stores brought the deck down to the waterline. Cases were piled almost everywhere and dogs were tied up around the decks.

At 2.30 on the morning of August 17 the *Gjoa's* anchor was lifted and the vessel turned her head slowly toward the northwest. Perils of every sort lay ahead. They probably did. But the sun shone and Amundsen and his companions were in high spirits. They had made their last call and seen the last glimpse of civilisation they were likely to meet for many a long month. Overladed, cramped for space, crazily small for the weather ahead, the attempt to find the Northwest Passage had begun.

A fortnight's sailing followed. The usual Arctic weather conditions—fog, storm, and sleet alternating—prevented the days from being uneventful. Once the *Gjoa* grounded on a low island, but floated off without damage.

The expedition was now close to the Magnetic North Pole, and as Amundsen's plan was to winter at a suitable spot, if such could be found, about ninety miles to the west, those on board were congratulating themselves that, despite many dangers, they looked like reaching their first winter quarters on the edge of the world without serious mishap.

Hardly had the pleasant prospect been conjured up by their good progress when an incident occurred which very nearly brought disaster to the whole party.

On the night of August 30, 1903, Amundsen had retired to his bunk when he was aroused by a terrific shout from the deck above. Rushing up, he found the black night lit by roaring flames which rose through the engine-room skylight. A fire had broken out in the engine room, within a few inches of tanks holding over two thousand gallons of petroleum. And this on a tiny vessel alone in the Arctic wastes and with the long northern winter speedily closing in on them.

Once those petroleum tanks got heated, the *Gjoa* with

THE " GJOA " 6

In this herring-boat Roald Amundsen and his little crew of big-hearted men
discovered the North-west Passage.

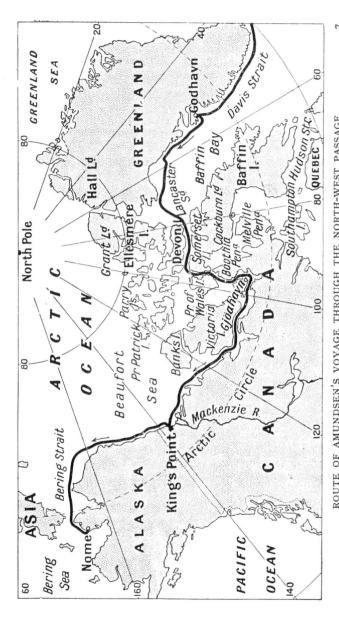

ROUTE OF AMUNDSEN'S VOYAGE THROUGH THE NORTH-WEST PASSAGE

every one aboard would be blown to smithereens. Wiik, a member of the expedition on duty as engineer, had pluckily stuck to his post and now others rushed to his assistance. Two fire-extinguishing appliances were on board and these were swiftly brought into use. For what must have seemed like an eternity to that desperate lonely handful of men the flames continued to rush skyward. Then the water got the upper hand and only smoke remained.

It was afterward discovered that the blaze had originated in some cleaning rags left lying soaked with oil that had leaked from one of the tanks. When the matter had been reported the previous day to Amundsen, he had ordered the leaky tank to be emptied. His command was promptly obeyed, and to this fact the expedition owed its safety, for had the tank nearest to those rags still been filled with oil when the fire broke out, nothing could have saved the ship from utter destruction.

Hardly had the little band recovered from this unpleasant thrill when they found themselves in extreme peril for the second time in one week.

The *Gjoa* grounded on a submerged reef not marked on the faulty maps of that almost unknown region, drifted off, and finally grounded fast for a second time and could not be moved.

Loaded as she was, the *Gjoa* drew over ten feet of water, and, after soundings had been taken, it was found that on all sides she was surrounded by shallow channels fringed with rocks. The prospect was serious, but with characteristic energy Amundsen set to work to get his ship afloat again.

The first thing to do was to lighten the vessel. Twenty-five precious cases of supplies, each weighing four hundred-weight, were thrown overboard. The rest of the deck cargo was then pushed to one side to get as big a list as possible on the vessel. That accomplished, there was nothing to do but wait until high tide and hope that the depth of water would float her off.

Alas for hopes. Late that night high tide had come and the *Gjoa* had not moved a single inch. She was still stuck fast. To add to their troubles, the wind, which had been calm, freshened, and at daybreak the following morning a full gale was blowing.

What followed may best be described in the very words of Amundsen's own diaries, published in his book "The North-West Passage."

I took counsel with my comrades, as I always did in critical situations, and we decided as a last resource to try and get her off with the sails. The spray was dashing over the ship, and the wind came in gusts, howling through the rigging, but we struggled and toiled and got the sails set.

Then we commenced a method of sailing not one of us is likely to forget should he attain the age of Methuselah. The mighty press of sail and the high choppy sea combined had the effect of lifting the vessel up and pitching her forward again among the rocks, so that every moment we expected to see her planks scattered in the sea. The false keel was splintered and floated up. All we could do was to watch the course of events and calmly await the issue.

Still the end of that terrible reef was not reached, although the water got shallower, and the *Gjoa* pitched so violently in the gale that her crew had hard work to prevent themselves from being flung overboard. Amundsen found himself faced with the twin alternatives of abandoning the *Gjoa* and taking to the boats, or to risk the vessel being smashed to pieces under their feet.

One and all decided to stand by the ship. In a final effort

to save her, the remainder of the deck cargo was thrown overboard as the boat reached the shallowest part of the reef, beyond which lay deep water and safety.

How the *Gjoa* got over those last terrible yards of rock is related in the words of the commander of the expedition.

The spray and sleet were washing over the vessel, the mast trembled, and the *Gjoa* seemed to pull herself together for a last final leap. She was lifted up high and flung bodily on to the bare rock, bump, bump, bump—with terrific force. In my distress I sent up (I honestly confess it) an ardent prayer to the Almighty. Yet another bump, worse than ever, then one more and we slid off.

Once safety had been reached the vessel was guided into deep water and then anchored, so that the worn-out men might sleep before taking soundings and finding a safe passage through the channel to open sea.

The Arctic is no place for tired men, and that night Amundsen and his band discovered it. Hardly had they gone to sleep when the gale returned with redoubled force, so that there was every probability of the vessel dragging her two anchors and being broken to pieces on the reefs which still surrounded her.

Nothing could be done except to set the tiny engine running at full speed to relieve the strain on the anchors, and fill the lifeboats with provisions and water, in case it became necessary to abandon ship.

Tired out, in the last stages of mental and bodily exhaustion after their struggles when grounded the previous night, Amundsen's men were called upon to face another night of terror—and another. For five days the gale persisted. Every minute of that time the anchors might have snapped. There could be no rest beyond a few minutes snatched while others watched. Nor was it possible to do anything to avert the threatened peril.

At last the gale moderated, and after a week of terror the *Gjoa,* battered but triumphant, crept out of the reef-strewn channel and continued her voyage in search of winter quarters.

A suitable spot—a natural harbour—was found in King William Land, and this Amundsen decided to make his main headquarters for one or two winters, while he carried out the scientific work which he had planned to accomplish before attempting to complete the passage of the Northwest.

All the members of the expedition had been working very hard and sleeping little for weeks past, and rest was imperative. Moreover, winter was approaching and there were winter quarters to prepare, and hunting to be done before the snow and ice came back. Otherwise they would have to face a meatless winter.

By October 1, the *Gjoa,* resting at her anchorage fifty yards from the shore, was encased in ice. Amundsen's first winter in the Northwest Passage had begun.

The following months were spent in sledging expeditions, hunting, and scientific work of the greatest importance in connection with the Northern magnetic pole.

It is easy enough to write down those facts, but how difficult the task of each member of the party must have been in the conditions that accompany an Arctic winter.

Temperatures of from sixty to seventy-nine degrees below zero were common, and the ice and snow penetrated everywhere. In the bay, christened Gjoahaven, the ice on the water was twelve and a half feet thick! Even the cabins on board the *Gjoa* were encrusted with ice, while the ceilings were filthy with lamp smoke.

Outside, the sledging journeys, undertaken at the first signs of spring to lay depots for the supply of later parties that were to try and fill in the blanks on the maps of that region, were carried out under conditions that demanded the last ounce of strength from every member of that expedition.

Even the early spring temperatures did not rise above twenty or thirty degrees below zero. That meant halting for the day with an hour of daylight to spare in order to build an igloo, or Eskimo snow hut, in which to spend the night. Tents were too cold in that low temperature.

Great care had to be exercised, too, against frost bite; to take a glove off for an instant necessitated violently exercising the whole hand to avoid its being frozen stiff. It can be imagined how difficult progress was under these conditions. Can it be wondered at that it took Amundsen on one sledging journey two and a half days' hard effort to travel seven miles?

On these journeys members of the expedition met several Eskimo tribes and got to know them quite well. Later in the season many of the men worked for Amundsen, or hunted food for him in return for presents of needles and iron.

It was while on a visit to one of these villages—in reality a settlement of perhaps half a dozen snow huts on a snow-white plain—that Amundsen saw a number of Eskimo children playing football within the Arctic circle.

The rules governing this remarkable game were difficult to discover, but the football looked very much like the English variety, and was made of laced-up reindeer skin. Propelled by arms and legs the ball passed from side to side of the white field. Presently the women joined in the game; indeed, they seemed to Amundsen to be the better players. He found that the Eskimo will play football thus while halting on the march wherever there is a level stretch of snow or ice, which in winter means in almost any part of the vast and inhospitable land they inhabit.

Through the efforts of their Eskimo allies, and the prowess of the huntsmen of the expedition, a varied diet was maintained during the following summer of 1904, and the second winter.

Fox steak, reindeer tripe, and many other strange dishes figured on the menu and were much appreciated.

During all this time all members of the expedition were kept busy on the work of surveying the unknown world by which they were surrounded, and the making of scientific observations.

For two winters and a summer the expedition remained at Gjoahaven. The summer was spent in long sledge journeys, and the autumn and winter in astronomical observation and hunting.

When spring came in 1905, the little *Gjoa* still had the hardest part of her journey before her. So far Amundsen had followed in the footsteps of the famous British explorers, Ross, Parry, and the ill-fated Franklin Expedition which had been lost in 1845 with every one of the one hundred and thirty-four members of the expedition almost at the very spot which Amundsen made his headquarters. Away to the west lay narrow, winding channels running eastward to meet them from the Behring Sea. But between lay the secret of the Northwest Passage—the link which no explorer had ever passed over to join up East with West.

On the night of July 31, 1905, Roald Amundsen hoisted the Norwegian flag at his masthead, left the soil of Gjoahaven for the last time, and turned the bows of his tiny ship toward the unknown West.

The sledge journeys made the previous summer had explored some of the many channels and islands which lay in their path. Everything which the mind of the greatest organiser of our generation could suggest had been done to increase their chances of success.

And yet there were many times of uncertainty, many moments when the fate of the entire expedition hung on a thread. It is in just that way that the world of ice keeps you thinking and guards her secrets.

Dropping the lead continually to test the depth of the water, using her tiny engine to smash through the ice in her track, the *Gjoa* crept forward over waters that no boat had ever penetrated since the beginning of the world.

Anything might have happened at any minute. There were no charts to help them. Depths varied from seventeen fathoms to five fathoms in a few minutes. Reefs stretched out in every direction, hidden under the ice. It was a terribly anxious time even for the experienced men who were on that boat. Normally the working of the ship demanded eighteen hours' work each day. Sleep took another five and food one, to complete the twenty-four. But during that voyage through uncharted waters, no man slept except in hasty snatches.

Worse still, Amundsen found difficulties with his compass, so that over and over again he almost lost the sense of direction altogether. There was iron in the mountains that rose from some of the islands, and the iron affected the instruments on board.

In the midst of this chaos the *Gjoa* staggered forward like a drunken man. Inch by inch the boat crept on, from time to time her keel scraping on the rocks sticking up out of the bed of the sea.

Things got worse. The bumps from rocks below the water got so bad that, in Amundsen's own words, it was "like sailing through a ploughed field." A boat was put off to take soundings ahead. That meant all hands on deck all the time, with no sleep for any one.

More ice packed up ahead and made matters worse. The strain was beginning to tell on them all. But all this time they were progressing through the unknown belt that connected East and West up there in the Polar Seas. They were doing something that men had died in hundreds trying to do. And they were succeeding.

On August 17, after seventeen days of terrible toil and anxiety, the *Gjoa* dropped her anchor on the west side of Cape Colborne in order to carry out some needed repairs. That date will ever be memorable in the story of exploration—for it was the day when Amundsen reached the furthermost point ever penetrated in the Northwest Passage from the west side. The *Gjoa* had added the missing link! The Northwest Passage had been sailed!

True they had still many miles to go before the *Gjoa* had completed her journey and passed the full length of that voyage. But at least they had lived to find a way through those terrible miles that had always beaten the sturdy seamen who had come before them.

Nine days later Amundsen was roused by the shout of "Vessel in sight!" Dressing in haste he found a two-masted schooner approaching them from the west, flying the American flag.

The first ship they had seen for nearly two years! The first news from civilisation. No wonder their eyes were filled with tears at the emotion of that moment.

Launching a boat, they rowed to the stranger and scrambled on board. The American skipper met them.

"Are you Captain Amundsen?" he asked.

"I am," replied Amundsen.

"Is this the first vessel you have met?"

Amundsen told him that they were the first people other than Eskimo they had seen for two years.

"I am exceedingly pleased to be the first one to welcome you on getting through the Northwest Passage," said the American, shaking Amundsen warmly by the hand.

It was thus that Captain James McKenna, master of the American schooner, *Charles Hanson,* was the first man to learn that the problem of the Northwest Passage had been solved.

Amundsen had to spend a third winter in the Arctic after that meeting before he finally brought his expedition triumphantly to Nome, and civilisation. But the worst was over. The third winter was spent at King Point, in Northern Canada, close to the winter quarters of the American whaling fleet. They knew now that it was not possible for the *Gjoa* and all hands to be lost in those icy wastes without the world knowing what they had accomplished, or having the benefit of the work they had performed.

After meeting the American whaling fleet Amundsen found that their supply ship had been held up by ice and had not got through, with the result that flour was very short. He therefore gave ten cases, or about twenty-four hundredweight of flour to these ships.

I wonder how many of my readers will realise what a tribute that simple fact was to the masterly organisation of Amundsen. Here is a little herring boat two and a half years from port, during the whole of which time no extra supplies of food, other than meat, have been available. Within six months of sailing the whole of the deck cargo, including much valuable food, had to be thrown overboard to save the vessel from disaster. And yet at the end of their adventure, there is still a sufficient supply left to enable the *Gjoa's* commander to give over a ton of flour to vessels worse off than he is.

I mention this incident because there you have the secret which has made the name of Amundsen rank so high in the history of modern explorations. It is this genius for organisation which has resulted in the saving of all those with him over and over again when a tight corner has had to be turned. And it was never better illustrated than in this incident of the flour which he was able to present to the American ships.

Up to this point, every member of the expedition had, by careful living, kept in excellent health, but during this last winter in the North, Wiik, one of the gallant little band of seven, died and was buried on top of a lofty hill looking down on the waters through which they had victoriously passed.

Shortly after leaving winter quarters for the last stage of the journey, an accident happened which Amundsen had been dreading for months. The propeller of their tiny engine struck a submerged reef, and the engine stopped. Nor could the efforts of the two engineers on board make it go again.

They had now to rely upon sails only, a thing which would have meant disaster three months earlier, and even now meant every ounce of seamanship being exerted to keep the boat safe.

It is perhaps fitting that the *Gjoa* and her gallant crew were in peril up to the very end of their trip. Without any engine the vessel lay becalmed amid the ice when the wind dropped. And without the greatest care this means that the ice will hold you fast and while you are helpless, carry you steadily north—north—north until you, or your bones, are entrapped at the North Pole itself.

This was the situation Amundsen had to face. He knew the swift current that swept northward, knew he could not fight against it if the wind dropped.

To manœuvre a sailing ship in close ice needs years of experience. Fortunately Amundsen's men had had years with the whaling fleets and knew their work as well as their leader.

All sail was packed on the boat and her nose turned to the ice pack through which she must batter a way to reach open water and safety. Once, twice, the *Gjoa* charged, and each time her bows thrust a little farther into that icefield that held them prisoner.

At last there was little ice left to the south. Only two huge masses separated them from open sea and a clear homeward track. The vessel seemed to know that too. Again she charged, and inch by inch, with the aid of boathooks in the bows, the ice was smashed asunder. So open water was reached and the failure of the engine overcome by seamanship.

More storms lay ahead, but the route was clear, and after the perils of the past three years, storms did not worry that little band.

On August 30, 1906, Amundsen sighted the cape which guards the northern entrance to the Behring Straits. And south of the Straits lay Nome and the end of the journey.

It was blowing a gale at the time. It was impossible to cook that special dinner Amundsen had promised his crew. Impossible even to hoist the flag, which would have been blown to tatters in that wind.

All they could do was to propose a simple toast, and to shake hands. The passage of the Northwest, from end to end by one band of explorers in one keel, had been accomplished. Before them lay the reward—world fame, excitement, congratulations! But all that could wait. For the moment six of the seven men who had actually accomplished this voyage for the first time celebrated their victory, and raised their glasses to the seventh who lay beneath a cross, forever watching the waters they had conquered.

In June, 1928, since this book was first published, Roald Amundsen returned to the ice-bound North on what proved to be his last journey.

Accompanied by a pilot and five companions, he left Norway in a Latham seaplane to try to locate the survivors of the Nobile Arctic Expedition, who were marooned in three parties in the icefields following a disaster to the airship *Italia*. It was his intention to land, if conditions made it possible, and bring the weakest back to safety.

A desperate errand of mercy, but the old Viking, who knew both Arctic and Antarctic so well, did not hesitate when there was a hope of rescuing brother adventurers.

The aeroplane rose into the air and headed to the Great White North. The rest is silence. Amundsen never reached any of the Nobile parties. Nor was his seaplane seen again. In the following September a float of a Latham seaplane was picked up off the northern coast of Norway and identified as belonging to Amundsen's machine. But of the occupants no trace has been found.

Thus ended a career and a record unequalled in the story of exploration. Roald Amundsen spent the best part of thirty years in Polar regions. To him belong the triple honours of being the first to make the Northwest Passage by ship from end to end, the first to reach the South Pole, and joint leader in the first crossing of the North Pole by air.

CHAPTER II

MOST travellers into the wilds start out with some object in view. One wants to find a ruined city deep in the jungles, another is searching for a new way across a mountain or desert, a third is after some rare bird, or beast, or plant, while a fourth goes out with a moving-picture camera, intent on filming shy wild creatures. There is, however, a small remainder who are driven by the spirit of pure adventure. They start off into unknown countries simply because some instinct forces them to do so. To these it seems to make little difference where they go; their urge is to get right away into the unknown. They are happier in the heart of the jungle than in the comfortable security of an English town with a sturdy policeman at each street corner.

The lady whose wonderful adventure in Central America is described in this chapter is one of these. Seen in the peaceful surroundings of her flat in London you would never take Lady Richmond Brown for an adventurer of the Elizabethan type. She is not big or masculine or loud-voiced, but on the contrary rather small, very nice looking, very quiet in speech. It is difficult to imagine her in boots and breeches tramping through the tropical jungle, and still more strange to picture her in the midst of savages who had never before seen white folk; savages, perhaps stricken with terrible diseases, whom she doctored and nursed and helped in all sorts of ways.

In 1921, recovering after a severe illness, Lady Richmond Brown was travelling from London down to her Hampshire home when she met at Waterloo Station an old friend, Mr. Mitchell Hedges. He was then preparing for a fresh expedition to the Caribbean, that deep, warm sea which lies between the Antilles and the Central and South American mainland, and which contains a wealth of tropical life unknown in any other part of the ocean. The two travelled together and had a long talk, and there and then Lady Richmond Brown made up her mind to go with him. Mr. Hedges laughed. He thought she was joking. When he found that she was really set upon it he began to tell her what tropical travel really was. He spoke of the torture of mosquitoes, sand flies, ticks, and other terrible insects; of snakes, of fever, of fearful heat, hunger, thirst. Then as the lady did not weaken he shrugged his shoulders. "Very well," he said, "but you had better put all your affairs in order and make your will before you leave."

So presently it was arranged and they left for Jamaica. From Jamaica they crossed to Panama on the Pacific side of the Panama Canal, and from there returned to Colon on the Atlantic side of the Isthmus. Then it was that Mr. Mitchell Hedges told his fellow explorer of his plans. He had heard of an Indian tribe that had probably never seen white men. They were, he said, an absolutely primitive people who carefully guarded their territory against any invasion. He did not know whether it would be possible to get in touch with them, but he intended to try to do so. The difficulty was to find a means of getting to them, for the journey would have to be made by sea and the whole coast was such a mesh of coral reefs that a mere sailing boat was of no use at all. It was absolutely necessary to get a boat with some sort of an engine.

The two were deep in discussion of this difficult matter when a friend, Major Fitzwilliam, came in. "I have to go home at once," he told them. "My boat is for sale. Do you care to buy her?" This boat, the *Cara,* was a twenty-ton motor yacht able to travel at ten knots, and perfectly suited for their purpose except for one thing. She had no sail. "So if the engine breaks down," said Mr. Hedges to Lady Brown, "we are stranded, and shall stand a precious good chance of staying stranded for the rest of our lives. It's too risky for you. I shall go alone."

But Lady Richmond Brown had other ideas on the subject, and in the end the *Cara* was purchased. The very next day Lady Brown became ill again and had to go to hospital, where she remained for three weeks. But her resolve to go never faltered and while she was laid up Mr. Hedges made all preparations for the journey and engaged two men as crew. One was Robbie, the original engineer of the yacht, a coloured man, the other an old native called John George who had been up and down the coast on a schooner and so could act as pilot. A big medicine chest was one of the chief parts of the cargo, for Mr. Hedges well knew how far a little doctoring goes with savages.

If you study a map of Central America you will see that the Canal cuts the isthmus not from east to west, as might be expected, but from north to south. Some way east of Colon lies Cape San Blas and beyond it is an archipelago of tiny islands, many of which have never been charted. This may seem strange because, as every one knows, this part of America was found and colonized by the Spaniards nearly four hundred years ago, and Nombre de Dios, the town which lies nearest to Cape San Blas, is very old indeed. But the fact is that the sea is so shallow and so sown with reefs, and the mainland is such impenetrable jungle, that it has never seemed worth while to explore that part of the coast. So when the little *Cara* poked her nose around Cape San Blas she was entering waters as little known as any on earth.

The first experience of the travellers was an electric storm so terrific that the whole sea and sky were one blaze of lightning. It was so bad that the dynamo of the *Cara* was fused and even the magneto of the engine upset. It took hours to repair the latter, then when they started again the little boat was plunging in a terrible sea. The travellers at last reached Nombre de Dios and there found shelter behind an islet where the water was calm. Lady Richmond Brown wanted to bathe, but the sea was infested with stinging seaweed and sea centipedes, the latter horribly poisonous. On the following night they had an even worse storm, of a sort which the natives called a *chuquesana*. The wind blew a hurricane and when next morning the *Cara* pushed out to sea the waves were at least twenty feet high. The yacht had to pass through a channel between huge jagged reefs over which the seas broke with a terrible roar, but this risky business was managed in safety and next day they reached the first of the islands, and saw an Indian village. Men paddled off in canoes and the chief, a very fine-looking man, came aboard. He and his headman dined aboard the *Cara* and though they had never before seen a table knife or fork, their manners were wonderfully good. After this the travellers passed several deserted islands, then came to another village where again they were received in friendly fashion. Here they went ashore and were horrified at the amount of sickness in the place. Many of the Indians had a form of itch; others had old cuts which had festered. One man had a great thorn deeply embedded in his foot, yet. in spite of the pain, sat perfectly stolid and

LADY RICHMOND BROWN AND MR MITCHELL HEDGES ON THE STEPS
OF A PREHISTORIC RUIN IN THE JUNGLE SOUTH OF PANAMA

LADY RICHMOND BROWN WITH A GROUP OF CHUCUNAQUE INDIAN WOMEN AND CHILDREN

still while it was cut out. Sulphur ointment and permanganate of potash were in great request. The natives were
intensely interested at seeing how a little permanganate
coloured clear water. Island after island was visited and at
each the people were quite friendly and brought presents of
all kinds of fruit. At one island Mr. Hedges caught a huge
shovel-nose shark with hook and line. The Indians, who
had never before seen modern shark tackle, were greatly
surprised and delighted. In each village they visited the
travellers were careful to instruct the medicine man in the
use of such simple remedies as sulphur ointment and cas-
tor oil, and in each case the medicine man was proud as a
peacock of his new knowledge, and of course became their
firmest friend.

To say truth, all this was done with an object. The
travellers knew very well how quickly news spreads among
natives and hoped that the unknown tribe on the mainland
whom they wished to visit might come to hear how the coast
Indians were being doctored, and so be induced to allow a
visit. But time went on and there was no sign, and they had
begun to despair when at last, at a place called Oostoppo,
they found waiting for them half a dozen strange-looking
Indians who stared at them in amazement, for none had
ever before set eyes on a white person. These were an embassy from the Chucunaque tribe, sent to ask the white
healers to visit them. That night all was made ready and
next day the adventurers started in the frail dugout canoes
of the Chucunaques. They took with them rifles and medicines, and Lady Richmond Brown carried in a parcel a thin
white dress, together with a necklace of huge imitation
pearls and some great glass earrings, while Mr. Hedges
packed some red flares.

The first part of the journey was up an uncharted river,

c

the mouth of which was choked with a mass of great dead trees washed down from inland by floods. Once in the stream itself they travelled up a green tunnel, for the trees met overhead. After paddling some ten miles, the stream became too shallow for their canoes, and the party landed, and went on afoot. The heat was frightful, the ground across which they had to tramp terribly rough so that, after a few miles, they were quite exhausted and forced to rest. The track rose steadily, the trees thinned, and they came to a gully running up into steep hills. They went on until they were quite worn out, then camped for the night. Or rather they lay down on the ground and slept the sleep of exhaustion. They were so weary that not even the mosquitoes could keep them awake. In the morning they breakfasted on hot tea and cold corned beef out of a tin, and went on until they came to a jungle that was like a solid wall, but the Indians took them by a tunnel-like track through it. Once a deadly snake crossed their path; in another place were the fresh pad marks of an enormous jaguar. The temperature was ninety-five degrees and the air thick with humming, stinging insects.

All of a sudden they were met by four of the strangest figures imaginable. These were men dressed in robes entirely covered with strange cabalistic figures. Each held a stick of office, the tops being carved to represent figures, birds or grotesque animals. With them were two *contoolies,* or medicine men, who wore towering headdresses made of brilliant feathers and round whose necks were hung necklaces of bones, dozens of them, which jingled as they moved. These contoolies carried rattles, the head of each formed of a calabash filled with dried seeds. Behind the chiefs and the medicine men were about fifty Indians armed with clubs made of dense, heavy *lignum vitæ,* spears which were also made of wood, and bows. Some of these bows were not less than nine feet long and the arrows matched them in size, each arrow having several prongs barbed like fish hooks. Not one uttered a sound. They simply formed up, turned and escorted their visitors to the village. The two travellers were taken straight to the chief's house, where he sat in a hammock, the material of which was woven in a beautiful design of blue, yellow, red, and white. They were given stools facing him, then for some minutes there was a deadly silence.

When meeting savages white visitors must never speak first. This Lady Richmond Brown knew well, so simply sat still and watched the chief. At last the chief spoke and the language he used was so like that of the Indians of the Islands that the visitors were easily able to understand. The Spirits, he said, had commanded that no stranger should ever come inside their country on pain of death. This sounded anything but cheerful, and what made the two explorers feel still more uncomfortable was the fact that the two contoolies were quite clearly egging on the chief to get rid of them. The fact was, of course, that they were jealous, for if these white visitors started making cures they, the medicine men, would lose face and have to take second place.

But Mr. Mitchell Hedges was equal to the situation. Rising to his full height he stretched out his hand, then in a voice which rang through the hut said, "We, the healers, will confer with the Great Spirits." Lady Brown added sternly, "We must be left entirely alone." Then she and he together walked calmly out, no one making the least effort to stop them. A hut was cleared for them and food was brought, an extraordinary mess steaming in a great earthenware pot. They did not ask what it was made of but ate, then as they were both worn out, dropped into their hammocks and went to sleep. When they had rested they went straight back to the chief. The headmen were still there and the contoolies. The medicine men were triumphant, for by this time they had the chief under their thumb and quite clearly meant to force him to kill the strangers. Mr. Mitchell Hedges marched straight up to the chief.

"Listen to me," he said sternly. "At dark every single one of you—man, woman, and child—are to gather in the open in front of our dwelling. You will then be shewn a sign. Fail to do so and you and all your people will be burned up in a fearful fire which will rise from the ground."

Then he stalked off again, followed by Lady Richmond Brown and leaving the natives in a very nervous state.

"I am going to use the flares," Mr. Hedges told Lady Brown, as the two reached the hut.

"And I will put on my white dress and stand in the middle," said Lady Brown.

While they were making their preparations some of the Indians came to them in a terrible fright, and said that they knew that what Mr. Mitchell Hedges had told them was true and that there was no need for the sign. The answer was that the gods had spoken and that their orders must be obeyed. The messengers went off in a dreadful fear and as darkness fell there was wailing all through the village.

When night came the Indians came drifting up. The white people's orders were obeyed to the letter, for every mother's son was there, including even the tiny children and babies in arms. The travellers were in no hurry and waited until it was pitch dark before touching off the flares. As the flares blazed, flinging out crimson flames and masses of ruddy smoke, Lady Richmond Brown, who had been lying flat on the ground, rose quickly and stood erect. She was wearing the white dress and with her stage jewels glittering in the red glow, must have presented a rather startling figure. At any rate the Indians thought so, for with shrieks of terror they fled in blind panic. So frightened were they that some burst right through their own lightly built huts, making great holes in the walls.

The flares died down and the velvet darkness of the tropical night settled over the clearing. The silence was broken only by low moans, and when at last the two adventurers went out to explore they found the ground littered with sick folk. These had been carried from their beds by their relatives in order to see the sign given by the white visitors, then left behind by the Indians in their terror-stricken flight.

"Now we are in a mess," groaned Mr. Hedges, and indeed it seemed that he was right, for there were literally dozens of sick Indians lying all over the ground, and it was out of the question to carry them back into their huts.

"I will change my clothes and then we will see what we can do," said Lady Richmond Brown.

It was a terrible job. The wretched invalids were so terrified that they tried to crawl away and hide when the white people came near them, and among them were small children, many of them in a terrible state. So pitiful was the whole business that Lady Richmond Brown, who, as she says herself, does not easily cry, was reduced to tears.

The night seemed endless and when dawn did at last come the village was still deserted. There was nothing for it but to go out into the jungle and try to find the fugitives. A slight movement in the thick foliage caught their eyes; they called and the chief appeared, followed by the witch doctors and headmen. They were still shaking with fright. They crept up like beaten dogs and it was a long time before they could be made to understand that nothing dreadful was going to happen to them. When at last they were re-assured it was an easier matter to collect the rest of the fugitives. Then Mr. Mitchell Hedges addressed them and told them that he and Lady Brown had been sent to save them and cure them of their illnesses. He added that they would give knowledge and medicine to the contoolies so that they would be able to continue the healing.

This bit of diplomacy cleared up the situation, for the contoolies were so pleased to know that their power would not be taken from them that they were ready to help in any way they could. From that minute on they obeyed every order given them by the visitors without the slightest hesi-tation.

But the task that lay before the travellers was a terrible one, for in all the tribe there was hardly one who was sound. The chief himself, his wife, children, and practically the whole tribe were suffering from a form of itch so terrible that their whole bodies were raw. Some had lost all their hair from this complaint and in other cases the eardrums had been attacked, leaving the sufferers stone deaf. Sulphur ointment was the only remedy for this mal-ady, and fortunately a large supply had been brought. But there was worse than itch, for smallpox in its most deadly form was raging in the village. Four unfortunates, three men and a woman, had died of it that morning, and their bodies were lying in their hammocks. Many were afflicted with trachoma, an infectious disease which affects the eyes, and some had been blinded by this. Jiggers had attacked many. The jigger is an insect which is common all through tropical America. It pierces the skin and lays its eggs in the flesh. The Indians of South America understand how to deal with this pest, and dig it out at once, a comparatively easy matter, but these poor people seemed to have no idea of helping themselves. They were covered with appalling sores. To add to all these dreadful troubles, the children were affected with hookworm and some of the people had consumption.

The fact was that the Chucunaques were living in a frightfully unhealthy country and under terrible conditions. They were crowded in one small clearing, and as for the food they ate and the way they prepared it, the description given by Lady Brown is almost beyond belief. Into the cooking pot was dumped anything they thought eatable. Lizards were a favourite food, and these were flung into the pot alive and uncleaned.

The doctoring was a shocking business. There were many cases which would have been beyond the skill of the best of specialists, but the travellers did what they could. They insisted, first, on cleaning and disinfecting, and were successful in curing many of the less serious complaints. But the sights were so terrible that four hours at a time were all that Lady Brown could endure.

When the worst of the doctoring was finished, the explorers found time to study this strange race of people among whom they found themselves. In some respects the Chucunaques are as primitive as any people on earth. They have no metal or any idea of it. More than that, they do not even use stone, all their weapons being made of wood. Yet in many ways they are extremely ingenious. All use bows, arrows, and spears. The bows, made of black palm, are strung with vegetable fibres and the five-pointed arrows are barbed like fishhooks. They make blowpipes from hollow reeds and the darts blown through these are dipped in a virulent poison which is made by soaking rotten liver in the venom of serpents. They cultivate sugar cane and have devised an ingenious press for extracting the juice from the cane. They not only drink the pure juice, but pour it into the pots in which all their food is cooked, boiling it up with lizards, yams, pineapples, bananas and all sorts of stuff, into a regular witch's brew.

The women spend a great deal of their time in working the most extraordinary and intricate designs in needlework on cloth. During their stay with the Chucunaques, the travellers were presented with a large number of these strips, and some, when examined in London, were found to consist of a velvetlike material of great age. Several pieces were trimmed with Spanish lace at least three hundred years old, thus proving that at some period the ancestors of the tribe must have been in touch with the Spanish conquerors. These embroideries form a sort of pictorial record or history of the tribe and prove that the Indians who made them understand, among other things, the length of the solar year.

Among these people the wife rules the family. True, the chief and the contoolies are supreme, but in all smaller matters the woman is more powerful than the man. It is she who orders the building of a new house, the getting of firewood or food, and the husband does none of these things unless his wife first orders him to do so. Each family has its own god carved out of wood. The carving is done partly by the use of fire and partly with the aid of the teeth of sharks or of wild animals. There are no flints such as most savages possess. These wooden *ju-jus* are most curious. Some have wings and several show the figure of a man wearing what appear to be a top hat and frock coat. Yet most certainly none of these people had ever seen either of these garments.

When at last it was time for the travellers to return to

the coast the Indians were very sad and unhappy. The whole village turned out and the children were brought to Lady Brown so that she might pat or touch each one in turn. Then as their visitors left the village the people all raised their terrible death wail, a most creepy and awesome sound.

The quantity of presents given to Lady Brown and Mr. Hedges by the Chucunaques was so great that it took quite a large party of men to carry them, and the dugout canoes had to make no fewer than three journeys to carry them all out to the yacht. The *Cara* herself was so loaded that there was very little room left for her crew.

Their Indian friends on the islands were greatly pleased to see them again and celebrated the event with a dance. The orchestra was of eight men who played homemade reed instruments, while some others beat wooden tom-toms. This went on half the night until in fact the dancers were quite tired out. Next day there was a sort of review at which the two travellers were paid the great compliment of being made chiefs. They were presented with necklaces and three small golden images made in the shape of toads.

After another day spent in doctoring the Indians, they said good-bye and started back. Every Indian who could find room in a canoe lined the shore of the island, and the rest, with the women and children, stood on the beach or waded waist deep into the sea. "Their pathetic cry of farewell," says Lady Richmond Brown, "haunted us for hours, and it is the dearest ambition of my life to return."

CHAPTER III

ONE evening in 1925 a dinner was given in London in honour of a French explorer whose name ranks high in the annals of Antarctic exploration, but whose exploits are still very little known to the public in Great Britain. This explorer is Commandant Jean Charcot, the famous French sailor and scientist, who has made no less than four journeys to the unknown South, in two of which he commanded expeditions which succeeded in discovering many things which the world did not know about that region.

Commandant Charcot, who was welcomed in London on that occasion by Captain E. R. G. R. Evans, another famous Antarctic explorer whose exploits are recorded in this book, was the second Frenchman to cross the Antarctic Circle. He led his first expedition to the South Polar regions at the end of 1903 and explored a vast stretch of unknown coast line. There he wintered in the ice and brought back a rich harvest of scientific results.

But it is about his second expedition, which began in 1908 and ended in 1910, that you are to read in this chapter. These were the years during which Captain Scott and Amundsen were contemplating their famous dashes to the South Pole, and Charcot might have been excused if he, too, had put aside thoughts of scientific work in the South and preferred instead to join in the race for the honour of being the first man to reach the Pole.

But Charcot is before all else a scientist. His aim was

to enlarge our knowledge about this vast unmapped region of the earth's surface which had then been visited by fewer than a dozen men, each of whom had only touched the Antarctic Continent at one or two points. So he decided that instead of approaching the Antarctic from Victoria Land, the route chosen by the ill-fated Captain Scott, he would go instead to the icebound and unknown quadrant of land lying below Cape Horn, in South America, and finish there the scientific work which he had begun in 1903. This, thought Charcot, would avoid having two expeditions cover the same ground and learn the same things, and enable all the expeditions to gain fresh knowledge of immense value to the whole world. No wonder Captain Scott called him "The gentleman of the Pole."

During the two years that the expedition was away from France, Commandant Charcot did not therefore join in any hair-raising adventures. He did not try to reach the South Pole, nor did he try to sail completely round the world. He made no record sledge journeys. Instead, he was content to finish his scientific work which, like the scientific work done by Amundsen in the Northwest Passage, and Scott and Shackleton in the Antarctic, has proved of immense value to weather experts, geologists, map-makers, navigators, and many other people.

In collecting the information which he brought back, however, Charcot and his little band of men were many times in great peril from storm, ice, and hunger. Not once, but many times they thought they would never see France again alive. During all the time they were away they were sailing in perilous seas, and among ice-girt lands, and it needed all their skill and knowledge of navigation to save their little ship and the crew from destruction. That they did so, and were able to bring back this story of fine seamanship amid great dangers, proves that Jean Charcot has well earned the high position among the heroes of modern adventure which his fellow explorers have given to him.

And now let us tell you the story of the voyage of Commandant Charcot, with a crew of thirty-one seamen and scientists, on board the good ship *Why Not?* It sounds a funny name for such an important ship, but Charcot so christened it because he did not see why such a little ship should not go to the land of ice and come back safely. "Why not?" he said, when people smiled at the little ship he had built to carry him there. And the *Why Not?* it remained.

The ship was most carefully built in France, for it had to carry the expedition to a region where there is ice everywhere and where the coast line is fringed with high mountains that are insurmountable.

The *Why Not?* was fitted with a strong engine of 459 horse power to drive it through the ice and had room in her bunkers for two hundred and fifty tons of coal.

Directly she was finished, the work of equipping her began, and because the task of fitting out a Polar expedition is an adventure in itself, we will tell you just what Commandant Charcot took with him.

First of all, of course, were all the scientific instruments which they would need for their work. These were housed in two laboratories specially built on board for the purpose. Then they took no fewer than three thousand books. It sounds a lot, but you must remember that down there in the great White South there is hardly any daylight during the long winters, and often it is impossible to move about on shore for days, owing to the fierce tempests. Men who had nothing to read would go mad with the monotony of life.

For the same reason Charcot fitted his ship with an electric lighting outfit—the first time electric light had been taken to the Antarctic, and thus during the long winter nights they had plenty of bright light to help them at their work and play.

Many lifeboats they took, for use in penetrating into the icepack where the *Why Not?* could not go, and also ice saws, chisels, ice anchors, ice hooks, crowbars, shovels, and spades.

For possible sledge journeys they had six tents and six special portable kitchens, together with utensils, sleeping bags, and other equipment.

Nothing was forgotten. Special clothing, special boots, sledges, and tons of tinned foods. The deadly snow blindness was averted by taking specially prepared glasses to protect their eyes from the dazzling light. Thanks to these glasses not a single man suffered from this terrible malady during the whole of the expedition.

Thus fitted up for a three years' journey, the little *Why Not?* dipped her flag and slipped out of Havre Harbour on August 15, 1908, with thirty-two souls on board. These were Commandant Charcot, seven scientists, and a crew of twenty-two. They crossed the Atlantic in fair weather, and four months later, on December 16, 1908, said farewell to civilisation when they steamed out of Punta Arenas, in Chile, and turned the bows of the ship toward Cape Horn and the silent South.

The first big adventure came when they were nearly caught in the great piles of drifting ice at Wandel Island, which had been Charcot's winter quarters in his former expedition.

The little *Why Not?* was saved from this fate and sailed on to a point of the Antarctic called Port Circumcision. The ice is too thick beyond this point for the *Why Not?* to force a passage without grave risk, but the neighbourhood needed to be explored and charted so that future explorers might have reliable maps. To do this work, Charcot and two of his lieutenants set out in the picket boat, which is really a motor boat similar to those seen at any seaside town, to reconnoitre along the channels and islands round about the point where their ship was anchored.

As they expected to be away from the *Why Not?* only a few hours, they took enough food for one meal only, and no extra clothing beyond what they stood up in.

For a time all went well, and many new details were filled in on the draft maps. Then ice became thick, and once the motor boat was nearly smashed between two icebergs that threatened to collapse upon the little boat.

After one or two moments of great peril such as this the three adventurers reached Berthelot Island, and there climbed a large mountain which would give them a view to the south.

Imagine what that means. Three men, part of a little band which had come on the only ship for hundreds of miles around, stood on top of that mountain and looked at a view of the eternal ice stretching right from Berthelot Island to the South Pole. And they knew that they were the first men ever to see that mighty scene. No wonder that they decided to celebrate it by eating a meal, when, at ten o'clock that night, they returned to their motor boat and prepared for the return journey to the ship.

There, on the shore of the island, they had a meal of soup, meat, chocolate, jam, and biscuits—a wonderful meal for that part of the world. And hardly had they finished it when snow began to fall—snow that shut out the view and made it impossible to see the channels through the ice.

It damped their spirits, but they started off on the return journey, only to find that the pack ice had drifted in solid between them and the spot where they had left the ship and that it was impossible to force a way through it.

There was nothing to do but return to Berthelot Island. From there they made a fresh start to find a channel between the ice. There was no darkness in the South at that time of the year, but the snow and an icy wind left them numbed and weak after all the hard work they had done since leaving the *Why Not?*

For hours they searched among the constantly moving ice for some way of making progress, while the rising wind constantly shifted the position of the ice floes. At last they gave up the attempt to break through. The ice had blocked them in!

They found it hard to keep awake now. One of the planks of the motor boat had been stove in, while others had been cracked and torn by contact with the ice. Their position was one of high peril. Add to this the fact that there was no room in the boat in which to lie down and sleep, and that their clothes were soaked through with icy water—not to mention that all the food they possessed for three men was one tin of beef, two sticks of chocolate, two biscuits, and a flask of rum—and their plight may be imagined. It meant that right at the beginning of the voyage there seemed every prospect of Charcot and two other members of the expedition dying from hunger and exposure, before help could reach them.

Sleep proved impossible owing to the frightful cold, and as the ice pressed harder against the little boat, they turned back once more to Berthelot Island.

There they spent the next day, still hemmed in by solid ice, which prevented any boat either approaching or leaving the island. Their one meal on this day was a cake of chocolate and one biscuit divided among the three. Imagine that as a day's ration for a healthy man in the frozen South, with the temperature never rising above zero, or colder than on the coldest day of an English winter.

To make matters worse, the little motor boat ran ashore on a rock and was wedged fast for the best part of the day. By the time they had managed to refloat the boat they had been three days without food and were rapidly growing weaker. You can imagine, therefore, with what joy they saw ahead a clear channel through the ice which had been holding them fast.

Joyfully they set out—and had hardly started before the engine failed. Not once but twice they coaxed it to go again, but they had not gone far along the coast before it finally broke down.

The moment had arrived for a quick decision. The motor boat was too heavy for them to row in their weak state, even if they could have got through the ice before the channel closed up again.

The only thing to do was to abandon the boat and try and make their way on foot to Cape Tuxen from which they might signal to Port Circumcision, where the ship lay anchored. This meant a ten hours' tramp across the ice and snow, a terrible journey for hunger-weakened men.

At 10 P. M. they were ready and after having a last small meal of the remaining meat and chocolate they set out. It was snowing again and bitterly cold, but it was their last chance of reaching safety. Another three days without food and they would be lost.

As Charcot stepped out of the motor boat and began that walk a sound reached them—the first sound apart from the noise of sea and ice since they had been imprisoned by

JEAN CHARCOT
Captain Scott called him " the Gentleman of the Pole."

THE LITTLE "WHY NOT?"

This little vessel carried the intrepid band of French explorers farther south
below Cape Horn than any ship had sailed before.

the ice pack. It was the sound of a ship's syren. The *Why Not?* was searching for them. Rescue was at hand!

Climbing a rock that gave a view of the surrounding sea they saw her. The gallant little boat was smashing her way through the ice in the effort to reach Berthelot Island, where they were thought to be. How the three castaways shouted, and did not stop shouting until three blasts on the ship's syren told them they had been sighted.

Soon they were on board, changing into dry clothing and eating warm food again. The first adventure had ended happily.

Hardly had they eaten that meal when the next adventure began. With a great shock and crash the *Why Not?* ran aground on a submerged rock.

Her position was one of great danger, with her bows in the air and her stern submerged. All that day they worked to get her off without success. The sea was calm, and so in a final effort they launched all the lifeboats, and filled them with deck cargo, thus lightening the ship considerably.

At last the *Why Not?* slid off the rock and was safe. But still there was no rest for Charcot and his companions, for all the stores which had been put into the lifeboats must be taken on board again and stowed safely away.

Imagine the terrible weariness of these men. For six days they had had hardly any sleep; three of them had been practically without food for three days, and forced to wear clothes saturated with freezing water. And then, just when rescue had been effected, they must toil for another twenty-four hours without once stopping, to save their ship. It is this sort of thing which demands so much of the man who would go to the silent South.

During the days which followed, the scientists aboard the *Why Not?* were kept busy at their work of map-

D

drawing, charting, and geological work as the vessel slowly made her way through almost continuous ice. Some idea of what sailing a ship in that part of the world means may be gathered from the fact that Charcot sighted over ten thousand icebergs in one summer in that region! In winter, of course, the South is one solid ice field for thousands of miles.

On January 14, 1909, the little *Why Not?* passed the last point ever reached by former explorers in that part of the world, and penetrated into a coast which did not appear on any map. The ice was getting steadily thicker, the bergs bigger and bigger as the summer advanced, and the danger of this voyage of discovery is well illustrated by an incident recorded by Doctor Charcot himself in his account of the journey entitled "The Voyage of the 'Why Not?' ":

I was writing in my cabin, he states, when a noise like a big explosion of fireworks, accompanied and followed by a loud rumbling, brought me in a few strides on deck just in time to see the magnificent spectacle of the iceberg splitting open and capsizing. Enormous spurs of glaucous hue jump out of the water, and even rocks are uplifted as if by a submarine mine; the sea boils fiercely and in a few seconds its surface far and wide is covered by debris of all sizes. The iceberg has lost a third of its bulk.

That is what happens when an iceberg splits into two or more parts. You can imagine what would happen to any little ship which had the misfortune to be too close when that occurred. Indeed, but two hours later another iceberg split into two pieces so close to the *Why Not?* that it touched the stern of the ship and smashed one of the lifeboats to atoms.

As no safe harbour could be found in this unknown coastal region for winter quarters, the expedition was

obliged to turn north again and go back to Petermann Island, which they had passed that spring, and where the
ship would be safe during the Antarctic tempests which
would have to be faced before the spring break-up of the
ice made further voyaging possible.

This harbour was reached safely, and the task of building huts on shore to live in, and for astronomical and
scientific work, was soon in full swing.

The work which Charcot and his comrades did here
during the winter, although too technical to explain in this
book, was of the greatest value to science, and it was to
enable this work to be done that both the French Government and the learned societies of that country had contributed large sums toward fitting out the expedition.

It was a winter of hardships bravely borne. In the first
place the necessity of saving the small stock of coal meant
going without any fire in the cabins until the thermometer
fell to a few degrees below zero. Fancy eating your supper
and trying to read in a room in which there was about
thirty-six degrees of frost!

Then there was trouble with icebergs that drifted in
to the little harbour and threatened to smash the *Why Not?*
To save the ship it was necessary to build a defence across
the mouth of the harbour to keep the ice out. Nearly every
gale—and winter in that part of the world is one gale after
another—destroyed the defences, and they had to be built
again. And while all this was being done the scientific work,
which was Charcot's real task, went on without interrup-
tion.

What this meant may be realised by the fact that one
early winter storm lasted for three weeks without respite,
during the whole of which the expedition worked amid
snow, mist, and driving ice carried by the wind, which made

it torture to go out in the one or two hours of grey gloom which is all the daylight experienced during winter in that latitude.

To make matters worse, a new form of scurvy, the disease which is the curse of explorers far from fresh food, appeared before midwinter. This new disease was caused by a diet of preserved foods, and Charcot himself was one of the first members of the expedition to go sick.

The only remedy was to stop eating tinned foods and find seal meat instead. Hunting excursions were therefore organised and in this way the patients were cured. But without fresh food and vegetables it was impossible to stamp out the disease, and it reappeared from time to time for the rest of the winter, causing the victims much weakness and pain.

Despite these troubles, the little band not only carried out its valuable scientific work, but managed to keep wonderfully cheerful by organising special days for sports and other festivities. One of these was celebrated on July 14, the French national holiday, when the cook surpassed himself by serving up the following wonderful dinner amid the Antarctic ice and storms:

Soup
Lobster salad
Gelatine of Chicken
Filet of beef with mushrooms
Artichokes
Plum pudding
Compote of fruits
Champagne

These amazingly cheerful men, ignoring the terrible cold and illness, even managed a few days after this dinner to

produce an original play in honour of their Commandant's birthday. These things are mentioned to show the
wonderful courage which the explorer must have if he can
face the hardships of a voyage to the land of ice.

Later in the winter long sledge journeys were made to
survey the coast line and the interior of the surrounding
ice-locked land, and in these Charcot was too ill to take
part. When these journeys were undertaken the weather was
still so bad that after struggling forward over the ice for
twelve hours daily the sledging parties could only cover
two miles a day. It is a miracle that in such bad weather they
managed to complete the maps of the region before the
coming of spring enabled the *Why Not?* to sail again from
her harbour.

With the coming of spring the thick coating of ice which
had encrusted the ship began to thaw, and large pieces would
fall on the deck from the masts and rigging. As far as
possible the crew dodged these ice falls, but there were a
few accidents, for some of the ice was heavy, and the work
of packing the stores on board again had to be completed
whatever the dangers.

At last, on November 25, after nine months of almost
continuous blizzards and gales, the little *Why Not?* was
able to sail away from Petermann Island for the second
part of her task, which was to go farther south toward the
Pole than any other ship had done.

In forcing her way through the ice the previous year
the bows of the ship had been badly battered, so that further
shocks might send the *Why Not?* and all the expedition
to the bottom of the sea, but Charcot was determined to continue his work of exploration as long as his coal lasted, and
very early in the new year he had his reward, for he sighted
a new land not marked on any map.

The ice barrier to the southward made it impossible for the *Why Not?* to reach this new country, although the attempt was made, but Charcot got near enough to survey its coast line and to feel the thrill of looking at a land which no man had ever seen before. The wonder of that discovery was worth all the hardships they had endured, and later the importance of it was recognised by the new land being christened Charcot Land.

Later in the voyage, the expedition sighted Peter Island, which had not been sighted since 1821, nearly one hundred years before.

The voyage had now added much to what is known about this far edge of the world, but the little *Why Not?* had reached a position of grave danger, for in pushing on so far she had sailed right into the thick ice pack, and it needed all the skill of Charcot and his expert navigator to get her out without disaster.

For all one day and the following night they groped their way through thick fog, which hid a sea almost covered with great icebergs. Hour after hour Charcot was on the bridge as the little ship crept forward, turning first this way, then that, to avoid collisions which would have sent her to the bottom. It was a nightmare journey. A dozen times they were within an ace of destruction. Great icebergs almost touched the yardarms and threatened to topple over and smash the ship and all in it. So the mad race to safety went on until the next day, by which time the *Why Not?* had sailed into clearer seas and the worst of the ice was behind. But it is certain that if the boat had not turned back when it did, nothing could have saved them from the sudden masses of ice that piled up in their track.

Once in safety Charcot decided to steer a course for Punta Arenas and home. The little *Why Not?* had now been among the ice for eighteen months. Her stock of coal was almost exhausted. Her crew were many of them sick and weak. The ship itself had been so badly battered by the ice that she must be completely overhauled. But their work was done.

So the *Why Not?* came home again victorious. First the tiny vessel was overhauled in South America, and the damage done in charging the icefields put right. And then the little ship which had sailed farther south from Cape Horn than any other recrossed the Atlantic and, on June 5, 1910, arrived back in France, where a great welcome awaited the greatest of all living French explorers.

While Peary, the American explorer, had been making his dash for the North Pole, and Shackleton journeying across the Pacific to attempt to reach the South Pole from the other side of the world, Commandant Jean Charcot and his gallant band had penetrated a great distance into unknown seas in one of the stormiest spots on the whole globe, had collected scientific facts of great importance, and had brought their ship safely back to port. It is because of the brilliant way in which he led this daring expedition that to-day the name of Charcot ranks among the great explorers of our time.

CHAPTER IV

THE story of how Sir Alan Cobham rose to fame is one to delight the heart of every boy. It begins not very many years ago when the airman was a flying instructor in the British Royal Air Force during the Great War. Then he began flying for the first time, and after the War he decided to take up flying as a career.

It was slow work in those early days, for there was very little civil aviation and numbers of experienced pilots were unemployed. But Cobham had faith in the future of the aeroplane and was quite content to wait his chance.

He began by organising "joy flights" up and down the country, in coöperation with another pilot. With their small savings they bought an aeroplane and set out to open their first show at Newbury.

According to Sir Alan himself, they arrived in that town "complete with one aeroplane (running well), one hammer, some copper wire, a tank full of petrol, a few shillings in our pocket and a big overdraft at the bank."

They had advertised their visit beforehand, and a small crowd gathered to see them arrive. That morning they took up sufficient passengers to buy some more petrol. They had begun—and they never looked back.

From Newbury they went on to other towns, gaining in experience day by day until when some time later they arrived at Nottingham they were taking up passengers by the hundred, and thousands of spectators visited the flying ground daily.

Money was coming in, so they helped to keep the crowds amused between flights by employing a band of twenty musicians to play each day. They also organised sports in an adjoining meadow, giving free flights as prizes, and they were the first to demonstrate the stunt of walking on the wings of the aeroplane while in flight.

Even in those days flying had its adventures. There were no advance weather forecasts to help those who were trying to keep interest in aviation alive, and when they flew across country from town to town they simply had to chance what weather they might meet on the way.

Sir Alan had his first experience of flying over mountainous country in bad weather when they moved from Stoke on Trent to Chesterfield, a route which took them over the Peak district.

Soon after starting he ran into low clouds, and as the ground became higher it necessitated flying in mist without any view whatever. Suddenly the pilot was confronted with a solid wall of cliff directly ahead. The mist hid the summit, and as he was unable to see the top, it was impossible to tell whether he could avoid it by rising. Instead Sir Alan banked hard to the left, and the aeroplane spun round and missed the cliff by a matter of feet.

That experience taught Cobham the danger of flying over high ground in a mist.

During 1919 the two airmen toured over fifty-seven different towns, finishing up with a three-weeks' Christmas show at Edinburgh. During the year they had given over ten thousand people their first experience of an aeroplane ride without mishap, a record of which Sir Alan is still rightly proud.

While they were engaged in this "joy flying" the new air routes to the Continent were being planned, and in the following year Sir Alan began his career as a long-distance civilian pilot which has since carried him to nearly every part of the world.

His first big overseas flight was made in 1921 when the company for which he was working as a pilot was asked to supply an aeroplane to carry a passenger for a tour of Europe. The first call was at Brussels, where pilot and passenger had light refreshments, arriving in Amsterdam in time for lunch.

The following morning they flew to Hamburg, where they spent a night before going on to Copenhagen and Stockholm. In Sweden Cobham found the air amazingly clear, and they were able to see cities over two hundred miles away quite clearly.

Berlin was the next stop and then Warsaw. From the Polish capital they pushed on to Prague, in Czecho-Slovakia. Vienna came next; then Milan in Italy. Afterward they flew along the blue Riviera.

That trip took three weeks, during which time they had visited fourteen countries and covered over five thousand miles, with but a small portion of each day taken up by travelling.

After this first trip Cobham made many others. Some took him to far-away Morocco; others were spent racing against the clock to get exclusive pictures of big events to some London newspaper office in record time. In all these trips he was successful. And the reason for that success was, and is, that above all things Sir Alan is a great organiser. Before making a flight over a new route he learns all about it—the contour of the land, the probable weather conditions, the landing places, the danger spots. By the time he starts off he knows all there is to be known about that particular district. It is this capacity for taking pains over the smallest journey which has since carried him safely across the world, and which will, we hope, enable him to do even greater feats for British aviation in the future.

This brief outline of Sir Alan Cobham's early days as a pilot has been written to inform you as to the experience which he had when he set out on his first really great flight. This was the record journey of over seventeen thousand miles from London to India and back—a flight which marked another milestone in the history of flying and which first showed that long-distance air routes to link up the British Empire were a possibility.

It was in November, 1924, that Cobham left London on the long air trail that carried him across Europe, Asia Minor, Irak, India, and the Himalayas to Burma and back, and which he has described in his book "Skyways." [1]

With Sir Sefton Brancker, Director of Civil Aviation (who later lost his life in the R101 disaster), as a passenger, he flew to Berlin, where he met the German Air Minister, who had several times been over London as a Zeppelin Commander. The next stop was at Warsaw, and at Lemberg they encountered fog. Here Sir Sefton Brancker decided to go on to Bucharest, in Roumania, by train in order to keep several appointments while the aeroplane was held up by the weather.

On the third morning a message came from Bucharest saying that the weather there was good and that a track had been cleared of snow on the aerodrome on which he could land, so Cobham decided to push on without delay, despite the continued fog at Lemberg.

According to his original plans, he was to follow the

[1] London, Nisbet & Co. Ltd.

valley of the river down to the plain on which Bucharest is situated, thus avoiding the Carpathians. The low levels would be wrapped in fog, but the peaks of the mountains would give him his direction, and, with fine weather at Bucharest, an easy landing should be ensured.

For a while all went well. Hour after hour Cobham flew over mountain ranges while below were the fog-filled valleys. Then to his dismay the pilot discovered that the great plain of Roumania was covered with thick fog also. From the aeroplane all he could see was a sea of cloud stretching to the horizon in every direction. And somewhere beneath that blanket lay Bucharest and the aerodrome at which he was expected to land.

There was only one chance of safety; that was to land somewhere up in the mountains where there was no fog. After a search, Cobham found a field where the aeroplane could land on soft earth without overturning. This safely accomplished, Cobham left his mechanic, Mr. A. B. Elliot (who was afterward shot by a wandering Arab in Irak during the flight to Australia), in charge of the machine while he went in search of a post-office from which he could send a message through to Bucharest, explaining his plight.

He found a post-office about two miles away, and when he entered in full flying kit, the excitement was great. The postmaster turned all customers out of the office, locked the door, and pulled all the plugs out of the telephone switchboard, thus clearing the line to Bucharest by the drastic method of cutting off every other connection.

Cobham and his engineer had to wait for two days before completing the journey down to the Roumanian capital in bright sunshine. At Bucharest they landed in the cleared way at the aerodrome, between walls of snow piled twenty feet high.

From there they flew over Bulgaria to Constantinople, and then over Asia Minor to Konia. They were now approaching a difficult stage of the journey, for their route lay across the Taurus Mountains, a wild spot where for miles the earth is a series of towering peaks and giant chasms and where there is not an inch of level ground on which an aeroplane could land without disaster.

In foul weather, with driving rain, they flew over the region, through the one and only pass, down a steep mountain gorge, with the high rocky precipices towering above and the rock walls of the chasm only a few feet away on each side of the wings. It was like driving a motor car at terrific speed down a narrow alley. Yet the bottom of that alley was five thousand feet below them, and the thick clouds hung only just above their heads.

At last they won through this region and prepared to land at Alexandretta. It was a wicked place for flying, for the currents of air from the mountains behind them caused violent bumps, during which the baggage in the cabin was moving about, despite scientific packing, and the passengers' heads were constantly hitting the roof.

However, a good landing was made, and the following morning they flew on to Aleppo, afterward going by easy stages to Bagdad and Basra.

Here Cobham experienced carburettor trouble which baffled the airman and his engineer for some time. It was not until they had dismantled the petrol system that they discovered the cause; a spider had crawled into the air intake during the night and had got lodged in one of the jets.

The bad weather which had persisted all the way out from England still continued, and they crossed the desolate swamps of the Persian Gulf in low cloud and fog. For a hundred miles there was scarcely any sign of life. The coun-

try was just one great swamp, with an occasional lonely
hut dotting the landscape. It would have been terrible country in which to land and no one was sorry when they reached
Bushire.

They had still fifteen hundred miles of travelling to do
before reaching India, but the worst of the journey was
over.

Near Bundas Abbas they passed over a district where the
oxides in the soil had turned the earth into vivid colours.
One hill would be amber; close by a mountain loomed brilliant blue, and another shone jade green in the sunlight.
It was that Cobham describes as "like a gigantic builders' colour yard."

As they neared India the weather began at last to im-
prove and Karachi was reached in brilliant sunshine, with
cloudless blue skies.

In India they visited Delhi, Allahabad, Calcutta, and other
cities. At Calcutta Sir Sefton Brancker was taken ill with
a severe chill, and while waiting for his recovery Cobham
decided to survey the possibilities of an air route to Dar-
jeeling, the town up in the Himalayas to which white people
in India go during the hot weather if they possibly can.

Elliot was sent ahead to report on a possible landing
place at Jalpaiguri, a town at the foot of the mountains,
and upon hearing that this was possible, Cobham flew north.

It was the first time that an aeroplane had been seen in
that part of the world, and the natives came for miles
around to examine the curious machine. When Cobham
landed, their enthusiasm could not be kept within bounds,
and they broke through all the barriers and rushed for the
aeroplane.

A handful of Gurkha soldiers fought hard to keep them
back when it looked as though the wings would be dam-

aged, but it was not until a detachment of elephants had been rushed to the scene and these huge beasts walked gently round the aeroplane that the crowd was pressed back.

The following morning Cobham set out on an aerial reconnaissance of Mount Everest. He flew quite close to the mountain, but a rising bank of cloud made flying dangerous at such an altitude and on the principle of "safety first," they returned to the aerodrome after a flight of four hours, during which a magnificent view of the great Himalayas had been obtained.

Back at Calcutta, they picked up Sir Sefton Brancker, now happily recovered from his illness, and set out for Rangoon, in Burma. For a day they were flying over dense jungle which grew right to the water's edge. Toward evening Rangoon came into view, with its wonderful gold pagoda lit up by the rays of the setting sun. Here they landed. They had reached the end of their outward journey. For nearly eight thousand miles they had flown over deserts, mountains, and ocean without a mishap to man or machine.

After a halt of two days the journey home was begun and this was accomplished in record time. At one stage they crossed the Libyan Desert in absolute comfort in six hours —a journey which ten years ago took a motor car thirty hours of hot dusty travel.

The whole of that great flight was made in one aeroplane with the same engine throughout—a wonderful proof of the superior quality of British engineering. The flight proved that a skilled pilot could fly continuously in bad weather with perfect safety. Neither rain nor cloud held up Cobham at any stage of the journey.

It is not surprising that Cobham should wish to repeat

his fine achievement. How he did so is now history. First came the great flight to South Africa and back across uncharted Africa, and then the greatest flight of all—on which this one pilot flew the same machine with the same engine from London to Australia and back.

It was early in the Australian flight that Mr. A. B. Elliot, the engineer who had made the Indian flight with Cobham, was shot by a wandering Arab who, startled at the sudden appearance of an aeroplane in the Irak desert, fired at it. This tragedy greatly upset Cobham, but he did not abandon the flight which so many millions of people both at home and in Australia were following with such interest. After delays, he pressed on again, and Sydney was safely reached.

On the way back bad weather forced him to land his seaplane on the sea beside a lonely uninhabited island in the Pacific, where terrific rains which obscured his view held him up for precious days.

For one whole day the famous pilot was "missing." No one knew where he was, or whether he was safe. But happily, as soon as the weather made flying possible, he pushed on and reached the aerodrome toward which he had been flying when forced to descend on the sea.

For this magnificent achievement, together with his Indian and African flights, Cobham was made a Knight of the British Empire—an honour which every one agreed to be richly deserved.

It is a long way from those early days of "joy riding" described at the beginning of this chapter to the world-wide fame which Sir Alan Cobham now enjoys. But he is not yet contented. It is his belief that the day when the farthest parts of the Empire will be linked by regular air lines is fast approaching, and he is planning fresh flights which

SIR ALAN COBHAM   54

LIEUT.-COLONEL P. T. ETHERTON PHOTOGRAPHED
IN SIBERIAN DRESS 55

will help to blaze the trail for the pilots who are to operate these air routes of to-morrow.

These fresh flights will be as carefully planned as those of the past, and they will be as useful to the future of aviation. For Sir Alan does not believe in "stunts." To fly over the Atlantic Ocean in order to create a sensation does not seem worth while to him, but to fly from Ireland to Canada to survey a possible route for an aeroplane service linking London with Ottawa may be one of the flights he will attempt in the near future.

Meanwhile he has well earned his popularity, for among all the famous airmen of to-day none has rendered finer services to his country or to the cause of aviation all over the world than Sir Alan Cobham.

CHAPTER V

O F all living travellers and explorers there is none
who knows more about the unknown heart of Asia
than Lieutenant Colonel P. T. Etherton, F.R.G.S.,
F.Z.S., the British soldier who has travelled extensively in
every corner of the world, and whose greatest feat was a
wonderful journey of four thousand miles across the Roof
of the World through India, Kashmir, Gilget, Chinese Turkestan, Mongolia, and Siberia.

Among other fine feats of exploration, Colonel Etherton
is one of five white men who have visited Ordam Padshah,
the Holy City of Central Asia. Only the modesty of this
traveller has prevented his name from becoming a house-
hold word. But Colonel Etherton has confined his lectures
to the learned societies and apart from his two books
"Across the Roof of the World" and "The Heart of Asia"[1]
this was the first account of his adventures to be published.

It was on March 15, 1909, that Lieutenant Colonel
Etherton bade good-bye to his comrades of the Indian
Army and set out—on a bicycle—over the first mile of
his record journey across the heart of the most unknown
and difficult country in the world.

Before him lay certain difficulties. The path of his expedition lay across the Pamirs, that vast mountainous region fitly termed "the Roof of the World," and having an

[1] Constable and Company, Ltd.

average height of thirteen thousand feet. Hundreds of miles farther north were the Thian Shan, a grand chain of mountains rarely visited by white men. Beyond these were the wind-swept plains of Northern Turkestan and the desolate Mongolian steppes. Truly it was an awe-inspiring journey.

Of necessity, the watchword for the expedition was "mobility." Everything taken was cut down as low as possible to facilitate rapid marching. For his personal use the traveller took butter, pearl barley, jam, baking powder, corn flour, custard powder, soup squares, cocoa, vermicelli, tinned fruits, jellies, Bovril, and saxin, or sugar in tabloid form.

Tents, cooking utensils, medicines—everything was cut down to a minimum and loaded on to yaks, the beasts of burden in this remote part of the world.

Add to these supplies an orderly, a cook, and an odd man, and the expedition was complete.

The orderly selected by Colonel Etherton was Rifleman Giyan Sing, and he was the only man to remain with the traveller from the first step to the last. Eleven and a half months after the start, Colonel Etherton and Giyan Sing arrived at Flushing, in Holland, and the Indian orderly saw the sea for the first time. A day or so later he was astounded at the "discovery" of London, with its vast population of more people than he had imagined existed in the world.

The first stage of the journey lay across the Tragbal pass to Gilget. This route, because of the danger of avalanches and snow slides, is not used before May. But Colonel Etherton had secured permission to make the attempt earlier in order to get as far as possible before meeting bad weather, and after climbing four thousand feet in eight miles, with his stores carried by coolies, he began the ascent of the Tragbal Pass on March 31.

It is a lonely region, over eleven thousand feet above sea level. There are no tracks except those made by the footsteps of the post-runners who carry the mails through during the bad weather.

Part of the way the path lies through a narrow ravine, the sides of which are so precipitous that it seems impossible that snow could cling to them. Here it is said that even the vibration of the air caused by speaking is sufficient to dislodge and bring down an avalanche of snow from the sides of the hills, and the expedition had to file through the ravine in complete silence in order to reach safety.

During the night it freezes hard in this region and there is therefore less chance of being buried by avalanches during the first hours after dawn. The next morning, therefore, the expedition set out at four o'clock in the hope of doing a long march before the sun brought down snowslides. The going was heavy. Frequently the men had to climb over avalanches of snow which had fallen during the previous few days.

More than once new avalanches, big enough to have engulfed a house, just missed the little band, but Etherton pushed steadily on, determined not to waste time.

The night was spent in a small telegraph hut used by those whose duty it was to repair the telegraph lines when broken by avalanches and landslides, and at six o'clock the next morning they were off again.

The track led them into deep valleys, shut in by towering mountains, and the leader knew that at any moment a thundering roar of flying snow might bring the expedition to a sudden end.

It was late in the day when it happened. Suddenly a huge mass of snow came thundering down just as the four men were passing, cutting off Colonel Etherton and his orderly from the coolies following behind. The great white mass came hurtling down in one irresistible sweep, bringing in its wake trees, rocks and *débris* of all descriptions. Luckily Etherton and his orderly were able to race out of the way in the nick of time, while the coolies found shelter under the lee of a depression in the hillside.

Later, Colonel Etherton heard that a few hours before he passed through that valley two post-runners had been overwhelmed by a similar avalanche and killed.

There was a second peril to be faced in this region. This was the crossing of the rivers by means of snow bridges, which are simply masses of snow and drift ice that have fallen into the rivers and frozen solid.

A few hours after escaping the avalanche, the expedition was crossing one of these bridges when it collapsed, and left them all struggling in the foaming torrent below. Fortunately all escaped without anything worse than bruises due to being dashed against rocks and boulders during the scramble ashore.

Once through the mountains, the expedition reached Gilget, the remote region northwest of Kashmir which in winter is often shut off from the world for weeks at a time.

There Colonel Etherton was entertained by the Mir of Hunza, the local chieftain, before turning his steps toward the Pamirs, and the Roof of the World.

A few miles beyond the Hunza Valley the expedition reached the Kanjut River and crossed the mighty Batur Glacier. This wall of advancing ice threatens to block up the whole valley. Year by year it creeps steadily onward, nothing being capable of stemming its irresistible march. The crossing took some time, the surface being much broken with crevasses and cracks of a forbidding nature.

The whole region is a fearsome place—enclosed in towering heights which form a mighty canyon, which, were it more accessible to travellers, would be one of the sights of the world. The whole region is almost barren. There are no trees, and wood is brought up from the river banks lower down the valley. Bare rocky mountains and the entire absence of foliage make it a place to get out of as quickly as possible.

Beyond the valleys the route led across the Roof of the World by way of the Mintake Pass, one of the only two passes over the Pamirs. Fortunately, after cold weather and snow which had sent the two coolies down with fever, the sun came out on the morning that Colonel Etherton had decided to cross over the mountains, and at noon the expedition reached the summit, 15,430 feet above sea level.

Standing on the crest line Etherton saw the cairn of stones erected to mark the boundary line between the British and Chinese empires. He had reached the farthest point of British influence; ahead lay the weird dominions of the great Yellow Empire. And the road leading to it consisted of a vast inhospitable region of mountains piled range upon range.

The cold in this region is extreme, while winds of hurricane force are frequently experienced. Here, among the scattered inhabitants of the region, it is a case of the survival of the fittest, for only the strongest constitutions can resist the Arctic severity of the long winter months.

After sliding and tobogaining down from the summit the expedition found the first Chinese official, who had secured yaks with their drivers as transport for the stores. There Colonel Etherton paid off his coolies.

The yaks soon proved their worth, for a short march farther northward the party came to a river swollen by melting snows and running with the force of a Niagara.

Standing on one bank it seemed impossible for man or beast to secure a foothold in that rushing torrent. Yet crossed it must be before the journey could be resumed.

Colonel Etherton led the way and with the aid of the yaks the raging cataract was safely crossed. At the spot chosen for the crossing the ravine rose on either side in solid walls fifteen hundred feet high, while the noise of the river was so deafening that to make oneself heard at all needed a voice like a foghorn.

A valley littered with great boulders through which even the yaks found it difficult to pick their way was the next problem which the explorer had to solve, and then came the crossing of the Yarkland River, after which the road lay open to Chinese Turkestan.

The expedition was now crossing the Roof of the World and each day's march meant much climbing up and down. Going up was bad, but going down was worse, for the tracks zigzagged so steeply that there was a danger of boulders dislodged from above falling on to the leaders of the party below.

Added to this were the difficulties caused by the rarity of the atmosphere at this height, which put a great strain upon men and animals alike, and caused their hearts to beat like sledge hammers. Often Colonel Etherton found it difficult to breathe after the slightest exertion.

Before they had reached the topmost summit of all, one of the ponies had to be left behind, as, although walking unladen, the poor beast could not gather the energy to get along in the rarefied air.

The last four hundred feet meant a supreme effort, for the slope approaching the summit was so nearly perpendicular that it seemed impossible to climb it with the laden beasts. But patience and perseverance had their reward and at a quarter past four that day Colonel Etherton stood on the summit and after taking reckonings with his instruments found that he was 17,400 feet above sea level—an achievement of which the most experienced climber might well be proud.

From the summit of old Asia a grand view was obtained, a mighty panorama of peaks and glaciers stretching away north and south as far as the eye could reach. Snow-capped heights towered up to twenty-six thousand feet.

The descent was made in drifting mist which shut out every view and made the going even more treacherous than it is in fair weather. One yak, laden with valuable stores and photographic plates, missed its footing and crashed down into the ravine hundreds of feet below, but this was the only casualty and at last, after sixteen hours' continuous heavy work, the little band was able to camp with the knowledge that the highest pass had been conquered.

The next day Colonel Etherton paid off the carriers who had left their homes to cross the roof of the world and "signed on" a fresh batch with new yaks in place of the travel-wearied beasts. It was well that he did so, for that day the track he had to follow compelled him to ford one river no fewer than twenty-six times before nightfall.

However, to set against this inconvenience was the fact that down in the valleys the air was warmer and breathing easier.

At the beginning of the next climb—to the summit of the Kara Dawan or Black Pass—shepherds were met who told Colonel Etherton that he was the first white man ever seen in that region. Upon learning that he was making the journey in order to explore the region and shoot game, they expressed great surprise that any one should undergo such hardships for the sake of "having a look round."

The next day the expedition crossed the Black Pass, fourteen thousand feet high, and also the Sandal Pass, which meant a climb of sixteen thousand feet above sea level. The crossing of these two passes in one day was a record, and the reader will realise how great was the endurance necessary to travel from the one camp site to the other between daylight and dark. Frequently for miles there was no suitable level ground on which even the smallest tent could be erected, and to be caught in such a region before the journey's end meant a night of discomfort.

Fresh yaks were again secured and shortly after crossing the Sandal Pass the track fell to six thousand feet and brought them into the climate of a perfect English summer day, with their road leading through trees and cultivated land—a strange and welcome contrast to the lonely gaunt regions of mountain and snow which they had been traversing for so long. How restful it seemed to the weary white man and his Indian orderly,—and how pleasant to reflect that they had accomplished their first objective. They had crossed successfully the bleakest and most desolate spot on the face of this globe.

Even where the sun shines on green trees, however, the weather plays strange tricks in unknown Asia, and the next morning the march was interrupted by a sandstorm which made any progress impossible. The clouds of whirling dust often left the travellers in utter darkness and made it impossible to do anything but turn the ponies round and sit covered with coats to keep out the driving grit. Even so, Colonel Etherton spent some time after the storm had abated picking stones and dirt out of his eyes! He had exchanged the mountain pass for the desert and now he did not know which he liked best.

A few more marches, and the crossing of the Yarkland River in flat-bottomed boats brought Colonel Etherton to Yarkland, in Chinese Turkestan, where he caused a sensation by going to dine with the Chinese Governor in the full uniform of a British Army Officer—a sight rarely seen because of the arduous nature of the journey from Kashmir.

Now began marches in strange contrast to the climbing of a fortnight before. For some days Colonel Etherton and his companions covered over thirty miles a day, mounted on ponies. They were weary days spent travelling over the same sand and scrub-covered plains with occasional stretches of muddy and swampy ground. It was heavy going and tiring for both men and horses, and the traveller was not sorry when he found himself approaching the Great Yulduz Valley, despite its reputation for being the haunt of robber bands.

In the Yulduz Valley the lone white traveller wished to buy a fresh batch of horses. At first sight that seemed an easy matter, for the whole valley was filled with horses, but upon enquiry Colonel Etherton was informed that they were all the property of the Khan, the local chieftain, and the Khan lived at the other end of the valley, some miles away.

There followed a day and night journey to the Khan's camp in order to arrange the purchase. The Khan was away from home on a mysterious visit, which was not so mysterious when Colonel Etherton learned that it is the custom to poison each Khan when he attains the age of twenty-five,—just the age the Khan had reached two days after he disappeared! However, the Khan's mother proved an agreeable old lady and Colonel Etherton got the horses he needed.

While travelling down the Tzanma Valley—the next

stage of his journey—Colonel Etherton met a Kazak native who rode up to him and enquired whether he were Russian. Upon learning that he was British, the man shook him warmly by the hand and said, "During my travels in Russian Central Asia I have heard of the might and power of Britain and I always wanted to meet a native of that country." The incident is interesting, showing as it does how the good name of the British Empire has spread to the most remote parts of the world—further than newspapers—further than posts or telegraphs.

In this region Colonel Etherton stayed for some time, hunting wapiti and ibex, and getting good sport, and the season was well advanced when the expedition turned northward once more.

The weather was cold now, and often more suited to the Arctic Circle than Central Asia. Apart from rains and frost, however, the marches were uneventful during the closing days of October and until the expedition climbed the Talki Pass and gazed down beyond on the Sairam Nor, a vast sheet of blue water surrounded by high mountains and forming an inland sea over twenty miles long which few Europeans have ever seen. On the shores of this lake wild horses were sighted but it proved impossible to get within four hundred yards of them.

Beyond this inland sea Colonel Etherton entered some of the most desolate country in the world. For mile after mile there was nothing but low rocky hills—without a bush or blade of grass; without a bird or an animal. Day after day there was nothing to temper the loneliness of that desolate region. The silence became oppressive and in the month of November, with the country already in the grip of winter, the solitude seemed accentuated.

This was Western Mongolia, and during November and

December, while the expedition slowly made their way across this region, the wind shrieked and howled across the desolate plains as it can do only on the steppes of Central Asia.

Midway on this march a halt at the town of Chugachak, just across the Russian border, was a welcome relief, and the white traveller was hospitably received by the authorities, who warned him, however, of the risks of proceeding farther northward now that the snows had come and winter in its full severity gripped the land.

Colonel Etherton's intention was to continue his journey until he reached the Trans-Siberian Railway, and he therefore thanked his Russian friends for their advice—and set off northward.

The ground was now frozen hard, and all the rivers solid smooth ice over which the pack ponies slipped and slithered at every step. Eighteen miles a day was a good journey for this region—to be followed by nights when frequently, despite the stoves found in every wayside house, the traveller slept with over thirty degrees of frost in his room!

Day after day the expedition pushed across the frozen plains in temperatures averaging fifteen degrees below zero. It was just mile after mile of desolation relieved only by the ruins of villages deserted owing to frequent attacks from robber bands which had driven the former inhabitants away.

Blizzards reminiscent of the Antarctic persisted, and by now Colonel Etherton realised that the journey from India to Siberia is one that cannot be conveniently made in a single year. However, having got so far, he decided to complete his march across Asia.

The daily marches had to be carefully planned now, for there was an almost total absence of wood for fires, and to be caught out in the open without means of obtaining warmth might easily have meant death.

It was during nights spent in Mongol camps in this region that Colonel Etherton saw for himself the sturdy upbringing which had made the Mongols the hardy race they are. More than once he saw children of six and eight years of age sleeping peacefully and apparently comfortably in fifty degrees of frost—a temperature which would cause a British boy of an older age to huddle over a fire all night.

The expedition had arrived at the Black Irtish Valley when the caravan men—Kazak natives whom Colonel Etherton had hired to lead the ponies and handle the stores —struck work and declared that they would go no farther.

They commenced to throw the stores to the ground. It was an anxious moment, for mutiny amid the steppes might easily have meant death to Colonel Etherton and his orderly —the only man upon whom he could rely to stand by him.

In desperation the solitary white man thrashed the ringleader among the mutineers. The action had the hoped-for effect, the rest of the carriers changed their minds and decided to continue the journey.

Christmas Day was spent at Shara Sumbe, a small village at the very foot of the Great Altai Mountains, the last great range which the expedition had to cross. Colonel Etherton celebrated the festival "far from the madding crowd" by calling on the Hsei Tai, or officer commanding the garrison, who in turn honoured the first British officer he had ever received by ordering his bugler to blow a tune of welcome on an old German bugle which gave forth curious and ear-splitting noises.

After leaving this interesting and isolated township the

weather became steadily worse, ending in a blizzard, which caught the expedition out on the open steppes.

The strength of the wind was terrific, driving the snow in dense clouds so that the ponies, unable to stand such a battle of the elements, turned round and refused to face the blast. It seemed impossible that anything could withstand such a wind, and hardly any progress was made before nightfall caused the temperature to drop still lower.

At last Colonel Etherton reached a small log hut which offered some shelter from the storm. By that time Giyan's hands were badly frost-bitten and several of the carriers declared they were too ill to proceed further.

The next day several of the invalids, and particularly the orderly, were so bad that it became necessary for Colonel Etherton to retrace his steps to Shara Sumbe in order to get fresh passports which would enable the expedition to reach Zaisan, a small Russian military post where medical aid might be secured.

It was a dreadful ride across frozen plains, and before reaching the shelter of the town Etherton was suffering severely from frost bite in the right leg and knee, and also hands.

The local commander called in a Chinese doctor to attend to the white invalid. The yellow medico came armed with weird plasters and poultices which did not, however, prevent the frozen limbs from swelling most painfully.

When at last a start was made for the Russian military post, Colonel Etherton was so badly off that he had to obtain a carriage drawn by two horses in which he could ride. The local roads, however, made that method of progress rather more painful than walking, and after the vehicle had capsized twice, it was abandoned, and he finished that day's march on foot.

The rest of that last march is a story of long weary treks across endless snow-bound plains, every minute of which was made agony by the frozen limbs and the intense cold.

At last they reached the frontier of Siberia and were able to secure fresh horses and sledges, on which the remainder of the journey to Zaisan was safely accomplished.

There a doctor was found, and Colonel Etherton underwent operations to save his frost-bitten limbs by the grafting of new skin. It was largely due to the skill of this Russian surgeon that neither the Colonel nor his gallant Indian orderly suffered any amputation of limbs after their terrible experience.

Once the invalids were well again, arrangements were made to complete their record march across unknown Asia by a sledge journey to the Trans-Siberian Railway. Travelling by sledge was a delight after the terrible marches across the frozen steppes that lay behind, although temperatures of seventy-six degrees of frost were met with before the railway was reached.

This last stage meant sledging for eight hundred miles through a most inhospitable region, but the smooth hard snow made the route an easy one. Owing to the low temperatures, however, Colonel Etherton was frost-bitten again before he reached the end of the journey. No number of fur coats and rugs seemed able to keep out the intense cold.

Further days spent travelling through dense forests inhabited by packs of marauding wolves brought the weary traveller at last to the railway.

"As the sledges neared the station," Colonel Etherton wrote in his diary, "I realised the long journey was over. For nearly a year I had been marching across mountain ranges, over interminable plains, and across the mighty steppes of Mongolia and Siberia, lands of desolation, as they might well be in midwinter. I mentally reviewed the results of such an undertaking, the regions I had traversed, the strange and interesting tribes I had encountered, the superb shooting I had enjoyed in the heart of Asia, the journey accomplished which no man had ever done before.

"The bell warned travellers to board the train. The last good-byes were said, and the next moment the train rumbled out of the station over the silent snow-covered wilderness on the way to Moscow—and England. The long trek was over."

NATIVE PORTERS CARRYING THE EQUIPMENT OF THE
EXPEDITION OVER THE PAMIRS, 17,400 FEET ABOVE
SEA-LEVEL   70

SEALS BASKING OFF CAPE EVANS—THE ICELOCKED POINT IN THE ANTARCTIC NAMED
AFTER CAPTAIN EVANS

CHAPTER VI

O F all the stories of real life adventure of our generation there is not one that equals, as a simple story
of courage, heroism, and endurance, the immortal
story of the Scott Expedition to the South Pole, in which
Captain Robert Falcon Scott succeeded in reaching the
Pole with four companions only to perish with that brave
little band amid the silent wastes of the Antarctic Continent on their way back.

Do you remember those last lines, written while Scott
was dying in the frozen South:

Had we lived, I should have had a tale to tell of the hardi-
hood, endurance, and courage of my companions which
would have stirred the heart of every Englishman. These
rough notes and our dead bodies must tell the tale, but
surely, surely a great rich country like ours will see that
those who are dependent on us are properly provided for.

The story of Captain Scott's dash for the Pole, and
the disaster which overtook the tiny band on their way back
has been told many times. It is not included in this book
because every British boy has read it, or heard it.

In this chapter you are going to read the story of another member of the Scott Expedition who was the last
man to see Scott alive, and who, after nearly losing his own
life, lived to take command of the survivors and bring the
expedition safely back to England.

F

This is Vice-Admiral E. R. G. R. Evans, one of the greatest of living British explorers, who after taking part in several Antarctic expeditions, and being the hero of the *Broke* fight off Dover during the war, when he won the Distinguished Service Order for fighting and sinking two German destroyers with his one little ship, became captain of H.M.S. *Repulse*.[1]

Evans has faced death many times in his life. He faced it when he went to the frozen South for the first time at the age of twenty-one and was nearly drowned through falling off an ice floe. He faced it in the Pacific when he swam to a steamer piled up on the rocks to get a line on board to save its crew, and thus won the only Gold Medal for life-saving ever awarded to a sailor by Lloyd's. And he faced death many times during the Great War.

But never has this daring explorer been quite so close to a terrible death as he was during the record sledge journey that he made to within one hundred miles of the South Pole with Captain Scott and his companions. It is the great story of that long, long march that you are going to read.

It began on January 4, 1912, when, in the midst of the white silence that surrounds the neighbourhood of the South Pole, Evans and his two companions, named Tom Crean and William Lashly, stood watching Scott and his band pushing southward to the Pole, and gave them three cheers—little realising that those cheers were the last sounds of the outside world those ill-fated men would hear.

Captain Evans and two companions had hauled a loaded sledge for seven hundred and fifty miles across the

---

[1] When this chapter was written Vice-Admiral Evans held the rank of Captain, but it should be noted that at the time when he was serving with Scott he was still a Lieutenant.

ice and snow so that the food depôts might be prepared for the return journey of Scott's party. Just before saying 'Good-bye' Scott had asked Captain Evans to give up one of his men to increase the chances of the South Pole being reached. Thus Lieutenant Bowers had joined Scott's little band, and Evans was left with his two companions to face the lonely trail of seven hundred and fifty miles back to the ship lying at the edge of the ice—and safety.

They were then over ten thousand feet above sea level, upon the bleak, silent plateau that is the very edge of the world. There the three men stood by their sledge and watched the Polar party, little black specks in the snow, until Scott and his men disappeared and they were alone.

After the first day's march towards home Evans realised that with only two men, nine hours' sledge-hauling each day would be insufficient to get them back to the ship before food ran out. He explained the position to his two companions and they agreed cheerfully to march for twelve hours each day. It was a tremendous feat in such a climate, but it was necessary if they were to complete the main part of their journey while fit and thus provide for emergencies in the shape of ice crevasses, scurvy, blizzards, and other things which might delay them later on.

Day after day they fought their way northward over the high polar tableland. The silence was ghastly, for beyond the sound of their own voices and the groaning of the sledge runners when the surface was bad, there was no noise whatever to remind them of the outer world.

Three days after saying 'Good-bye' to Scott they encountered a blizzard and were forced to continue their marches although faced with navigational difficulties which made it impossible for them to maintain more than a rough northward direction.

Muffled up tightly in their windproof clothing, they did all in their power to prevent the dust-fine snowflakes which whirled around from penetrating into the tiniest opening in their clothes. The blizzard blinded and baffled them, forcing them to turn their faces from it, for the stinging wind cut and slashed their cheeks like the constant jab of a thousand frozen needle points.

At the end of the blizzard they found themselves considerably out of their course, but in spite of the blizzard, a temperature of twenty-eight degrees below zero, and the fact that these men had already trudged for seven hundred and fifty miles across the ice and snow, they had covered nineteen, nineteen, and sixteen miles on three successive days of terrible weather.

The blizzard was followed by some days of hazy weather, during which it was difficult to find the course, and when the weather cleared, Captain Evans and his two companions found themselves at the top of the Shackleton Ice Falls— high cliffs of gleaming ice—which barred their path and which, had they been able to keep to the correct route, they would have avoided.

Now came the first adventure. Far below them was the Beardmore Glacier, which they must reach to descend on to the ice barrier and thus get home. But it was hundreds of feet below, and they must choose one of two alternatives: either to march right around the ice falls and thus lose valuable days which they could not spare if food was to last, or to take their lives in their hands and toboggan on their sledge right over the falls and trust to luck that they would reach the bottom alive.

To go over the falls meant terrific drops in places, but they decided to risk it and with sinking hearts the descent of the ice falls was begun, with special ice spikes strapped

CAPTAIN EVANS IN POLAR KIT   74

THE CAMP UNDER "CLOUDMAKER" MOUNTAIN ON THE BEARDMORE GLACIER to their fur boots to help them to obtain a foothold and steady the sledge.

Carefully they guided the sledge through the maze of hummocks and crevasses, or chasms, in the ice. They were still harnessed to the sledge, because it was their one chance of life if, as was probable, one or the other slipped down a crevasse. So when the sledge got on to a nice shiny piece of ice and charged forward, it would sweep them off their feet. Thus they encountered fall after fall, while bruises, cuts and abrasions were collected with startling rapidity; but they stuck to it patiently because it meant saving three whole days, and that might mean saving their lives if they were delayed by weather or accident later on.

The whole morning was spent working toward the more even surface of the glacier itself, but the actual steep part of the Shackleton Ice Falls was accomplished in under half an hour, during which they dropped many hundred feet.

At one time during the thrilling descent the speed of the sledge was over sixty miles an hour! And this amid yawning chasms in the ice which might swallow up sledge and adventurers at any moment.

It was impossible to brake down those steep blue ice slopes for the sledge had taken charge and any attempt to stop it would have meant broken bones. So they held on for their lives, lying on the sledge face downward. Toward the bottom of that slope the sledge leapt into the air—they had left the ice and shot over a deep crevasse which they did not know existed. For one second they were in the air. Then they crashed on the ice ridge beyond the crevasse, the sledge capsized and rolled over, dragging the three men with it, and finally came to a standstill.

How they ever escaped uninjured was a miracle. They examined themselves and found no bones broken. Then they looked over the sledge and found that a piece of ice had caught into a ski-stick during their "flight" and torn it from the straps that held it. That ski-stick had dropped down the deep ice chasm over which they had come, and they looked oddly at each other as they thought of what might have been their fate.

When Evans had taken stock of their position, he found that they were almost back on the Beardmore Glacier again and that their bold escapade had saved them three precious days of foot slogging—and that amount of food.

So to celebrate it, they pitched their tent, had a good meal, and then, delighted with their progress, marched on until 8 P. M.

That night in their sleeping bags they nursed their bruises, but being in perfect condition, these did not prevent them from sound slumber. And in the morning, when they looked back at the treacherous "Crystal Palace" over which they had come, the troubles and bumps were forgotten. The first stage—and the worst stage—of their march was over. So they thought. And so it would have been but for bad luck which lay ahead.

It was a wonderful day, and they were off at 4.45 A. M. on the next lap of their journey down the Beardmore Glacier. Six hours' hauling on the sledge brought them to the Upper Glacier Depôt, where they replenished their stores, and soon started on the march again.

It was very warm that night, for the temperature rose to zero, or only thirty-two degrees of frost. The warmth caused the three tired men to sleep soundly, and it was eight o'clock before they got away the next morning. However, the surface of the ice was in fine condition and at the end of the day they had covered twenty-two miles.

The next day they did between eighteen and twenty miles

and camped among pressure ridges and huge crevasses, but still only fourteen miles from the Cloudmaker Depôt, the next supply dump, which Evans expected to reach easily the following day.

Consequently they were all very happy at the thought of their fine progress, and with the added luxury that the warm weather had dried their clothes and sleeping bags. Before turning in Captain Evans took a look out of the tent. Although it was then 10 P. M. the sun was still visible at the southward and there was not a cloud in the sky.

By 6 o'clock the next morning the tent had been struck, the sledge packed and they were on the march again. Another day had begun—a day which, although it was before the war, none of those three men are likely to forget.

They began unluckily, for low clouds had spread like a tablecloth over the glacier and filled it with mist. This added tremendously to the difficulties of steering, for they had no landmarks by which to correct their course. They could judge the approximate direction with the aid of the sledging compass, and had to be content with that. And a sledging compass is not a sure guide when you are making for a tiny dump of stores fourteen miles away, in the midst of a mighty land of eternal ice.

Because of the mist it was impossible to keep the sledge on the clear blue surface, down which they could have made their way had the weather been fine and a clear view obtainable. Instead, the party soon found themselves going over rougher ice, while the air remained thick with tiny ice crystals, through which great hummocks of ice loomed weirdly.

Soon Captain Evans realised that they were getting into trouble. They fell about a good deal and to his consternation the surface got steadily worse. Huge crevasses began to loom up and all signs of anything like level ground disappeared. Imagine trying to man-haul a sledge weighing four hundred pounds over a surface of this description. It was terrible work. Every yard meant patience and tireless effort, but the three hardened explorers achieved by stubborn purpose what would have been impossible to the ordinary man.

It was no good going back, and they could not tell whether the good track was on the right or the left of their line of advance. So they pressed on and hoped that the sun would disperse the mist and enable them to find a way out of the terrible ice before their strength failed. The uncertain light worried all three and they had to take off their snow goggles to see to advance at all. But those three men had the hearts of lions and they just would not let bad luck daunt them.

At midday the mist showed signs of dispersing, and as they were by that time pretty near exhausted, Evans decided to camp and eat lunch while waiting for the mist to disperse.

With the greatest difficulty they found among the hummocky ice a place to set up their tent and gloomily they sat down to a cooker full of tea.

An hour later the mist had partly cleared and they could make out the shapes of high mountains which so few human eyes had ever seen. Warmed by the tea and cheered by the better weather, they repacked the tent and started off once more. Evans did think about going back, but it was clearly impossible. For one thing they simply had to reach the next supply depôt and get food. For another they were now too exhausted to haul the heavy sledge up to the place where they had camped the previous night, even if they could have found it.

For hours they fought doggedly on, sometimes overcoming crevasses by bridging them with the sledge. If the crevasse was too wide to be crossed they worked along the bank until they found an ice bridge along which they could go to the other side.

As the sun's rays grew more powerful, the visibility became perfect and their hearts sank. Around them, stretching as far as the eye could reach, was the most disheartening wilderness of pressure ridges, ice disturbances, and broken surface. They were in the heart of the Great Ice Fall which is to be found halfway down the Beardmore Glacier. Still they struggled on, though if they had not been in superb physical training, all three would have collapsed. Again and again they literally carried the sledge over the rough ice—and it weighed nearly four hundred pounds!

Hours later they were still in the same plight, while the crevasses became wider and wider, necessitating long journeys to the right and left of their line of march in order to find some means of crossing them.

At 8 o'clock that evening they were travelling on a ridge between two stupendous open gulfs, and they found a connecting bridge. Cross that bridge they must in order to reach the undulations which terminated the broken ice, for it would save them a mile or two of marching, and by this time their legs were giving way under them. But it was a precarious proceeding.

They paused for a breath and then placed the sledge on the ice ridge which connected the two sides of the crevasse. The ridge was so narrow that Lashly, who went first, dared not walk upright or look down into the black chasm below. He actually sat astride the ridge and was paid out at the end of an Alpine rope.

Eventually he reached the other side and climbed the slope before him. The next task was to get the sledge across. This was done by Lashly pulling gently from the opposite slope, while Evans and Crean held on the sledge sides, balancing it carefully, and pushed it across. It was one of the most exciting moments in their lives, as Captain Evans still admits, for at any moment the sledge might have toppled off that narrow ledge and carried Evans and Crean into the depths of the crevasse in its fall.

Inch by inch, with infinite care, they got it across those terrible feet of ice until at last they reached the other side and Lashly held the sledge while Evans and Crean crawled up beside him. Then all three pulled the sledge on to firm ice. We have mentioned before that the sledge weighed four hundred pounds, and the strain of hauling it up on to the ridge tested the three exhausted men to the limit of their strength.

Without stopping to rest they "harnessed up" again and tramped on. The outlook was still black. Food was nearly gone. They were all exhausted and their eyes pained horribly from the glare and glint of the sun's reflections from that awful maze of ice falls.

There seemed no way out of the wilderness of crevasses and broken ice. No room could be found to pitch the tent and to stagger farther with that laden sledge was impossible. To leave it behind hundreds of miles from help meant death.

Evans now realised that if their lives were to be saved there would have to be a change of tactics. Accordingly he ordered a halt. Each began to wonder what was in store. Their throats were dry and they could not speak. They were done. The great strength of perfectly fit men, hardened by months in the Antarctic, had been used up to the last ounce, and still they had not reached the depôt where the food they needed would be found.

Captain Evans got up from the sledge, took off his harness, and said, "I am going to look for a way out. We can't go on."

At first Lashly and Crean tried to persuade their commander not to leave the party. It was too dangerous, they said, to walk about such treacherous ground unroped; but Evans pointed out that it was impossible for them to continue in their exhausted condition.

If only they could find a camping place and rest, they might gather strength for one final attempt to reach the depôt. At any rate, in their state at that moment they were quite unfit to face the final stage of that nightmare journey.

After some twenty minutes' hunting round Captain Evans came to a great ice hollow. Down into this he went and up the other side. On the summit he looked back toward where he had left the sledge. There two figures were silhouetted against the skyline—his companions who had shown such tremendous loyalty during that terrible day.

Down into the next hollow he went and then stopped. For in this hollow, unlike the others, there were no crevasses. The sides of the depression met quite firmly in smooth blue ice.

In a flash Evans called to mind seeing this ice fall from the glacier on his outward journey with Scott. He remembered quite well the huge frozen waves. If he was right, then it meant that they were on the very edge of the broken ice, and might still reach the supply depôt before their strength gave out.

For some minutes Captain Evans surveyed the valley, checking off landmarks with his memory. Then he fell on his knees and prayed that it might be proved that he was right

—that this valley might show them the way to safety.

Rising to his feet he hurried on boldly up the opposite slope. From the top frozen waves of ice continued into the distance, but each one less in magnitude than the last. Beyond lay the smooth shining bed of the glacier itself, and away to the northwest the curious reddish rock under which they had placed the Mid-Glacier Depôt when marching southward. That prayer uttered amid the wilderness of eternal ice had been answered and they were saved.

Captain Evans had considerable difficulty in making his way back to his companions, but he reached them at last, and told them the good news.

His reconnaissance had occupied just one hour, but it took them three times that long to get the heavy sledge over the last of the ice valleys on to the glacier itself. There they camped and made tea before marching on to the depôt itself. They ate their last biscuits and finished everything in the food bag. Then, full of hope and joy at their deliverance from the nightmare of being lost amid the ice, they marched to the depôt itself. They reached it soon after midnight, and they had been going since six o'clock in the morning, with two little halts for meals. No wonder those three intrepid men turned in and did not wake up until late the next day.

The following morning Captain Evans found that he had a bad attack of snow blindness, due to having to keep his goggles off to pick a way for the party the previous day. This was painful, but fortunately the march that day over the smooth ice of the glacier was easy.

Averaging seventeen miles a day, the little party made good progress down to the ice barrier—a rate of progress which surprised the men themselves, for on February 1, 1912—in the middle of that homeward march—Evans and

CHRISTMAS EVE IN THE PACK 82

THE DIVIDE OF THE QUIMSA CRUZ, BOLIVIA 83

It was along such switchback trails—in parts only a narrow ledge bordered by a precipice—that Colonel Fawcett journeyed. See Chapter VII.

Lashly had been sledging exactly one hundred days. Crean had not been on the trail quite so long, because he had come out with Captain Scott's party, which had started later than Captain Evans' depôt-laying expedition, and caught them up later.

Think of the standard of fitness demanded of men who had to cover an average of fifteen miles a day over endless ice, through blizzards, at a temperature below zero, and pulling a sledge weighing four hundred pounds for all those miles. That march of fifteen hundred miles under such conditions was the ultimate test of endurance. No man of our generation has done anything finer. Down there, on the edge of the world, those members of the British Antarctic Expedition had reached the limit of human endurance. They worked, trudged and pulled over those miles of ice until the very last ounce of their strength was reached—and passed.

For some days following their departure from the Mid-Glacier Depôt Captain Evans had been feeling uncomfortable, and it was just about the time when he celebrated the hundredth day of that great journey that he made the unpleasant discovery that he was suffering from scurvy—that disease dreaded by all explorers far from fresh food or medical aid.

It came on with a stiffening of the knee joints. Then he found it impossible to straighten his legs. Finally they became horrible to behold, swollen, bruised, and green.

As day followed day, his condition became steadily worse; his gums were ulcerated and his teeth became loose. Then came the last straw—hemorrhage, or bleeding due to weakness and the need for rest, good food, and a doctor.

During those terrible days Lashly and Crean were unremitting in their care of their sick commander. But gradually they lost hope that they could nurse him back to health and they realised that other help must be obtained; somehow Evans, however sick, must be got over those miles of ice which still lay between them and the main depôt of the expedition, where they might find food and help.

The heroism of E. R. G. R. Evans in those awful days deserves to be remembered with the moving story of the last desperate hours of Captain Scott's party. For hundreds of miles he trudged on, each step hurting him more than the last. He had done too much on that outward journey, pulling a sledge for miles daily and then building depôts and erecting landmarks by which they could be sighted. Now he had passed the limit of human endurance and was paying for it.

He suffered agonies and eventually became so bad that he could only push himself along by means of a ski-stick. Somehow he stuck it out, waddling along with his companions until one day he fainted when striving to start a march.

Crean and Lashly rigged up the tent and, having brought the sick man back to consciousness and made him as comfortable as possible, held a council of war. It was clear that even to escape death on the ice, their companion could not crawl another step. Evans begged them to leave him and make their own way to safety; but it was useless to argue. Gallant fellows, those two men decided that "stick together" was going to be their motto.

They put their commander on the sledge, sleeping bag and all, and strapped him there with their own sleeping bags spread out under him to ease the bumps. Then they set out, going ever northward toward safety.

How weary those marches must have been. Yet those wonderful two pulled the sledge for ten miles each day. Nobly they fought a great fight against disaster until one day a blizzard came and completely spoilt the surface of the ice.

Lashly and Crean had now been marching nearly the whole fifteen hundred miles and great though their hearts were, they had to give up. Their strength was spent. In vain they tugged at the sledge with their sick companion on it. They could move it no farther.

Sadly they re-erected the tent and put the invalid inside. Then they went out and talked things over together.

They were discussing which should try to reach help and which should stay with Evans. It was decided between them that Crean, as the fresher man of the two, should attempt to reach Hut Point, thirty-five miles away, and there get relief to come to them.

Failing relief there, he would have to go a further fifteen miles to reach Cape Evans, named after the sick man in the tent, and the headquarters of the expedition.

Crean said good-bye to Evans and Lashly and started upon his wonderful march for help. Lashly held the little round tent door open so that the sick Evans, lying in his sleeping bag, could see the last of him. And both wondered whether they would ever again see that figure that strode out so nobly.

Left alone, Lashly made porridge out of some oatmeal picked up at the last depôt, and fed the invalid. Then he laid him on Crean's sleeping bag, which helped to make Evan's own bag seem softer for his sore body after being dragged for a hundred miles on a jolting sledge.

Warmed and comforted, Evans slept and awoke to find the faithful Lashly keeping watch over him. As Captain Evans expressed it later, "Few wounded men in the Great War were nursed as I was by Lashly amid that great white silence."

A couple of days passed, and as Evans grew steadily weaker, Lashly would every now and then go outside to scan the horizon for signs of relief.

The end had nearly come, and Evans was past caring; they were without food but a few biscuits soaked with parafin, and Lashly himself, whatever might happen, had become too weak to attempt the march to safety. He took it very quietly—this noble steel-true man—when death seemed but a matter of an hour or two for both his commander and himself. And then, when everything looked blackest, relief came.

Suddenly the baying of dogs was heard—first once and then again. Lashly, who at the time was lying down beside Evans, talking quietly to him, sprang to his feet, looked out and saw a glorious sight.

A dog team was galloping at full pelt for the tent. Relief!

What a wonderful moment that must have been for pain-racked Evans, and for despairing Lashly, who had never let his companion guess that his hopes were failing. What a wonderful moment for the men who galloped up just in time to save those two gallant lives from the fate that had overtaken Captain Scott and his gallant party farther out in those wastes!

The leader of the dogs, a beautiful grey dog named Kris-ravitsa, seemed to understand the situation, for he came right into the tent and licked the face and hands of the sick man, as though to let him know that at last their troubles and anxieties were ended.

Doctor Atkinson and Dimitri the Russian dog-boy had come over hotfoot to save them, and of all the men in the expedition, none could have been so useful at that moment as Atkinson, the clever naval surgeon.

After resting the dogs, and telling the men the story of Crean's wonderful march through the snows—eighteen hours without stopping—and giving them a carefully prepared meal, the doctor put Evans into his own sledge, and Lashly into the second sledge driven by Dimitri, and the dogs were given their head.

In three hours the party arrived at Hut Point, where Evans and Lashly were greeted by the overjoyed Crean and heard from his own lips the story of his great march for help.

It was months before Captain Evans was able to stand, and for some weeks there was a doubt as to whether he would recover from the terrible attack of scurvy, but thanks to Doctor Atkinson's careful nursing his life was saved and he had the honour, after the tragic news of Scott's death, of taking command of the expedition, and bringing it back to England.

But the final chapter in this wonderful story of bravery and pluck in the face of superhuman difficulties was not written until the summer of 1913, when, after their return to England, Captain E. R. G. R. Evans had the honour of telling the story of that record march to King George V. and presenting to him those two wonderful companions, Tom Crean and William Lashly. They had been summoned to Buckingham Palace with the surviving members of the expedition to receive their white-ribboned polar medals. In addition his Majesty showed his appreciation of that deathless march by presenting a further honour to Captain Evans, and the Albert Medal to both Lashly and Crean for saving the life of their commander at the end of that long, long march.

G

CHAPTER VII

A FINE, upstanding man of immense strength, Lieutenant Colonel P. H. Fawcett was one of the greatest of modern travellers. Beginning life in the Royal Artillery, he served in Ceylon, where he did much exploring in the jungles amid the ruins of ancient civilisations. Returning to England, he was lent by the British Government to the South American State of Bolivia and headed a commission to delimit the frontiers of that wonderful country. In spite of the dangers and hardships of this work, Colonel Fawcett became so deeply interested in South America that he has spent nearly twenty years in making one expedition after another into the mysterious heart of the continent. From the last of these, begun in 1925, he and his elder son have failed to return, and although no definite news has been obtained of their death, hope of their survival, after several years of silence, is but slender.

Bolivia is one of the strangest countries in the world ; it is so situated that it can be reached only by crossing the great Andes Mountains or by taking a very long and difficult journey through the Argentine Republic. It lies between Peru and Chile on one side and Brazil, Paraguay, and the Argentine on the other. It has all sorts of country from ice-clad heights to steaming swamps, all kinds of vegetation, and nearly all kinds of minerals ; it is four times as large as Great Britain but has a population only one quarter that of London.

When Colonel Fawcett first went to Bolivia much of the country was unexplored and the southern swamps had hardly ever been seen by white men, much less surveyed or mapped. His work included crossing the giant Cordilleras no fewer than six times, exploring that gigantic lake Titicaca which lies on a plateau nearly thirteen thousand feet above sea level, ascending the rivers La Plata and Paraguay nearly to their sources, and struggling through jungle so thick that sometimes a whole day's journey was only five hundred yards.

The Altiplanicie, the great tableland at the top of Bolivia, has a bitterly cold, intensely dry climate. There are cutting winds, and occasionally fearful electric storms. The view from these barren heights is magnificent, ridge after ridge dropping to the blue sea of forest in the depths below. A road, or rather track, crosses these heights to the western seaboard, which runs through Sorata under the towering heights of Illampu, a mountain 20,952 feet high. All along this trail travels a constant stream of mules and donkeys carrying rubber and other goods out of Bolivia to the coast, and along this track Colonel Fawcett made his way into the country.

Snowstorms were frequent while the dry air cracked the lips of the travellers and made their eyes bloodshot. The mules were as fractious and obstinate as only mules can be. Colonel Fawcett's first adventure with these beasts was near to being his last. As a snow squall blew up he started to put on his *poncho* (cloak) and the mule at once seized the opportunity to buck furiously, flinging his rider to the ground. When Colonel Fawcett picked himself up the mule had vanished over the edge of a three hundred feet precipice, and with it had gone, beyond recovery, five hundred pounds in gold which was in the saddlebags. Around a bend in the track Colonel Fawcett heard screams, and hurrying to the rescue found a Bolivian lady clinging to the neck of her mule, the hind legs of the animal being actually over the edge of the pass. He was just in time to save her before the beast went to its doom.

In most places the trail is a mere shelf of rock with nothing between its edge and a drop of anything up to two thousand feet.

Here and there the trail rises to fifteen thousand feet above sea level. Here the mules must be stopped every few minutes to breathe them. If pushed, they die. The whole trail is lined with the whitened skeletons of pack animals, and the losses are simply incredible. A transport company lost over twelve hundred mules in a year, and on one occasion an Englishman in charge of a convoy saw thirteen loaded mules go over the precipice, one after another, before he himself could reach the spot and stop the rest from following. "It is," says Colonel Fawcett, "a heart-breaking business to see a mule go over the edge with a blood-curdling scream, and fall bumping from ledge to ledge, scattering precious stores as it falls." Some parts of the trail are so bad that nervous riders have to be blindfolded before attempting to pass them. The worst is the Tipuani Trail, a hundred miles of the most perilous going that can be imagined. Avalanches or great boulders sweep down from above, or a sudden snow squall blinds the riders. In places the trail itself may have crumbled away in the abyss. One of the chief dangers is for two convoys travelling in opposite directions to meet in one of the bad places. It is impossible to turn, and almost equally impossible to pass.

Another danger of the *punas,* as these great tablelands are called, comes from that huge vulture, the condor. The condor, which may have a wing-spread of ten feet, will sometimes swoop at a traveller and with a blow of its great wing knock him over the edge into the depths below, then leisurely descend to feed on his remains. The condor's strength is prodigious. It can carry a sheep or even lift an Indian. The natives all believe that these birds have a king and a regular organization. A German, settled in Bolivia and well known there as a business man, told Colonel Fawcett that once, when out shooting in the mountains, he saw a great concourse of condors, several hundreds in number. In the middle was one pure white in colour and on either side of this a bird with white wings. The German had never seen or heard of a white condor, so crept up and fired at it, whereupon the others instantly attacked him. The only thing he could do was to fling himself down on his back on the ground and fight them off with the stock of his gun. The battle went on for two hours, bird after bird swooping at him and when at last help came and the condors were driven off, the man was utterly exhausted. As Colonel Fawcett says, these birds are better not interfered with. He himself saw an Indian rope a condor but even then the man could not hold it and had to fasten the rope to his mule in order to do so.

On the punas are seen great herds of llamas as well as woolly alpacas and slim, long-legged vicunas. When an electric storm sweeps the heights, deafening and blinding travellers with its fury, the llamas gather in a dense herd and lie flat on the ground with their heads towards the centre. Cases have been known of a whole herd being electrocuted.

The hills are full of metal, silver, gold, copper, and tin. The mines at Potosi have produced silver to the value of more than six hundred million pounds since 1545. Colonel

Fawcett says that the Indians know of many old mines unworked since the days of the Incas. Occasionally an Indian would disappear for a few days, returning with his pocket full of nuggets. But the Indians will hardly ever reveal their knowledge for they believe that the penalty would be the death of themselves or of their families. One of the few exceptions was when an Indian, in return for the present of a cow, showed a Peruvian the entrance to an old mine at Domingo in Peru. This mine turned out amazingly rich.

In the hills the Brujas have their home. This tribe is one of the strangest in South America; instead of remaining in one place they wander like gipsies all over South America. Like European gipsies they are horse traders and are also known as wizards. Several cases of Bruja occult knowledge came to Colonel Fawcett's notice. The child of a wealthy planter was dying of some unknown disease, and a Bruja offered to cure her. He dug up the dead body of another child, burned a part of its flesh mixed with earth from the grave and administered the powder to the sick child. This terrible remedy was successful and she recovered.

Dropping down from the Altiplanicie, Colonel Fawcett travelled through a country with a lovely temperate climate, where English plants and vegetables grow well, down into the terrible jungle of the deep river valleys. This country is most unhealthy, being haunted by many diseases, including yellow fever, from which, if a patient recovers, he often loses all his hair, and terciana, a deadly form of ague which returns every third day. The usual way of travel in the valleys is down the rivers on a sort of raft called a *balsa*. "Balsa" is really the name of a tree of which the wood is so soft and light that you can cut one down with a penknife. A balsa is made of seven balsa logs keyed together. Three balsas joined together make a *callapo,* which requires a crew of four Indians. The rivers are one mass of rapids, falls, and whirlpools, making navigation most dangerous. On the Mapiri River Colonel Fawcett's party travelled down a series of tremendous rapids at a speed of something like forty miles an hour and reaching the bottom got into a *remanso,* or whirlpool, in which they were spun round at fearful speed and only by desperate efforts saved themselves from being sucked down into the depths.

Reaching less rapid water they took to a bigger boat called a *batelon* which drew three feet six inches of water but had only four inches freeboard. Fourteen Indians paddled it. Here the chief danger was from snags, that is, sunken logs, of which the river was full. Three times the batelon ran upon a snag, each time knocking a hole in her hull. The first two times she was beached and repaired, but on the third occasion there was no beach near and the Indians had to strip off their shirts and plug the hole with them, after which one sat on the hole for two hours until the Colonel could find a place to land and make repairs.

The Eastern side of Bolivia borders upon the Brazilian province of Matto Grosso, a country of narrow valleys, swift rivers, and dangerously savage Indians. The party came to a place called Bella Vista which was formerly the capital of this province and which then had a population of no less than forty thousand people. But the town proved so dreadfully unhealthy that it was abandoned, and Bella Vista is now a collection of ruins inhabited by about a hundred Negroes. Most of these die of a disease known as corrupcion, a disease so dreadful that the symptoms cannot be described in print. It does not appear to be known anywhere else than at this particular place. The old church still stands guard over the ruined city and in it still remain chests of silver plate. Bella Vista means, of course, "beautiful view," but the view is mostly forest and swamp into which it is most dangerous to penetrate, for the Indians who live in the neighbourhood are some of the most savage and bloodthirsty in the country; they not only kill travellers who fall into their hands, but very frequently torture them.

The tribe called the Parecis are the most dangerous Indians of Matto Grosso, while in Bolivia the worst are the Guarayos. Colonel Fawcett had a brush with the latter. He and his party were travelling up a narrow river when an arrow shot from the bank struck the batelon, penetrating the solid timber to a depth of an inch. He called out to the natives that he was not hostile, but the Indians refused to show themselves and his own men wanted to turn back for they said they would certainly all be killed if they went on. After some delay Colonel Fawcett decided that there was only one thing to be done; he landed on a sand bank, then, quite unarmed and with his hands up, walked deliberately toward the trees behind which the Indians were hiding. It was a desperate risk to take and he has told me that he felt very uncomfortable, not to say frightened, more especially when he actually entered the bushes. But it worked. When the Indians saw that he was really unarmed the chief came forward and within a few minutes he and the Colonel were fast friends. The Indians then brought food and all went well.

The Indians have never forgotten the horrible cruelties of the Spaniards who first conquered the country, and there are tribes who kill all strangers on sight. Some years ago an expedition of forty Portuguese headed by a couple of Americans from the United States went into Matto Grosso to look for rubber. When they failed to return search was made and forty skeletons were found, fastened to trees. None but the Indians know what horror these unfortunate folk suffered before their deaths. A rubber trader travelling up the Madeira River was treacherously murdered by Indians. His brother, when he heard of it, vowed vengeance, and travelling up to the spot where the other had been killed, left a barrel of poisoned whiskey among the trees. The Indians found and drank it, and no fewer than eighty died.

There are tribes in these vast forests which have never yet been seen by white men. One of these tribes which goes by the name of "the Morcegos," a word meaning "Bats," are said to hide by day and hunt by night, to have blue eyes, red hair, and skins the colour of putty. The other Indians dread them. Colonel Fawcett met a man who had been prisoner among them and who escaped by climbing into the trees and swinging from one tree to another until he had baffled pursuit.

Travel in the Brazilian forest is very slow. In 1911 Colonel Fawcett's party, working up the valley of the Canpolican River, actually took a month to cover thirty miles. They were soaked to the skin day and night, and were in constant danger of starvation. Game is very scarce in these jungles. True, there are tapirs, peccary, and deer, but these are very rarely seen and very difficult to kill. A party travelling in the wilds have to depend on tortoise, armadillo, and the brush turkey, with an occasional monkey. Sometimes even these fail; then the explorers are driven to eating snakes, which are everywhere terribly plentiful.

On the high ground are found rattlers, on the lower slopes that terrible creature the bushmaster, and in the swamps the water python or anaconda. The bushmaster rivals the king cobra of the East as the largest poisonous snake in the world. It grows to ten, twelve, even fifteen feet in length, is of a bright yellow colour, and has a most evil temper. While most snakes do not strike unless attacked or trodden on, the bushmaster will attack any one or anything that comes near it. On one occasion Colonel Fawcett, walking on the edge of the bush, close to a high bank, heard a sharp hiss and saw a bushmaster flash out of the scrub straight at him. By a sort of miracle the brute, which was eleven feet long, went right between his legs and over the bank into the creek bed below. Any person struck by a snake of this size is certain to die, for the amount of poison injected by the huge fangs is so great that no antidote is of much use. The wild Indians have certain cures for snake bites, but no bribe that can be offered will induce them to part with their knowledge.

The anaconda grows to a prodigious size. In 1907, when descending the river Abuna, Colonel Fawcett and his party saw a huge snake coiled on a dead tree by the water's edge. *"Sucuri!"* cried his Indians in a tone of terror, and begged him to turn back. Instead, he ordered them to go on, and taking up his heavy rifle, fired at the monster and broke its back. The creature was measured and found to be roughly sixty-five feet in length. Its skin of course would have been a trophy of incalculable value, but its mere weight would have sunk the canoe. Besides, the Indians were terrified and almost beyond control, for they believed that the mate of the great snake was sure to be close at hand and that she would attack them. Colonel Fawcett has seen in the swamps the tracks of snakes even larger than the one killed. He thinks they must be at least eighty feet in length.

In the great Beni swamp there is said to live a monster not yet described by science. A party going down a creek in this swamp saw a huge head rise out of the reeds, but before they could fire it sank down again and vanished. By the sound of its moving away they gathered that its weight must have been measured in tons. There are several varieties of pythons, among them a black snake known as the dormidera, or snoring snake, which makes a loud snoring sound. All these pythons give out an abominable odour, yet their flesh is eaten by the Indians, and Colonel Fawcett says that it is infinitely better than that of the poisonous snakes. The Indians speak of a snake which they call the salamanda, which they say is thirty feet long and as thick as an alligator. There is a very large variety of snakes most of which are poisonous. Many of the swamp vipers are specially deadly.

Some of the rivers hold good fish. The toro weighs up to one hundred and fifty pounds and the capibi up to forty pounds. The marmore, a scaled fish, is excellent eating. The Indians catch these fish by bruising the wood or leaves of two trees called the marnuna and the barbaso and pouring the sap into the water. This stupefies the fish, which rise to the top and are then raked out with barbed spears. There are also dangerous fish such as electric eels and the terrible piranha. The latter is a small fish, but has jaws like those of a bull dog, teeth like lancets, and a horrible passion for blood. It goes in great shoals and will devour even a creature as large as a bullock in a very few minutes. The colour red violently excites it and Colonel Fawcett tells a terrible story of a Portuguese soldier wearing red trousers who, being upset from a canoe in a river haunted by these fish, was torn to pieces in a few moments by a shoal. Nothing could be done to save him.

Unfortunately there are many streams which hold no fish at all and the banks of which are empty of game. These are waters which are poisoned with mineral, usually copper, and more than once when Colonel Fawcett was obliged to make his way up or down such a river he nearly starved.

His worst experience was when he, Mr. F. G. Fisher, and six *peons* (Indians) travelled up the Rio Verde (Green River) in Matto Grosso. They took a supply of provisions but found it out of the question to carry them, so decided to leave them and live on the country. But the water turned out to be bitter and there was no fish or game. The only food they could find was the cabbage palmetto, the centre of which can be boiled and tastes rather like a cabbage, and a little nengri-nengri, a kind of lichen which is edible. This gave them at most one meal a day, and that very scanty and with precious little nourishment. The travelling was dreadfully bad, for every foot of the way had to be cut through virgin forest. Day after day they struggled on, getting weaker and weaker yet somehow still moving. At the end of six weeks they were so feeble that they fell down every few steps. Then at last Colonel Fawcett sighted a deer and though his hands were shaking with weakness, managed to shoot it "at an almost impossible range." The others literally wept with joy at sight of fresh meat and it was hard to keep the Indians from killing themselves with overeating. Colonel Fawcett and Mr. Fisher both made themselves quite sick with eating sugar when at last they reached a settlement. It is curious that sweet things were missed most during this awful journey; they used to dream at night of cakes, puddings, and chocolates. As for the Indians, four of them died after the hardships of this trail.

The worst of travel in Brazil is the awful plague of insects. Mosquitoes of course are everywhere, but there are other pests much worse than these. First, the polverina, or powder fly, which is so small that it can hardly be seen, yet bites most vilely. That worries the traveller by day, and the gehene, equally small and equally poisonous, flies by night. Worse than either is the marigui, or pium, which haunts rivers with muddy banks and is at its worst in the dry season. It, too, is very small, but its bite raises a blood blister. Very soon all parts of the body exposed to it are covered with blackish blisters and the irritation is perfectly maddening.

Then there is the tabana, a kind of fly whose wings make no sound at all. It alights silently and buries its lancets in the flesh, making a wound from which the blood spurts. It, like the others, has a poisonous effect. In places small bees swarm in countless myriads. They do not sting but cover face and hands in a mad effort to suck the salty perspiration from the skin. They get into eyes, ears, and nostrils and blind and almost choke the traveller. They are a most intolerable nuisance. A large wasp stings savagely and its poison is so severe that the person stung is affected by a sort of fever and is sometimes very ill indeed.

Ants swarm. There are all sorts from the great black tucandera, an inch long and very poisonous, down to small red ants which bite like fire. One of the worst of the Brazilian ants is the so-called palo santo, or fire ant. It colonizes trees, and the insects drop like rain upon any intruder, biting furiously. Indians have been known to tie their captives to a tree inhabited by fire ants and leave them to be eaten alive. All living things avoid those parts of the forest tenanted by fire ants. Jiggers are a fearful curse. They bore under the skin, especially the skin of the toes and lay their eggs in a little sack. These soon hatch out, and if not removed cause dreadful sores. In Matto Grosso is found a white tick called the guanoco which bites, then falls off, leaving a dark patch on the flesh which may fester and leave an ugly wound.

Perhaps the most dreadful, certainly the strangest of

Brazil's dangerous insects, is the sututu, a moth which leaves on the clothes a drop of liquid containing an egg. This egg within a few days hatches into a tiny worm which enters the skin through one of the pores, and grows into a maggot from half to an inch in length. A large swelling arises, and if this is touched the maggot grips the flesh with its pincers, causing intense pain. The Indians took seven of these creatures out of various parts of Colonel Fawcett's body. Their method is extraordinary. They make a kind of sucking sound with their lips whereupon the maggot thrusts its black head out of its blow hole and wags it about. It is then seized and withdrawn. Only the Indians can extract them. Colonel Fawcett himself did his best to imitate their method, but without success. If the creature is not extracted a terrible ulcer results. Dogs suffer shockingly and frequently die. White men, too, die unless they have Indians to help them.

Vampire bats are common in many parts and there are regions in Matto Grosso where it is impossible to keep cattle or horses because of these pests. They frequently attack human beings, drawing so much blood as to weaken them terribly. Colonel Fawcett says that he can testify to the curious drowsiness produced by the rapid whirring of these creature's wings. A mosquito net is the only means of guarding against their attacks.

It will be seen that tropical South America is quite the most difficult and dangerous country for the explorer. The African bush may be dangerous and unhealthy, but at any rate in Africa native carriers can always be had. But as the Indian flatly refuses to act as carrier the explorer must take all he needs on his own shoulders, and so loaded be prepared to march through the worst forests in the world.

CHAPTER VIII

THERE is no other desert in the world like the Sahara. It stretches across the whole width of the great continent of Africa, and its area is larger than that of the island continent of Australia. It is so huge that a dozen countries the size of Great Britain might be lost in it, and much of it is still unknown and unexplored. Most people have but one idea of a desert. They picture it as a vast waste of yellow sand blazing under a fierce sun. It is true that the Sahara has great tracts of sand, but it has also many other kinds of country. There are, for instance, lofty mountain ranges, there are thousands of square miles covered with stones or broken rock, there are stretches of salt glistening like snow under the sun blaze, there are long ridges of dunes where the sand has been piled into hills by the action of the wind. And here and there are oases, tracts of fertile soil watered by springs or even lakes of sweet water where date palms and other fruit trees grow, and where the people are able to raise crops of maize, millet, and other grains with which to make bread.

Some of these oases are well known, others have hardly ever been visited by Europeans, and of all these the most inaccessible is that of Kufara which lies deep in the Libyan Desert, almost due south of the Gulf of Sidra. The journey to this oasis is at best a perilous one, for it means travelling across great expanses of country where the only water is contained in a few wells lying very far apart, and in any case difficult to find. If the traveller fails to find the well for which he is making, the chances are that he and his camels or horses will die of thirst. Nor is it easy to find the way in the desert, for terrible storms rage across the open plains, filling the air with blinding clouds of dust and rapidly hiding the track of former caravans. Also there is the constant mirage which deceives the eyes and so may lead the traveller astray. There are robbers, too,—bands of wandering Bedouins who will fall upon any party not strong enough to protect itself, kill every soul, and take all their goods.

But these are not the only reasons which make a visit to Kufara so difficult and perilous a matter. The chief cause is, in one word, Senussi. Those of us who are old enough to remember the Great War know that there was much talk at that time of the Senussi, and are aware that these are a fanatical sect of Mahommedans who have so bitter a hatred of strangers that they refuse to allow them in the country which they control. The sect was founded by Sidi Mohammed ben Ali Es Senussi who was born in Algeria in 1787. He became known as a teacher and prophet who lived a most ascetic life and who wished to return to the Islamic religion as preached originally by Mohammed and shorn of all modern additions. You might perhaps call the Senussi the Plymouth Brethren of the Mohammedan faith. The founder of Senussi was opposed to all forms of luxury and preached that his followers should have no intercourse with Jews, Christians, or infidels. He founded Zavias, or colleges, all across the Sahara, cleverly placing them at the usual stopping points of caravans. His success was enormous, and when he died in 1859 his eldest son carried on his work. To-day Senussi extends over the whole of North Africa and even into Arabia and has been the cause of closing the desert routes to the traders who formerly travelled them in great numbers. The Senussi do not merely stop strangers, they kill them; and it is impossible for any European to so much as set foot in the Libyan Desert without the permission of the Emir or his lieutenants.

In the year 1920 the English lady well known under the name of Rosita Forbes, having made up her mind to visit Kufara, if such a journey was in any way possible, landed in Italian territory at the port called Benghazi which is the capital of Cyrenaica. Benghazi is a bare little town standing on the coast, but has one fine building, the Italian Government House. At the time of her visit there were great doings there, for the head of the Senussi was staying with the Italian Governor, being on his way to Italy to visit the king of that country. The name of this chieftain, whose power extends over so vast a stretch of desert, is Es Sayed Mohammed Idris ben Es Sayed, El Mahdi Es Senussi, and unlike some of his ancestors, he is a highly accomplished and very charming person. "He has," says Mrs. Forbes, "the strange visionary eyes of the prophets of old. His lips are pale, his olive skin almost waxen and he looks out under a broad brow to realms even more remote than his own untrodden deserts." Rosita Forbes met him at a dinner given in his honour. Though her Arabic was halting, he listened to her with charming courtesy, and when he heard of her proposed journey said, "May Allah give you your wish." They dined on lambs roasted whole and stuffed with rice, raisins, and almonds; on strange, sticky sweetmeats and bowls of junket powdered with cinnamon. The meal was followed by delicious coffee, but the Emir ate little. Rosita Forbes sat beside the Emir and after dinner the latter turned to his followers and told them to salute the lady. All gave her the true Moslem salute. The Emir did

H

more. He wrote her a letter. It was not meant as a passport, but later it proved of immense value to her and her expedition.

The quartermaster-general of the expedition was Hassanein Bey. Without him the journey would have been impossible, for he knew the language, religion, and customs of the Arabs as no English person could hope to know them. Writing of him Mrs. Forbes says: "He was a chaperon when elderly Sheiks demanded my hand in marriage, a fanatic of the most bitter type when it became necessary to impress the local mind, my Imam when we prayed in public." His one weakness was a love for luggage and when the start was made from Benghazi Rosita Forbes was horrified to see the number and size of his leather bags. "They are all necessaries," he assured her, and just then an Arab dropped one and as it burst open there fell out a large bottle of bath salts, packets of salted almonds and chocolates, a pair of patent leather shoes and a brilliant blazer.

The first part of the journey was made on wiry little horses. They came to an encampment of half a dozen tents and stopped to see if the people would make them tea. At first they refused, but when they realized that Hassanein Bey was a Moslem they became more friendly. Then arrived a hard-faced man who glared at them, evidently thinking they both were the scorned Nasrani (Christians). When they told him they knew Sayed Idris he jeered. Then Hassanein Bey produced the letter which Sayed Idris had written and the atmosphere changed in a moment. One by one the Arabs kissed the letter and pressed it to their foreheads. They were ready to do anything for the people who possessed a letter from their beloved leader.

And so the party came quite safely and easily to Jedabia, where they were most kindly received by Sayed Rida El

Mahdi Es Senussi, younger brother of Sayed Idris, charming as his brother but much more human. He at once gave them a house, a cook, and servants, and asked them to dinner. The meal was of twelve courses, and lasted for three hours, from seven-thirty to ten-thirty. It ended with cups of delicious tea scented with mint.

This was all very pleasant, but the travellers soon found that it did not help them in their proposed journey to Kufara. It was forty years since any European had made the attempt to reach the unknown oasis. In 1879 the Germans had sent an expedition of four scientists headed by Rohlfs. This was backed by the whole power of Turkey. It was laden with valuable presents from the Kaiser, and hostages were held at Benghazi while the expedition went south with a hundred camels, and a large force mounted on horses.

Outside the oasis the travellers were held up by the Senussi who flatly refused to allow any Nasrani to enter their country. A large force of Arabs gathered outside the camp and openly discussed whether they should kill the hated strangers. For a month the travellers were kept prisoner in daily fear of death, when at last a friendly Sheik managed to arrange for the escape of the four Germans, and only just in time, for that very night the camp was attacked and looted. Every notebook and every scientific instrument was destroyed, so that poor Rohlfs could give no description or map of his journey.

Mrs. Forbes knew the whole story of this expedition, so she and her companion were well able to realize the tremendous difficulties that faced them. It was the friendship between Italy and Sayed Idris that helped them to reach Jedabia so easily, but after that they knew they had to fend for themselves. They dared not even tell their kind hosts anything of their plans, for they knew what horror they would feel at the idea of a young English woman venturing alone into the unknown. What made things worse for them was that Jedabia was full of spies. All sorts of people pretending friendship visited them and asked every sort of question as to their plans.

When they first arrived at Jedabia their idea was to hire a few camels and a guide and push off quietly into the desert. By the fourth day they discovered that there were no camels to be hired. The harvest had been good, and the Bedouins were so rich that they did not want to travel or work. Even if camels could be hired the owners would want to know where they were going, and that, of course, had to be kept secret, for the mere mention of Kufara would have finished everything. Since nearly all their servants were spies their plans had to be discussed in secret and that did not make matters any easier. Most people would have given it up then and there, but Mrs. Forbes is as determined as she is plucky. She set to work to make friends and, dressed as an Arab woman, wandered through the camps, reciting verses from the Koran. Soon the women became her friends and it began to be whispered, "She is a Moslem. She hates all European things."

To make a long story short a fine old Ekhwan (priest or teacher) named Haji Fetater vowed that he would take her to Kufara where she should kiss the holy Gubba and be a Moslem. He said he would send an expedition of his own to Kufara to bring back some of his belongings and that Rosita Forbes and Hassanein Bey could go with it. Even then, when all seemed settled, there were endless delays. They had to pack in secret and it was all that Mrs. Forbes could do to persuade Hassanein to pack his one suitcase with warm underclothes and necessaries instead of striped shirts and a lavender silk dressing gown. She dressed herself in Arab attire, consisting of trousers very narrow at the ankle made of white calico with a pattern of green leaves and a sort of shirt of dark red cotton with a blue pattern. Six sacks held their stores for the journey, and they themselves had to drag these out into the courtyard in the darkness. How they did it is difficult to understand, for Mrs. Forbes was suffering, at the time, from a badly sprained foot.

The start was to have been made soon after dark, but in point of fact it was a quarter to two in the morning before they at last got away. One thinks of the blazing heat of the desert but on this December night the cold was intense. A peculiar point about the Sahara is that it is often coldest when the wind is from the south. Mounted on camels they rode through pitch darkness and icy wind, but Yusuf, their guide, lost his way, and an hour before dawn they barracked (camped) on a bare sandy waste. The cold was so intense it was hopeless to try to sleep and when at last the rose of dawn lit the sky there was Jedabia still in full sight. They mounted and went on, Rosita Forbes suffering agonies from her sprained foot and Hassanein doubled up with rheumatism. It was three hours before Jedabia vanished behind the horizon, then at last they were able to rest and have some food and thaw in the warm sun.

Their party consisted of Mrs. Forbes and Hassanein, two Arabs, Yusuf the guide and Mohammed, and two coal-black Sudanese soldiers. The latter had brought no food with them, and as the amount carried was only enough for two people for a week the outlook was dark. The only thing was to travel as rapidly as possible, but when Mrs. Forbes suggested that they should start at once the two blacks rebelled. "We are not your slaves," they growled. "We are not going to overtire ourselves." But at last they were persuaded to reload the camels and they travelled until half-past two, when they camped again. There was a cruel gale that night but the travellers were comfortable in their thick sleeping bags. By the time they reached the well of Wadi Farig, some forty-five miles south of Jedabia, Mrs. Forbes was becoming badly frightened about the food. The blacks were the greediest of creatures, who wanted to eat all the food in one day. If the caravan which she expected to follow from Jedabia did not come up, it looked as if they would all starve. The water of the well was so salt that it was hardly drinkable and Mrs. Forbes found that her skin was cracked and dried, her nails breaking and her hair becoming brittle. Next day there arose a *gibli,* that is, a southerly gale with a dust storm. Dust drove into every box and bag. It filled hair, eyes, and skin. They had to stay in the tent all day, but at night came a piece of luck in the shape of a small caravan on its way south from Jedabia. It is the desert custom, when a caravan arrives at nightfall and finds another at the camping place, for the first arrivals to give a meal to the newcomers. Mrs. Forbes could not do this, so sent her apologies. A little later, as she and Hassanein were eating a scanty supper of corned beef and rice, a messenger arrived carrying two great basins of barley cooked with butter and sugar. Never was food more welcome. Next morning the kindly Arabs sent more food. Mrs. Forbes showed them Sidi Idris' letter and they were delighted. Other Arabs arrived and the travellers joined a caravan headed by a merchant named She-ib, who was going toward Kufara.

As in all uncivilized countries, there is a strange sort of wireless in the Sahara. The Arabs all knew of Mrs. Forbes' night flight from Jedabia and had made up their minds that she was on a political mission. She was no longer a stranger filled with a mad wish to penetrate the secrets of Senussi, but a mysterious messenger bearing sacred orders from Sidi Idris. The men of the caravan were most kind and when she tried to help to drive tent pegs would say, "Do not tire yourself, Sitt Khadija." This was the Arab name under which Mrs. Forbes travelled.

"Wadi Farig" means "empty valley" and from this point they climbed slowly to a bare tableland with long ridges and here and there a sand hill. Farther on, great rocks rose out of the desert and at last they came to a plain of white limestone and dropped into deep white sand where they saw clumps of low palm and sweet-scented feathery bushes. These gave fuel so that they could bake bread but food was getting terribly short. The blacks were still lazy and troublesome, and Mrs. Forbes did not trust Yusuf, who was a shifty-eyed fellow; but Mohammed was a fine man, faithful and helpful. All this time the two travellers were doing their best to write up their diaries and make their maps, but they had to be desperately careful. If any Bedouin, however friendly, had seen them taking a photograph or making notes, that would have meant a quick finish. As it was, some of Mrs. Forbes' possessions badly puzzled the Arabs. One midday when they stopped for a short rest she offered She-ib a cup of hot tea.

"How can there be hot tea," he asked, "when there is no fire, and we cannot stop to make one?"

The thermos flask from which the hot tea came proved a mystery which had to be explained in a hurry lest the owners thereof should be shot as magicians.

Beyond Wadi Farig was a stretch of deep white sand, and this was dangerous country infested by bands of robbers. Suddenly a party of eight men, six blacks and two Arabs, appeared from among the sand mounds. They had no camels, and this was a bad sign, for such are generally robbers.

"We are going to be attacked," said She-ib calmly, and every one pulled up and got their rifles ready. The display of force frightened the robbers, who scattered and vanished. The party pushed on toward an oasis called Aujela, but owing to the carelessness of the blacks the waterskins were nearly empty. A cruel south wind was blowing, blinding the camels so that they swung in circles, and the last part of the journey was a desperate struggle against cold, thirst, and hunger. They camped outside the village of Aujela but there was no food to be bought and they had to wait till next day before the Arabs brought them the usual presents, eggs, chicken, and flat loaves called *hubz*. Then came the greatest luck of all. The long-hoped-for caravan from Jedabia arrived; twelve camels well loaded and a dozen men led by Abdullah, a famous guide.

On December 19, they started again, making for the next oasis, Jalo. Here again they were received as honoured guests. Dates, native butter, goats' milk, and other food was presented, with eggs, tea, and sugar. Mrs. Forbes had some coffee which she had brought all the way from London. She boiled it over a little brush fire and the chiefs enjoyed it greatly. There was much talk and Mrs. Forbes learned the position of every well and what sort of water it held. She was told that in winter a camel can go as long as fifteen days without water.

Preparations for the new start were difficult. Before them was two hundred and fifty miles of desert with a seven days' waterless stretch. They had eighteen camels but some were small and weak. One in particular was an example of all a camel should not be. At four in the morning they were busy getting ready but it was half-past eleven before they

ROSITA FORBES IN THE DRESS WORN BY TURKISH WOMEN

at last got away, and the walls of Jalo were hardly out of sight before the worst *gibli* possible began to blow and everything disappeared in a whirling fog of driven sand. They piled the baggage to break the wind and lay with blankets over their heads and handkerchiefs tied over their mouths. Toward evening the wind fell, but it was too late to start again, so they camped for the night. Next day they reached Buttaful but there was not a palm or a tuft of brushwood. The well was full of sand and they had to dig it out. The water was good and they spent next day, Christmas Eve, in washing their clothes and themselves.

On Christmas Day a camel fell ill and appeared to be dying. It was a dreadful day but ended in the miracle of the camel getting quite well again. On the twenty-sixth they were off again with full water bags. The travelling was terrible and as the days went on they began to feel that they were lost. On New Year's Eve they had to cut the water ration. Next day Hassanein was in great pain with blistered feet, and had to ride, while Mohammed's eyes were bloodshot with the pain in his feet. By January 2, they ought to have reached Taiserbo, an oasis some distance to the north of Kufara, but a thick, bitterly cold mist covered the desert and they could see nothing so marched silently on, all knowing that, humanly speaking, death by thirst would be their portion within the next two days. The mist lifted at last, revealing nothing but a flat, pale, sandy waste without a sign of grass or brushwood. The sun blazed out burningly and mirages of hills and brushwood floated before their aching eyes. The men spoke in hoarse whispers of the fate of those lost in the desert, how one man had died within fifteen paces of the water he had failed to find; how another had been found dead beside a camel which he had killed to suck its blood. Mrs. Forbes gave the men her last bag of dates. The camels were ravenous and tried to eat the stuffing of the saddles. They ran to every dark patch of stones in search of grass.

At three on that dreadful afternoon two dunes showed on the far southeastern horizon. Every one hurried ahead, but the camels stumbled badly for it was their ninth day without water. Camels and men alike limped forward with parched mouths and bloodshot eyes, while in front the mirage showed tantalizing sheets of water and cool, dark hills. At last they reached the mound, and these at least were real. But no water—only a little coarse green scrub over which the camels fought madly. The men raced up the slope but Mrs. Forbes and Hassanein were at the end of their tether and fell behind. They saw the others clamber up the dune, watched them stand gazing, then sink motionless in silent groups.

Mrs. Forbes turned to her companion. "It is no good," she said; "they would be dancing if it had been the oasis."

Feeling utterly hopeless the two crawled slowly to the top of the ridge, not expecting for a moment to see anything but the same wide desert that lay behind them. Instead they beheld broken country, mounds and hillocks and a little way in front a clump of great green bushes. They stared at the Arabs, who crouched on the ground, the picture of despair.

"Surely there is water here!" Mrs. Forbes exclaimed.

The head man shook his head. "This place is El Atash (The Thirst). There is an old well but the water is bad. It would kill you to drink it."

It was not until long afterward that Mrs. Forbes found that the man was wrong. The well, which was filled with sand, held sweet water. That night they supped on malted milk tablets and the juice from a tin of carrots, and early next morning started again in the almost vain hope of finding water. At half-past two in the afternoon they saw palms and the men flung themselves down in a hollow and set to madly scooping up the sand. Water came, thick and muddy, yet drinkable. That afternoon Mrs. Forbes rested on her camp bed, drinking every few minutes and between times shaking the bottle to hear the delicious splash inside it.

On the following day they crossed a desert of black stones toward a line of distant cliffs, and on January 4 arrived at Buseima, a tiny village on a lake with gardens of dates, vegetables, and fig trees. It was the loveliest place, with its hills red as blood surrounding a lake as blue as the sky above and the green palms nodding in the desert wind. The Buseima folk were none too friendly, but luckily they were few. "We do not want strangers here," a woman said. "Make them go or they will suffer."

On the morning of January 8 as they made ready to leave on the last stage of their journey a spy arrived saying, "The Bazama family have returned from Jedabia, and tell us that strangers are coming into the country. We cannot believe that El Sayed has given permission to any stranger to visit Kufara."

This man made enquiries as to the strength of the party and all Mrs. Forbes' people were very anxious and troubled. The story the fellow brought was that Sidi Idris had sold Kufara and Buseima to Europeans and the Christian strangers were coming to gain information so that Europeans could occupy it. Mrs. Forbes knew that once this tale were spread in Kufara their lives would not be worth a penny. There was only one thing to do—hurry away and beat the man in a race to Kufara.

It was all very well to talk of hurry, but their way led

over real mountains rising to a height of two thousand feet. They did but twenty miles, then had to camp, and the night was icy cold. It was not until the eleventh that they reached Hawari, which is really a part of the great oasis of Kufara. Here they camped outside the town and waited. The people of Hawari were Zouias with mean narrow faces and cunning greenish eyes. Food was sent but next morning as the travellers started from their tent they were suddenly surrounded by a crowd of armed and angry Arabs.

"You shall not move till orders come from Jof," they cried. "We have been warned about you. Strangers die quickly here."

Hassanein spoke up sharply. "Is this the way you treat guests of the Sayed?" he asked.

A loud argument began. The Zouias were furious. "Why does not a messenger come from Jof?" they demanded. "Sidi Abdullah went last night and promised to send back news. We told him you should not follow till permission came." Then at last Mrs. Forbes understood what had happened. Abdullah had turned traitor and had gone on to Kufara to spread lies about the people whom he was paid to guard.

For a time it was touch and go. Mrs. Forbes had her revolver ready under the folds of her cloak. Hassanein saved the situation. "Do you wait for orders from Jof when your Sayed sends us here?" he asked. "Is this the insult you heap upon him when he trusted you to help his guests?" He argued with such skill that they gave in and offered food. But still they would not let the travellers move so that January 13, the day on which they should have ridden into Kufara, found them still prisoners in Hawari.

Meantime the treacherous Abdullah was busy at Jof, warning all there that two Christians disguised as Moslems were learning all about the country so as to conquer it later on. "They have watches on the feet of their camels and hang a strange thing on their tent to kill us if we come near." The strange thing was only a barometer, but Abdullah made it sound dreadful.

The *Kaimakan* (Chief) at Jof was impressed. He said, "The strangers must go back at once and you, Abdullah, must take the message to them."

Abdullah was horrified. The last thing the traitor wanted was to go back to the camp, but there was no help for it. He had to go, and his only hope was that the Hawari people had already finished his employers. Arrived, he told a lame story that Mrs. Forbes must not leave Hawari until a house was ready for her at Jof.

Mohammed came to the rescue. He vowed he would find the truth. He went off to Jof, learned the whole story of Abdullah's treachery, saw the Kaimakan, told him all about it and came back the same night, carrying a letter from the Kaimakan, offering all welcome to the honoured guests of the Sayeds, and asking them to come to Kufara on the morrow and honour the town by their presence.

And so at last all the difficulties were left behind and the travellers who had suffered and dared so much were able to reach the goal of their journey.

CHAPTER IX

MANY stately motor liners plough the waterways of the world, but the *Speejacks,* which recently made a journey around this planet, is a tiny craft of only sixty-four tons burden. She belongs to Mr. A. Y. Gowen of Chicago and her rather curious name is derived from the nickname of her owner when at school. The *Speejacks* is a stout little craft with copper bottom and teak decks, and is driven by two 250-horse power petrol engines. Her top speed is fourteen knots but her cruising speed eight. It takes two gallons of petrol to drive her a mile so that her cruising radius is only two thousand miles. Seeing that the Pacific is something like five thousand miles across, it would seem, on the face of it, that a vessel which can carry only four thousand gallons of petrol could not possibly tackle such a task as that of sailing round the world.

But this difficulty had been arranged for beforehand. Supplies of petrol had been placed on various out-of-the-way islands, and Mr. Gowen had settled that the yacht should be towed across the one stretch in the Southern Pacific where no islands were available.

It was on August 21, 1921, that the *Speejacks* left New York. She had eleven men aboard her and one woman, Mrs. Gowen. Running south down the American coast she passed round the south point of Florida, reached the Panama Canal, passed through the giant locks and was then taken in tow by the big steamer *Eastern Queen.* Being towed is never a pleasant business, and this tow of four thousand four hundred miles seemed endless. The Pacific is not always as calm as its name and, in so small a craft as the *Speejacks,* the pitching and rolling were terrible. It was so bad that when one day the sailors from the big steamer were sent over to make the tow rope more secure they became deadly seasick. On the *Speejacks* herself cooking was almost impossible, and all hands suffered severely. Mr. Dale Collins, who has written the story of the journey, says that members of the tramp's crew sent to watch the towline became sick from merely seeing the amazing movements of the tiny craft astern.

On October 3 they crossed the equator. It was so cold that every one aboard wore overcoats. Eighteen days out the water supply began to run short and all hands were cut to half a gallon a day for all purposes, including washing. On the twenty-first day the tow rope was loosened and the little yacht, under her own power, drove away towards Takaroa, an island in the Paumotu group. Imagine Mr. Gowen's disgust at finding no water at Takaroa! The island has no springs and there had been no rain. The only thing to do was to load up with green coconuts and make a dash for Tahiti, a run of 265 miles, and seeing that they had but twenty gallons of distilled water left, the risk was great. But luck and weather held and they reached their destination safely.

In Tahiti there is a law that no divorced person may remarry within six months. The very first thing that happened after the *Speejacks* reached the harbour was the arrival of a young American who wanted to marry a girl who had been divorced a short time before. Mr. Gowen asked how he could help him and the man answered that the marriage could be performed if the yacht was taken outside the

three-mile limit. Mr. Gowen agreed and the wedding party
came aboard, looking very spruce and happy. But when the
yacht had left the harbour mirth rapidly changed to gloom.
At best the *Speejacks* is not a steady vessel and she danced
so merrily that one of the bridesmaids sat on her new hat
and did not care a bit.

Leaving Tahiti the *Speejacks* started on a thirteen hundred mile run to Samoa, and on the second day out ran into
hurricane weather. The tiny ship was smothered in mountainous seas, then a great wave broke over her and short-
circuited the electric system, plunging everything into darkness, but the engine stood up nobly and after a fearful buf-
feting the yacht reached the lovely little island of Pago
Pago. This island belongs to America and wonderful work
is being done for the natives from a medical point of view.
The hospital, run by the United States Navy, is so much
appreciated that one of the native children was baptized
"Sick House Samoa."

At Apia, another of the Samoan islands, the anchor
dragged during a heavy gale and the yacht was saved with
difficulty from going ashore. The next stage was a six hundred mile run to Fiji. They passed Good Hope Island, which
is known as "Tin Can Island" because, having no harbour,
steamers anchor far out and fling the mails overboard in a
tin which also contains biscuits as a reward for the native
who comes out to fetch them. At Fiji they stayed eleven
days and were offered a feast consisting of raw fish, turtle
flappers, and kava, a national drink. They also saw the extraordinary ceremony of fire-walking in which native
priests strolled slowly across a sixteen-foot breadth of
white-hot stones, yet without blistering or scorching their
feet in the slightest. The native chiefs whom they met wore
dinner jackets and white shirts, but below the waist were

dressed in the *lava lava,* or native kilt, beneath which were black legs and bare feet.

New Caledonia was the next point for which they made and the eight hundred mile voyage ended on New Year's day. Noumea is the capital of New Caledonia and in the harbour they found lying a vessel which proved to be the *Snark,* once the well-known yacht of Jack London. The glass began to fall fast; there were whispers of hurricane and, to be on the safe side, the yacht hastily left the open roadstead and found safe anchorage. It was lucky for her that her skipper was so cautious, for the storm was a terrible one and many of the vessels in the roadstead were wrecked. The island of Noumea has so many deer upon it that there is a government reward of a franc for every tail brought in. The crew of the *Speejacks* went deer hunting, but as Mr. Collins says, it was more like massacre than sport.

Sydney, New South Wales, was next visited and after a pleasant stay in this wonderful harbour the *Speejacks* turned north for the long run up the Australian coast. For a thousand miles along the Queensland coast lies that wonderful wall of coral known as the Great Barrier Reef, between which and the shore is a channel of comparatively calm water. All their friends at Sydney had warned the crew of the *Speejacks* of the dangers of cyclone, but the yacht had wonderful weather all the way up and reached Northern Queensland in safety and comfort. Her crew visited various northern Australian towns and settlements, where the people flocked down to the water's edge, deeply interested in the tiny yacht. Many were anxious to join the party.

"It has always been my wish to enter a gentleman's home," wrote an Australian girl, "but I think your yacht

I

would be nicer. As my father is a seaman I should be a good sailor and I would be of much value to you in the sewing on of your buttons and other tasks, in addition to being a nice companion."

A young man wrote to Mr. Gowen: "It is my wish to join your party as cabin boy. I am a champion ukulele player and am also delightful with the piano. I would be prepared to polish brass all the morning and would guarantee to entertain you and Mrs. Gowen for the rest of the day."

"At one of the North Queensland towns," says Mr. Collins, "we nearly lost the ship. The Mayor and Council boarded her at the moment she touched the dock. There were thirty of them and their total weight nearly turned the *Speejacks* over."

Scores of lovely little islands seemed to float upon the blue sea. Lovely, that is, from a distance, but not so pleasant at close quarters. One night three of the *Speejack's* crew, including Mr. Collins, took the dinghy and left the ship in quest of turtles. They landed on a rocky beach and at once the largest mosquitoes in all the world fell upon them in a black cloud. "They would have carried us away bodily to their young had we dallied," says Mr. Collins, "but we did not dally."

Palm Island, off the Queensland coast, has been set aside by the Government as a reserve for Australian aborigines. The blacks are provided with food and clothing and each has a quarter of a pound of tobacco weekly. These people, of whom there are about six hundred, were delighted at the yacht's visit, and held a football match in its owner's honour. The game started under Rugby rules but fresh players crept in on both sides until the teams had swelled to about thirty each and the umpires lost all control. Then down came a sheet of rain, but play went on and when the white spectators were driven to cover, they left the entire population engaged in the game.

Sailing by the Hinchinbrook Channel they came to Dunk Island, where lives Mr. E. N. Banfield who wrote "Confessions of a Beachcomber" and "My Tropic Isle." He and his wife have a charming house and gave their visitors a splendid welcome. Dunk Island is a game sanctuary where no man may use gun or trap, and where, in consequence, birds and beasts are delightfully tame. Mr. Banfield came to dinner aboard the *Speejacks* and told his host that he had only been to two picture shows in his life and had never seen an aeroplane.

On March 12 the bow of the *Speejacks* was turned eastward through Cook Passage, one of the few gateways in the Great Barrier Reef, and presently the purple mountains of New Guinea came into sight. New Guinea is six times the size of England and Wales, and with its tremendous forests, lofty mountains, and impenetrable swamps remains one of the world's mystery spots.

"It is typical of New Guinea," says Mr. Collins, "that you can see a primitive native village within fifteen minutes of Port Moresby, the capital." This village, called Huanabada, has seven hundred people all living in reed and grass houses built out over the water on thin poles. The women wear *ramis,* or grass petticoats, and make wonderful pottery, which they exchange for sago, their staple food. Life in Huanabada goes on much as it did a thousand years ago.

As the *Speejacks* ran on down the coast fleets of outrigger canoes flocked out. Few of the men had clothes of any kind, but great brilliant flowers and bird of paradise plumes were thrust into their hair, while their faces and bodies were tatooed in strange patterns. They brought coconuts, fish, crabs, birds of paradise, fruit, and curios, all of which they were anxious to trade for tobacco. They did not want money. In fact, one old man clung to the side of the yacht, holding out four one-pound notes and begging them to sell him tobacco.

The port for which the *Speejacks* was making was Samarai, three hundred miles farther, and because of the dangers of the coast Mr. Gowen had promised the authorities not to land until they reached it. Samarai is very small but very beautiful. Native prisoners sweep and clean it every day. When Mr. Gowen wanted to get his hair cut he found that the only barber was the native prison warden, and he had to go to the gaol to be operated on. The place must be a heaven for the tired English housewife, for "boys," that is, native servants, can be had for only ten shillings a month. They make splendid nurses and every little white girl or boy has one to look after him or her. They look like gollywogs with their fuzzy hair, pierced ears and noses, and wrinkled faces.

Day after day they sailed slowly along the coast with tremendous, fantastically shaped mountains to their left, and in one quiet little harbour came upon a lugger in which a young Australian was prospecting for new trepang grounds. Trepang are sea slugs,—greasy, slimy-looking things which are dried and sent to China, where they are prized as delicacies. One fancies that the chief enemy of the diver is the shark, but in point of fact the native diver is far more afraid of the great codfish which lurk near the bottom. Some of these monsters weigh five hundred pounds, and will snap off a man's hand as easily as you or I would bite a biscuit. There are also huge rays similar to those caught by Mr. Mitchell Hedges, but even larger. Some are fourteen feet across and weigh two tons.

Beyond a place called Tufi the *Speejacks* struck a reef,

a great mushroom of coral. She floated off in safety as luckily she was going dead slow at the time, but damage had
been done, a blade of the starboard propeller having been
badly bent. Three of the crew had to go overboard, armed
with hammers, and beat it back into shape. While they
worked shoals of rainbow-hued fish darted around, and far
below through the clear water, long, slim, sea snakes were
visible, wriggling along the rocks at the bottom. The next
night they anchored at a place named Aku. An old native
with a queer, cunning face came hurrying down to meet
them.

"German fight, he feenish yet?" he asked eagerly. And
when the people of the *Speejacks* assured him that the Great
War was really over, "Who win—English?" he demanded.
Hearing that this was indeed the case, he grinned broadly.
"German, he feenish," was his remark. He went on to explain that he had returned from Port Moresby seven years
earlier and since then no news of the outside world had
reached Aku, so that all this time he had been wondering
who had won the great fight.

Few ships visit the low, mysterious islands of the Tro-
briand Group which lie to the north of New Guinea. A big
ship never comes there so that for once the *Speejacks* was
welcomed as a fine vessel instead of a tiny boat. There are
nine thousand natives in these islands but only twenty
whites. There are also forty thousand coconut palms. The
natives are a far finer type than those of the neighbouring
islands and are well looked after by the resident magistrate.
Kindly folk they are, for when Mrs. Gowen, tramping
across one of the islands, looked tired, the villagers at once
made a stretcher and six of them carried her, laughing
gaily as they tramped along. The danger of the islands is
malarial fever and even the babies have quinine rubbed into

their skins under the armpits to save them from this scourge. The captain of the *Speejacks* had a bad attack and it was thought best to leave at once. They headed for the wild Solomon Islands and ran into cruel weather, black storms in which the tiny yacht pitched among monstrous waves. It was difficult and dangerous, especially as the captain was still ill, but the luck of the *Speejacks* held, and at dawn on the second day the Solomons humped above the horizon.

It was principally to pick up petrol that the yacht had visited the Solomons, for a supply had been shipped from Sydney three months earlier by the schooner *William H. Smith*. The very first thing the resident told them was that the schooner had not arrived. "She is months overdue," he said. "I fear there is nothing to do but report her missing." This was a horrid shock for Mr. Gowen and his friends, for the tanks were empty and it looked as if they would have to wait months, since Sydney was the only place from which the necessary fuel could be obtained.

Then, as they sat with long faces discussing the position, a bowsprit poked around the coconut-clad point, and a sailing ship came bowling in before the breeze. Some one grabbed up a pair of glasses and focussed them. "It's—it's the *William H. Smith!*" he gasped. And so it was.

When she got in her skipper explained that it was not bad weather but calms that had delayed her. For twenty-six days she had been within sight of the southerly islands of the group. During that time her sails were raised and lowered forty-two times and she made in all twenty miles. The only danger had been from two huge waterspouts which had come curling across the hot sea, but happily missed the ship. The people of the Solomons are very black, and some are still head-hunters. But they are quieting down under

British rule, and have taken kindly to cricket. Even so, the Resident forbade the travellers to land on certain of the islands. The *Speejacks* visited Kieta on the island of Bougainville and found the entrance to the harbour a sweep of white foam, where great rollers broke on sharp-toothed coral. In a heavy rainstorm they blundered through in safety.

Maron in the Admiralty Islands is visited once in three months by a trading steamer and the people were speechless with excitement when the *Speejacks* arrived. The place is beautiful, but the heat intense and there is no amusement. Growing coconut palms provides the only industry, and one planter said, "I can tell you the number of palms on the sky line of the island opposite. There is nothing to do in the evening but sit and stare at them."

The natives were deeply interested in the Stars and Stripes. "What name belong this lap-lap (flag)?" they asked.

Maron formerly belonged to Germany and here a wealthy German, Rudolf Wahlen, built a real castle. It is the strangest thing to see this huge stone building with its high tower and broad stone verandahs rising in the middle of the palms. A queer place, Maron, with its huge yellow land crabs, thousands of lizards, iguanas and parrots. Mr. Collins was given one piece of information so odd as to be hardly credible, that there is in the island a grasshopper which only appears when a ship is about to put in. Sure enough the grasshopper had prophesied the coming of the *Speejacks*.

Hollandia, in Dutch New Guinea, was the next port of call. This is the centre of the cruel trade in bird-of-paradise plumes. Three hundred of the town's seven hundred people were out in the forest, murdering the most beautiful birds on earth for the sake of their exquisite feathers. Supplies of petrol were again rather low, but none could be bought in Hollandia. The tanks held 2080 gallons and the *Speejacks'* next run to Amboyna in the island of Ceram was a thousand miles. There would be absolutely nothing left over for bad weather or any emergency. A Dutch steamer offered a tow, but asked five hundred pounds and refused to take less. So Mr. Gowen resolved to take the chances and run on one engine only. The *Speejacks* crept along at five or six knots. The sea proved kind and they passed quietly down a mystery coast with headlands plumed with clouds and now and then flying fish flopping aboard out of the low wave crests. The sea was strewn with reefs, many quite uncharted, but the little yacht weathered them safely and reached Amboyna with a margin of a hundred gallons.

Now they were in the Dutch East Indies with white stone houses, cool and stately. They are great eaters, these people, and many of the foods were new and fascinating to the visitors. Breakfast was at six in the morning and the last meal at ten at night. Laundry men flocked out to the yacht, carrying testimonials. One ran:

"This man has done in my washing more completely than any fiend I have ever known. I sent him shirts and he gave me back cotton fishing nets. I sent him trousers and he gave me back kilts. May his God forgive him. I never shall."

Passing down a channel between cliffs where the current ran with mill-race speed, they came to Bouton where a Dutch commandant rules three hundred thousand people. Each native gives yearly twelve days' work to the Government and thirty to his village. The whole place is as clean as the proverbial new pin. Makassar had marble clubs and white villas. The richest man in the city was a Malay worth six hundred thousand pounds. In the Talor River near by are great crocodiles which are shot by torchlight.

Bali, the next stop, is famous for the beauty of its people. Their skin is almost the colour of gold. The island has two great volcanoes—Batoer and Kintamani, and the *Speejacks'* people climbed four thousand feet to get a view of them. After months of tropical heat it was strange to stand shivering in the bitter wind on the cloudy slopes. When Batoer last erupted a flood of molten lava poured down upon the village at its foot and it seemed as though it was doomed. In the path of the lava stood a temple and when the glowing tide reached the sacred building it stopped and the village was saved. Bali itself is lovely as its people, but even here the picture theatre has arrived. Mr. Collins saw a group of Balinese gazing at a poster outside, which showed gentlemen in dress suits firing revolvers and a lady fainting in the background.

Leaving Bali, Mr. Collins himself was steering the yacht through the blackness of a cloudy night when a Chinese junk, carrying no lights at all, banged into them. It was a miracle that they got off almost unhurt. They reached Sourabaya in Java and docked their battered craft for repairs. The workmen were an idle gang and fiddled about for days before any task was done. In the next dock lay a big cargo steamer with a gaping hole in her bow caused by smashing into a coral reef in the very waters through which the *Speejacks* had come unharmed. Meantime the crew of the yacht climbed the great gaunt volcano of Tosari. Reaching the top they looked down into a crater where hot mud bubbled and steamed and made hideous gurglings. The rock on which they stood quivered constantly.

There are thirty-five million people in Java, and the Dutch do not find it easy to handle them. Sugar is the chief crop and the workers get about twenty-five cents a day. But Mr. Collins says that it takes ten of them to do one man's work. There were horrors in the shape of lepers, poor creatures without faces or hands, some blind and dumb. At last the yacht was ready and after a call at Batavia where women washed clothes in the muddy canal running through the centre of the town, they coursed northwards to Singapore, crossing the equator for the second time. Some Chinese friends gave them a banquet of shark fin, crab, lotus seeds, and chrysanthemum tea. The dinner *ended* with soup. They met Chinese millionaires who lived in exquisite houses and were so rich they did not know what they were worth. The Sultan of Johore took them for a drive in a wonderful car which travelled along the crowded roads at the appalling speed of seventy-three miles an hour. The Sultan is a very good business man, very rich, very energetic. The contents of his palace are worth over a million dollars and he has a dinner service all of gold for one hundred people. His people adore him.

Along the coast of Sumatra the yacht ran through heavy weather. Before her was the long voyage to Colombo in the teeth of the monsoon. After much discussion they determined to try it and for four hours battled with a wild, grim sea. Waves broke all over the *Speejacks* and it was perfectly plain that the task was too much for her, so there was nothing for it but to take the risk of turning and going back. All the way back to Batavia they sailed and there made ready for the big jump. Thirty-two hundred gallons of fuel were pumped into the tanks and three hundred cases, each holding ten gallons, lashed to the deck. Five tons of water and a quantity of food were laid in and then the *Speejacks* started across the Indian Ocean for the Seychelles Islands.

All went well. The wind, strong at times, was behind the yacht and her people actually hoisted their little sail. The motion was tremendous, but they got used to it. On the morning of the eighteenth day the exquisite little Seychelles Islands rose on the horizon and that evening they bathed in a cool, fresh mountain pool. Time was drawing on; they could not stay and soon were running before a southerly gale up the African coast. The weather grew worse and a gust tore away the awning and sent it flapping off into the dark sky; they tried hard to find a harbour or any shelter, but it was no use and they were forced to drive to sea again into water fierce and angry as the heart of a whirlpool. At midnight the ship veered strangely; the steering cable had carried away. The hand tiller had to be rigged, a terrible task with the little yacht tossing like a chip on the huge seas. There was desperate risk of the workers being washed overboard, and it seemed hours before the task was finished. But finished it was in safety, then the break in the chain was found and mended, and next morning's dawn found them safely at anchor off Aden, the British port at the mouth of the Red Sea. Aden sizzled under the tropical sun, there had been no rain for seven years, yet the people carried on comfortably enough, even playing tennis and football.

The Red Sea is narrow but it is long, and very, very hot. When the *Speejacks* started away from Aden the heat was great, but so was the wind. It was like a blast from an oven dry and burning. Even on deck the temperature was 114 degrees, while at the same time the yacht pitched furiously in a heavy head sea. The fourteen hundred miles of the Red Sea took eleven days to cover and forty-seven hundred gallons of petrol. It was joy indeed to swim calmly through the placid waters of the Suez Canal.

It seemed as though the *Speejacks* had exhausted her luck, for when she drove out into the Mediterranean it was to meet with fierce head winds. In four days only three hundred miles were covered, and the storm grew so bad that she sought refuge under lee of the cliffs of Crete. Three pleasant days were passed ashore during which they enjoyed some good partridge shooting; then the sea smiled again and the *Speejacks* ran on to Athens. The Greek capital was crowded with four hundred thousand refugees driven out from Smyrna by the Turks. Some of these refugees had been rich men a few weeks earlier, but now had nothing left except the clothes they stood up in.

Leaving Athens, the yacht pushed through the Corinth Canal. The Roman Emperor Nero started to cut this canal in A. D. 67, but it was eighteen centuries before it was finished. There are fierce currents in the canal but the *Speejacks* got through in safety, only to run upon a reef on the far side. Happily she slipped off safely into deep water, and then they found that owing to magnetic attraction the compass was two whole points out. The voyage through the Mediterranean was peaceful. Italy was visited and Spain was reached without trouble. At Barcelona the *Speejacks'* crew attended a bullfight and saw bulls butchered and a wretched matador badly gored. Then they left for the last long stretch of their journey, which meant crossing the Atlantic from east to west.

In order to find calm seas Mr. Gowen ran down the coast of Africa for seven hundred miles, only to be buffeted by head winds and delayed for so long that the American papers announced that the *Speejacks* had been lost with all hands. Yet she came safely to the Canary Islands and thence to the Cape Verdes where she took in a huge load of petrol and started on the twenty-six hundred mile voyage to Porto Rico. With a deck load of sixteen hundred tins of petrol a gale would have meant disaster, but conditions were perfect. The ocean lay like glass, Porto Rico was reached in safety, and just sixteen months after leaving New York, she came into the harbour of Miami in Florida, and from that port ran up the coast to New York. The total mileage covered by the tiny yacht was thirty-four thousand, during which she had used seventy-three thousand gallons of petrol. The whole adventure had been a wonderful success.

CHAPTER X

FORTY years ago a young English doctor sailed from Great Yarmouth to begin an adventure which is still in progress, and which was destined to absorb his whole life and end by making his name known wherever the stories of gallant pioneers are discussed.

The English doctor was Wilfred Thomason Grenfell, and the adventure was the founding on the wild coast of Labrador of a medical mission which has since placed him in the front rank of modern pioneers and earned for him the name of "Grenfell of Labrador" and the honour of knighthood, which was bestowed upon him in 1927 at the opening of a new Grenfell Hospital in Newfoundland.

For five years previous to 1892, Doctor Grenfell had been engaged in medical work for the Royal National Mission to Deep-sea Fishermen among the fishermen of the North Sea and off the coast of Iceland. It was rough work, being afloat with the "gentlemen unafraid," as the English deep-sea fishermen were christened during the war, and the experience proved invaluable to Grenfell when he set out on the task of taking medical aid to the lonely fishers in the cold waters north of the "Roaring Forties" off the coast of Labrador.

The climate in that part of the world is about as bad as it could be. Long winters of storms, icy hurricanes, fogs, ice-cold bleak days, and freezing nights made it work from which the hardiest of adventurers might flinch.

But Grenfell went out to Labrador in the summer, when the seas were ice-free, and the coast looked most pictur-

GRENFELL OF LABRADOR   132

esque. Let us tell of his first glimpse of the land in which he was to work for the rest of his life by quoting the word picture which he wrote in his own life story "A Labrador Doctor":

A glorious sun shone over an oily ocean of cerulean blue, over a hundred towering icebergs of every fantastic shape and flashing all the colours of the rainbow from their gleaming pinnacles as they rolled on the long and lazy swell. Birds familiar and strange left the dense shoals of rippling fish over which the great flocks were hovering and quarrelling in noisy enjoyment, to wave us a welcome as they swept in joyous circles overhead.

That is how Labrador looked when viewed from the sea. But ashore conditions were terrible. Illness and disease were to be found on every hand, and there was no medical aid available for dealing with it. People just went sick and either lived or died, according to whether the illness or their own strength won. The only "cures" known for disease in Labrador at that time were superstitions as absurd as any believed by African natives. For instance, the fisher folk believed that the seventh son of a family possessed a wonderful power to cure certain diseases. They also believed in charms such as green worsted thread and haddock fins for keeping illness away. Prayer papers—rolls of paper on which prayers were written—were also used for the same purpose. Naturally, these "cures" usually failed to act, and the wretched patients died.

Doctor Grenfell had not long to wait for his first experience of disease in this remote corner of the world. On the very night of his arrival, before he had gone ashore, a half-clad man rowed out to the ship in a patched apology for a boat and asked the Doctor if he would attend a sick man without payment.

Doctor Grenfell went and found a tiny sod-covered hovel with one window of odd fragments of glass. The floor was made of pebbles from the beach; the earth walls were damp and chilly. There were six wooden bunks built in tiers around the single room and six neglected children huddled in the corner. In one bunk lay the sick man, seriously ill, while a woman tried to give him cold water out of a spoon. There was no furniture except a small stove with an iron pipe leading through a hole in the roof.

The sick man had pneumonia—in a land where up to that moment there had been no doctors, no nurses, no hospitals, and very often no money for medicines. He died because there was no hospital to send him to, but to-day, thanks to Doctor Grenfell and the band of doctors and nurses who have been toiling with him, the sick of Labrador are cared for in up-to-date hospitals built along the coast.

The building of these hospitals was Grenfell's first big task. Another doctor joined him from England, with two nurses, and a year later the first hospital was opened at Battle Harbour. Two years later a second hospital was opened, and since then five more have followed, dotted at intervals of two hundred miles along the wild coast line.

The building of these hospitals in Labrador was a very different task from building a new hospital in England. There are no firms of builders in Labrador, and if there had been there was not enough money to pay for the erection of hospitals. So Doctor Grenfell called for volunteers and organised expeditions to the woods. There a hundred sturdy Northern fishermen would work for a fortnight cutting timber and at the end of that time drag back enough material to build a hospital thirty-six feet long and as wide. The same men would then help in the building. It was a labour of love, for every one knew that one day it might be his turn to be nursed back to health within the walls he was busy erecting.

When the seas freeze over in the winter, the work of some of the hospitals thus built is moved to the winter quarters at the heads of the bays where the fishermen gather for winter trapping.

In this way Grenfell of Labrador has brought the "luxury" of a doctor within the reach of the hardy fishermen of the region. But he has done more. He has opened dental parlours to attend to their teeth, and arranged for an eye specialist to go to Labrador once a year. Previously a man had to go to Newfoundland to visit a dentist, while those who went blind from snow glare or other causes had to stay blind. Since the specialist began his work one man has recovered his sight after eighteen years and others have been restored to sight when they had lost all hope.

Such a work would have been enough to occupy the average man for a lifetime. But almost every year Doctor Grenfell found more and more work waiting for himself and his gallant band of helpers.

Here is a story told by Grenfell himself which shows how the two children's homes in Labrador came to be started:

I had been summoned to a lonely headland, fifty miles from our hospital at Indian Harbour, to see a very sick family. Among the spruce trees in a small hut lived a Scotch salmon-fisher, his wife and five little children. When we anchored off the promontory we were surprised to receive no signs of welcome. When we landed and entered the house we found the mother dead on the floor and the father lying on the floor dying. Next morning we improvised two coffins and contributed from the wardrobes of all hands enough black material for a seemly funeral and later, steaming up the bay to a sandy stretch of land,

K

buried the two parents with all the ceremonies of the Church
—and found ourselves left with five little mortals in black
sitting on the grave mound. Thus we began what developed
into our Children's Homes.

Doctor Grenfell also helped the people to revive their
home industries. Mat-making, basketry, toy-making—these
industries have once more provided interesting employment
during the long winter, when the seas are frozen over and
no fishing is possible.

Not content with doctoring the people, looking after the
orphans and encouraging them to work at home in the winter, Doctor Grenfell and his fellow workers set about the
task of enabling the people to buy the things which they
needed at reasonable prices by founding a chain of coöper-
ative stores. These are shops owned and run by the fishermen themselves, at which they can buy food, clothing, and
other necessities at cost price.

Those of us who live in towns are lucky in having plenty
of shops to choose from, when we want to buy anything,
from a motor car to a pencil. If one shop charges too much
we can go to the next. But in the wilds of Labrador the
fishermen had to trade at the only store available—often
tramping many miles to reach it. For this reason dishonest
traders could and did charge scandalous prices in many
cases, and the poor fishermen had to pay. They could not do
anything else—until Doctor Grenfell showed them how to
open shops for themselves; showed them where to buy supplies, and arranged for ships to bring goods to them from
the outside world.

During the twoscore years which have passed since he
first went to Labrador Doctor Grenfell has learnt much
about the people to whom he had given the best years of

his life, and experienced great hardships, which are, indeed, inseparable from work in that hard climate.

The most common disease there was consumption, due to the fishing folks' dread of fresh air. In the winter, when the thermometer often drops to thirty degrees below zero, they shut themselves up in their little houses and practically live in the same air all the season round.

If you do that in any country, you run a big risk of being ill at the end of the winter, and so Doctor Grenfell had to teach the people that fresh air, however cold, would keep them free from disease if only they would let it into their homes.

Among his patients have been many Eskimos who are very good when ill, but display great curiosity regarding the doctors, especially as to their work.

On one occasion, when an Eskimo girl had to have a toe amputated owing to frostbite, Doctor Grenfell borrowed an Eskimo hut to use as an operating room.

In an English hospital nobody but surgeons and nurses are allowed to be present, but in this lonely Labrador village every one took a special holiday in order to be present at the operation and gathered round the door dressed in their best clothes to see the show. There was nothing to do but proceed with the operation before this admiring audience, which the Doctor did. Happily the operation was successful and every one went home pleased.

Another story told by Doctor Grenfell concerns a clergyman who had arranged to go to a fishing village to marry an Eskimo chief. When he got there it was to find that the bride had changed her mind. The clergyman expressed his surprise, whereupon the chief replied, "Never mind, I will choose some one else." Which he did from among the women who had gathered for the ceremony.

Most of this visiting of the sick would have been impossible but for the little mission ship, which braved the storms and the drifting ice for as long as the seas were open in each year. The first ship used in this work was christened the *Sir Donald* and a second ship, named after Lord Strathcona, was built in 1899. Everything depended on these little steamers. If either of them had been wrecked, it might have been a year before another ship suitable for the work could have been found, and during all that time dozens of scattered settlements which could only be reached by sea would have been cut off once more from all medical aid.

First the *Sir Donald* and then the *Strathcona* enabled the doctors to reach the sick and to feed the hospitals along the coast. The ship found the derelict children and brought them to the home built for them. She was often a court of law where disputes were settled. At times the steamer was even loaned to several families of fishermen to enable them to bring home cargoes of wood fuel before the coming of the ice.

With so much depending upon the little steamer, the reader will be interested in the story of an adventure of a very different kind from the one related above, which Doctor Grenfell experienced toward the end of a Labrador summer, at a time of the year when the ice was almost due.

Doctor Grenfell was visiting a series of outlying townships in the *Strathcona,* which carried him up and down the coast, when it was found that her coal bunkers were on fire.

In the ordinary way the natural thing to do would be to anchor the ship close to the shore and fight the fire until it was subdued. But this would have meant a delay of days, a delay that would have prevented some of the fisher folk from seeing the Doctor before the storms came again and made travel impossible. So Doctor Grenfell ordered the ship to keep right on, and they fought the fire as they proceeded.

At the next settlement water was thrown on the coal while the Doctor was ashore, looking after the sick; then off they went again with the fire still smouldering.

A day or two later flames burst out again. Once more water was poured on the coal and the boat forged ahead while the Doctor and crew did not dare to think whether the fire was still burning deep down in the ship or not.

In all they travelled for ten days and covered over five hundred miles of coast line with the hold afire. And only then, with the Doctor's work done, could they spare time finally to stamp out the flames.

A year or two later, on Easter Sunday, 1908, Doctor Grenfell had another adventure which came near to costing him his life.

He had been called to attend a sick person some sixty miles to the north of the station where he was staying, and to get there he had to break through some bad ice while crossing an inlet or arm of the sea. He was alone except for a dog team, when he got onto a piece of ice which broke loose from the main ice pack.

In an instant he cut loose the dogs from the sledge, otherwise they would have been drowned. The "ice pan" on which he stood broke into two pieces, each too small to support a man, and the Doctor was thrown into the icy water and had to swim to a larger mass of floating ice; after scrambling on to this, he had to rescue his dogs.

This ice pan was about the size of a dining table, and on it he spent a night and day, clad only in a light sweater, vest, and boots, without hat, coat, or gloves—and that after being three times in the icy water.

The cold was intense and but for the dogs the Doctor

would have perished there and then. He killed three of the dogs and used their skins for coverlets, their bodies for wind shields, their harness for puttees, and their frozen legs as a flagpole on which he hoisted his shirt when daylight came, in the hope of attracting attention from the shore or some passing ships.

In this way he drifted some twenty miles without abandoning hope. The Doctor had heard too many stories of miraculous last-minute rescues among the fisher folk to do that. Fortunately, some seal fishers had observed the ice pan with its burden and reported it to the nearest village. In that village was a native with a telescope and after a close lookout he sighted the castaway and found that the wind was bearing him toward shore.

At first it was impossible to launch a boat, because the ice was breaking up all along the coast, but after a night of anxiety the villagers got together a volunteer crew at daybreak and, conditions having improved, succeeded in reaching the exhausted Doctor, when they bore him ashore in triumph, looking a weird sight tied up in rags and wrapped in the skins of dogs.

It is characteristic of Grenfell's love for all animals that before leaving the spot where he was rescued, he erected a memorial to the dogs who, by their deaths, saved his life while adrift on the ice pan.

In one winter at St. Anthony, on the north coast of Newfoundland, Doctor Grenfell covered over fifteen hundred miles with his dog team when upon errands of mercy in every type of bitter weather. During the whole of that winter he was only able to rest, at the trader's hut where he lived, on three Sundays. During all the others, there were sick people to be visited, often long distances away through dense woods or across the ice.

Sometimes during these trips the Doctor covered seventy-five miles in a day with his dog team. At other times five miles was covered in one day with difficulty. Winter travel in those wild parts often means hardships, as when the traveller loses his way and wanders for days hopelessly lost. In one case a white man was reduced to chewing pieces of green sealskin cut from his boots and to cooking his skin gloves over a fire which he succeeded in kindling.

It is not surprising, after reading of the care with which Doctor Grenfell and his helpers looked after the sick, to learn that even the poorest people in Labrador will not accept a penny payment when any of the members of the mission wake them up, perhaps late at night, to demand a meal and a bed before continuing their journey in the morning. That meal may mean short rations the next day; the bed may mean some one else sitting up all night, but the fisher folk know that the doctors are ever ready to set out on their errands of mercy at any hour, and they insist on repaying them in the only way possible.

Many fine men and women have eagerly gone to Labrador to help Doctor Grenfell in this great mission of healing. From the United States, from Canada and Newfoundland, and from Great Britain, men and women have gone out to serve in the hospitals which he founded. All of these men and women are highly trained and could easily have secured good positions in their own countries and lived comfortable lives. But they had heard of Grenfell's work and the need for helpers, and they sacrificed their comforts and went, just as noble souls have always gone, to the succour of the sick and weak.

The noble work begun by Grenfell forty years ago is now carried on, with the founder's assistance, by the International Grenfell Association.

Few lives are so inspiring as this fine record of real sacrifice for others, yet few people are so little known, for Grenfell of Labrador works far away from civilisation and newspapers, and during his rare visits to England he prefers to talk about anything but himself.

Since this chapter was written the greatest medical missionary of our generation has become Sir Wilfred Grenfell, K.C.M.G., and surely no honour bestowed by the King has been more richly deserved. For Sir Wilfred Grenfell's career lends lustre to the great tradition of those who, caring nothing for their own comfort and well-being, have gone forth into the far places, to make the world a better, kindlier place.

CHAPTER XI

IN January, 1922, a great whale swam into the mouth of the Panama Canal and was such a danger to shipping that it was killed with machine guns. The question was what to do with the body and this was towed to Cristobal Docks where an effort was made to raise it from the water. But even the great seventy-five-ton cranes could not lift it, so the carcass was towed out to sea and bombed to pieces by aeroplanes. This whale was ninety-eight feet long and must have weighed somewhere about a hundred tons.

Mr. Mitchell Hedges tells of this whale at the beginning of his book "Battles with Giant Fish," so as to give the reader some idea of the real size of the creatures which still inhabit the seas of the world. "There are," he says, "monsters beneath the waters of the Seven Seas of which science knows nothing. . . . Water beasts-of-prey beyond the imagination are waiting discovery and investigation, and I feel convinced that it is beneath the surface of the mighty ocean that startling discoveries will be made, to the great enrichment and advance of science."

In an earlier chapter the story has been told of the discovery by Lady Richmond Brown and Mr. Mitchell Hedges of an unknown tribe of San Blas Indians. It was in the course of this same journey that Mr. Hedges spent some months in successful attempts to capture great salt-water fish. His first experiment was made in the mouth of the

Black River of Jamaica, where he began by hooking a fine tarpon. He fought it for forty minutes then got it into the boat, but since a tarpon is not fit to eat he merely took a couple of its huge scales, each the size of a five-shilling piece, and let it go again.

Two days later he was fishing from a boat at the mouth of the same river with rod and line, his bait being half a mullet, when all of a sudden there was a strike and a great gleaming mass shot out of the water thirty yards astern of the boat. Then with a scream the line was torn off the reel as the huge fish rushed seaward. Griffiths, his coloured boatman, was so paralysed at the size of the fish that he blundered over getting up the anchor and hardly any line remained on the reel when, by a mercy, the great fish turned and went racing upstream. Griffiths paddled like mad, and presently the tarpon shot again into the air, falling with a crash which sent the spray flying. By this time hundreds of people were gathering on the river banks and yelling with excitement. An hour went by—two hours—three, and still the giant fought. Mr. Hedges was aching in every limb. Six times the fish had travelled from the sea a mile up river and back, a distance of twelve miles in all, and yet it seemed full of fight. At last it began to show signs of being played out and Mr. Hedges, staggering with fatigue under the blaze of the tropical sun, was able to reel in. Then, just as the victory seemed to be won, the line, twisted and kinked, gave way and the tarpon, possibly the largest ever hooked, disappeared. Of the many who saw this giant fish not one put its weight at less than two hundred and fifty pounds and the best judges vowed it was quite three hundred.

Such a disaster was enough to make many men give up but Mr. Hedges stuck to his guns, or rather his rods, only to meet with fresh disappointments. The next fish he hooked went straight away and, in spite of a sixty-pound pressure on the reel brakes, smashed the line. It was a shark, and afterward two more sharks took the bait. One broke the line, the next simply bit through the steel wire trace. The power of a shark's jaws is so great that they can nip the leg off a man as easily as you or I could cut a string with a pair of sharp scissors.

But the luck was due to turn and after a splendid fight Mr. Hedges captured a red snapper nearly five feet long and weighing one hundred two and a quarter pounds. A twenty-pound snapper is thought to be a good fish and this one was a world's record. Then on a fine December morning, while fishing off the mouth of the Black River, a monster seized the bait and went right out to sea, towing the boat like a chip behind it. Two hours passed in a desperate struggle and more than once the little dugout canoe was nearly swamped. At last the fish, a shark, was got alongside and Griffiths hitched a rope around its tail. Then began the slow and difficult business of towing it ashore and when at last it was landed, it proved to be an ugly brute of a shovel-nose, weighing two hundred and thirty-seven pounds. Mr. Hedges was very proud of this capture, for it was his record up to date. Later, however, as we shall see, he came to think such a fish very small beer.

On New Year's Eve, fishing near the same spot, he struck a leopard ray. All these tropical rays are terrible creatures, for they possess a very long whiplike tail in which is a dart or spear, dreadfully poisonous. The dart makes a most dangerous wound, and sometimes the victim becomes paralysed. This ray when landed weighed seventy-five pounds and was followed by one of eighty pounds.

This was nothing to what was to follow. There came a steady, heavy pull and, in spite of a fifty-pound pressure on the reel brake, the fish continued to move steadily away. At last Mr. Hedges managed to stop it and after a long time got it close to the shore. Then he himself landed from the boat and at last beached the brute. It was a sting ray, a hideous monster with a dirty brown back, raised, staring eyes and an immensely long tail. If the leopard ray is dangerous, the sting ray is much more so, for its dagger, hard as ivory, is about a foot long and the poison is deadly. After being struck the victim's body is twisted in dreadful contortions, black blood pours from the mouth, and death comes in three to six minutes. This terror weighed no less than two hundred and sixty pounds.

An even larger ray was hooked later. It weighed nearly three hundred pounds and had a double dagger. It was caught from the boat, and Mr. Hedges and his man had a terrible job to kill it. Even after it had received four bullets through its head from an automatic pistol it still struggled, lashing out with its fearful tail. Even this was not the record for, a few days later, while fishing from the boat, there came a rush which almost upset the dugout. Griffiths got the anchor up in a hurry and the fish towed the boat right out to sea. There was no question of playing it; the creature was far too heavy, and it simply towed the boat as it pleased. The breeze was strong, waves began to break over the boat and the case looked hopeless when suddenly the fish turned in a semicircle and went back towards the shore. The battle went on for over four hours and only those who have ever fought a big fish know how every muscle aches during such a struggle. At last the fish got into shallow water near the shore and suddenly rose to the surface, beating the sea into spray, while its long whip cut viciously in every direction. "How on earth are we going to land him?" groaned Mr. Hedges.

"We land him, boss," cried Griffiths. "We land him if stay all night."

At long last they themselves managed to reach the shore, but unfortunately Mr. Hedges had not got his pistol with him, and dared not try to drag the fish up the beach for fear of its poison-bearing tail. Two Negroes came to the rescue and, going off in their boat, fetched the pistol, and six shots through the ray's ugly head finished it. The monster was sixteen feet from head to tip of tail and seven feet six inches across. Its weight was four hundred and ten pounds. Mr. Hedges is a fairly powerful man, yet next day he was too stiff to move and had to remain indoors all day.

Some weeks later there was a terrible tragedy in Kingstown Harbour. A girl named Adelin Lopez was bathing near the Yacht Club and was standing in fairly shallow water when her father, who was on shore, heard her scream. He dashed in and, as he lifted his daughter out, found that her right leg had been bitten clean off. In spite of all that doctors could do for the poor child she died.

Mr. Hedges vowed vengeance. Getting five empty fifty-gallon oil drums he fastened them to the bottom with lines and to each attached a baited shark hook. Next morning one of the buoys was seen to be dipping and diving. The excitement was tremendous and such crowds poured down to the shore that, even with the help of police, Mr. Hedges had a difficult task to get to his boat. Plenty of help was ready to tow the captive ashore and this proved to be a shark which, though only eleven feet long, was no less than eight and a half feet in girth and weighed over seven hundred pounds.

April found Mr. Mitchell Hedges and Lady Richmond Brown at Colon. People who think that the sea is always

calm in these tropical latitudes would be surprised to know
how hard the northeast trade winds blow, and how ugly a
sea runs. Mr. Hedges began by catching a forty-two pound
barracuda on a spinning bait. The barracuda is a long, narrow pikelike fish with tremendously sharp teeth and the
Negroes dread it as much as they do the shark. There are
many cases on record of people being attacked by barracuda, among them a girl swimmer off the Florida coast
who was so badly bitten that she died from loss of blood.
After the barracuda had been dispatched, something seized
the spoon bait with a furious snatch, and to his amazement, Mr. Hedges found himself fast in a porpoise. He
was amazed because it is the rarest thing possible to hook
such a fish. The creature fought like a salmon and great
was the triumph when it was brought alongside, gaffed and
got aboard the yacht. It weighed two hundred pounds.

Off the San Blas coast our travellers startled the Indians
by catching with rod and line two nurse sharks, one weighing one hundred and seventy-five pounds and the other three
hundred and sixty pounds. Then, using a real shark line,
he hooked a monster which proved to be a shovel-nose
weighing no less than nine hundred and ten pounds. The
Indians were so delighted that they brought out a whole
boatload of pineapples and other fruit to the yacht.

The more Mr. Hedges fished the more certain he became
that there were far bigger fish to be tackled than any he had
yet landed, so when, a little later, he had taken his yacht, the
Cara, through the Panama Canal into the Pacific, he went
to the workshop at the Balboa docks and asked the superin-
tendent if he could make him some shark hooks. The super-
intendent said he would certainly do so but when he saw the
size of the hooks which Mr. Hedges had specified on a sheet
of paper, he burst out laughing. His men, too, fairly roared.

"What on earth are you going to catch?" they asked at last—"whales?"

"No. Sharks and sawfish."

"But they are no use. You can't sell them."

"I don't want to sell them. What I am after is records," answered Mr. Hedges.

In the end the man got quite keen and turned out the most amazing collection of fishing tackle. Some idea of it may be gained when it is said that each of the larger shark hooks, with the chain attached, weighed fourteen pounds, and that the fishing line was the strongest half-inch Manilla rope. The barbs of these great hooks were filed sharp as razors and the hooks themselves made of the finest spring steel. All the Panama people were hugely amused at the mad Englishman's tackle and the local paper had a full description of it.

Getting aboard the *Cara,* Mr. Hedges and Lady Brown started off to the island of Toboguilla, around whose shores the clear water was alive with fish. Suddenly out from the water sprang a big shark, coming down again with a thundering crash. The creature was trying to free itself of the parasitic sea lice which clung to it. Mr. Hedges determined to try for it and ran out four lines, each carrying one of the smaller shark hooks and baited with big Spanish mackerel. The fourth line was hardly out before the first was seized. Mr. Hedges grabbed the line and struck. He dropped it with a yell, for the pull was so tremendous that it seared his hand like a red-hot iron. He and the black engineer, Robbie, began to play the fish, while Lady Brown and the other man hauled in the other lines so as to get them out of the way, but before this could be done a second shark took hold. After a long and hard struggle both the sharks were drawn alongside, and a club was used to stun and kill them. When both were quiet and apparently dead the first was hauled on deck and Mr. Hedges was bending over it to get the hook out of its mouth when it lashed out its tail, striking Mr. Hedges across the shoulder and head and nearly knocking him overboard. These sharks weighed two hundred and sixty and two hundred and eighty pounds respectively, and Mr. Hedges set to cutting them up.

"What are you going to do with those great chunks of flesh?" asked Lady Brown.

"Use them for bait," was Mr. Hedges' answer, as he got out one of his giant fourteen-pound hooks and proceeded to bait it with a lump of solid shark flesh weighing seventy-five pounds. He laid out the bait, but nothing happened, so they had a cup of tea while they waited.

It was a long wait. Mr. Hedges had almost given up hope when suddenly the slack line began to slide slowly over-board. "A fish!" he shouted, as he and Robbie sprang to their feet. They had no idea what to do. As for striking, if they handled the rope the chances were that they would be instantly dragged overboard. The last of the slack ran out and the half-inch Manilla creaked as it tightened against the capstan; the yacht itself began to swing.

"Up with the anchor!" cried Mr. Hedges, and when this was done the twenty-ton vessel swung away like a dinghy in the wake of the monster. All four tailed on to the rope and pulled and pulled, but it was a long time before they got so much as a glimpse of the giant, and longer still before they got it alongside. Mr. Hedges then fired two expanding bullets through its head, but the only result was a furious rush. It was another half-hour before it gave up the strug-gle, then a third bullet finished it. Since it was out of the question to get it aboard, the motor was started and it was towed inshore and moored close to the beach, where the fall-

GIGANTIC SHOVEL-NOSE SHARK (WEIGHT 1460 LB.) CAUGHT OFF PANAMA BY
MR MITCHELL HEDGES

LADY RICHMOND BROWN AND MR MITCHELL HEDGES WITH THEIR RECORD CATCH—A SAWFISH WEIGHING 5700 LB.

151

ing tide would leave it dry. Two hours later Mr. Hedges was able to measure and weigh his greatest catch up to date; it proved to be a shovel-nose shark fourteen feet nine inches long and weighing nearly three quarters of a ton.

Such a catch only spurred Mr. Hedges to greater exertions, and presently he added to his bag two more shovel-nose sharks, one of eight hundred and sixty pounds, and the other nine hundred and twenty pounds. Between the islands of Taboga and Urava was a channel frequented by big fish, but here the bottom was all hard coral, making anchoring impossible. After searching for some time, Mr. Hedges found a spot of sand where the anchor would hold and there took a big sand shark. Cutting this up, he baited two of his largest hooks with slabs of flesh each weighing at least a hundred pounds, and rowing them out in the dinghy, dropped them overboard. The morning passed, nothing happened, they lunched on tinned meat and vegetables and fresh fruit, and still all was quiet. Then about three in the afternoon one line began to move. Up came the anchor, and away went the yacht. The fish swung round and made up channel toward some dangerous rocks, but luckily, when quite near them, swung again and went back into deep water. For an hour and a half the creature dragged the yacht as if it had been a toy, then at last began to weaken. Suddenly Robbie and the other man dropped the line. "Boss, it's the devil!" shrieked Robbie. "Cut the line!"

"Don't be a fool!" retorted Mr. Hedges who had not himself yet seen the fish. He got the men to work again but when for a second time the creature came to the surface he could only gasp with horror, for never before had he seen such a hideous monster. It was a hammerhead shark, a creature with a head shaped like a hammer, a monstrous mouth and great bulging eyes at each end of the hammer. Robbie

L

and the native were terrified and still anxious to cut the line, but Mr. Hedges told them fiercely to haul. He snatched up his rifle and as the ghastly looking creature came alongside, quickly put three bullets through its head. These finished it, and towing it astern they hauled it back to Taboga. Since the tide was low they had to manhandle the carcass ashore, and it took sixteen men to haul the creature on to the beach. It was the biggest hammerhead ever taken, being seventeen feet six inches in length and weighing thirteen hundred and fifty pounds.

But here is the strangest part of the business. Right across its body on both sides were fearful scars, showing quite clearly that some monster had seized it across the middle. The size of a creature big enough to tackle such a shark and the gape of its jaws can only be guessed at. It is, however, one more proof that stranger things live in the sea than man has yet seen or dreamed of.

Some days later the yacht was anchored close inshore and Lady Brown, who was keen on collecting shells, was standing in only about nine inches of water, bending down with her back to the sea when Mr. Hedges and two friends who were aboard were horrified to see a black fin cutting the sea and driving straight inshore.

"Don't move!" roared Mr. Hedges. "Look behind you. Don't step back!"

Quite calmly Lady Brown turned her head and saw the shark actually wriggling on the bottom in its frantic efforts to reach her. Its sabre-toothed jaws were barely a yard away. Lady Brown walked quietly up on to the beach, the shark still vainly trying to follow her.

"I'm going to get that fish," declared Mr. Hedges, and at once he ran out a big hook baited with a huge lump of sand shark. Within a very few minutes the man-eater took hold. It got short shrift and with half a dozen men on the line was hauled in close enough to be shot. It was a tiger shark weighing twelve hundred pounds.

There is no space here to describe many other exciting adventures with sharks and other fish, including a desperate but successful battle with a sand shark weighing no less than six hundred and twenty pounds which Lady Brown hooked on rod and line. It was over five hours from the time the creature was hooked until it was finally killed and fastened to the stern of the yacht. This was the largest sand shark ever taken.

The anglers visited the Pearl Islands and had fine sport, then returned to Taboga where Mr. Hedges caught another shovel-nose weighing thirteen hundred pounds. Later in the same day they had a big hook overboard when the bait was taken by a monstrous fish. The strain was so great that the anchor was torn from its hold, and the yacht towed rapidly out to sea. Time and again the three men gripped the line but without the faintest result. The fish went straight ahead for two hours, towing the *Cara* as easily as if it had been a chip, then all of a sudden the line went slack. They hauled in, to find that the hook itself had been bitten clean through. When you remember that the shank of this hook was made of half-inch spring steel, the jaw power capable of such a feat is almost beyond imagination. What the fish was no one will ever know.

There were sawfish in these waters, and a few days later Mr. Hedges went out in a *panga* (a flat-bottomed boat) with a harpooner to try to capture one of these strange fish. As they drifted slowly the harpooner, standing in the bow, suddenly called out "Back water!" Down shot his keen-pointed lance and next instant the line attached to the harpoon went flying overboard at tremendous speed. The pace at which the fish swam was extraordinary, and the water curled white under the bow as the panga shot out to sea.

"A big sawfish," the harpooner told them in Spanish, and certainly it was big, for when it sulked and went to the bottom nothing they could do stirred it. After a long half-hour it suddenly roused and began swinging back toward the shore, and at last they got close enough to the beach to scramble ashore. Before the fish could move again they fastened the line to a rock close to the water's edge, then the crew of the yacht joined them, and all set to hauling on the rope. Inch by inch, foot by foot, the monster was dragged in until at last Mr. Hedges was able to drive two bullets into it. It reared up, grunting hideously, then fell with a mighty splash and lay still. This fish proved to be twenty-four and a half feet long and seventeen and a half in girth, and it weighed one and three-quarter tons.

All up and down the coast the stories ran of the huge fish caught by the Englishman, and visitors came from distances to see. The British Consul, Mr. Ewing, and his wife arrived and Mr. Ewing was intensely pleased to catch a three hundred pound sand shark. He had hardly killed it before Mrs. Ewing's line ran out.

"Heaven knows what she has hooked," cried Mr. Hedges, "but it's no sand shark."

The anchor had to be got up in a hurry and for an hour and a half the great fish towed the yacht before it could be got alongside and shot to death. It proved to be a monstrous white shark weighing fourteen hundred pounds. The very next day news came that the President of Panama, Doctor Belisario Porras, was coming out in his yacht. He arrived just as Mr. Hedges' party were towing ashore two huge sawfish, the larger of which was almost exactly the same size as the first one caught. He was delighted and astonished.

"Never did I know that such fish lived here!" he exclaimed. "I must be photographed with them! I must be made immortal." And photographed he was, wearing a bathing suit and with a towel round his shoulders.

Fishing with Spanish mackerel as bait, Mr. Hedges had a blank day, catching nothing at all. The fact was that the bait was tainted, and that sharks do not like putrid fish. But the natives believed that the reason for the failure was that Lady Brown was not with them. They declared that she was a mascot in the matter of fishing. Curiously enough when, next day, she came out with them, the party made a record catch, taking in all sixteen sand sharks and a gigantic tiger shark, this latter barred and striped like a Bengal tiger. The weight of the whole bag was no less than sixty-four hundred and ninety pounds, a world's record for one day's line fishing.

The very next afternoon, when fishing from the yacht with the heaviest tackle, a fish seized the bait and towed the *Cara* right out to sea. Two hours and a half passed before those aboard got even a glimpse of the creature, then at last it rose almost under the yacht. The sight was paralysing, for the creature, a giant sawfish, seemed to be almost as large as the vessel itself. Inch by inch they managed to raise the colossal bulk and Mr. Hedges was on the point of finishing it with a bullet from his rifle, when it made a last fearful struggle. Its great toothed saw struck the bottom of the *Cara* with a force that jarred the whole craft, and sent a wave right over the deck. Then the line went slack, the hook had drawn and the great fish escaped. Later they found four holes driven clean through the copper sheathing at the bottom. This fish must have weighed well over two tons.

The next experience of Mr. Hedges and Lady Brown was while they were towing in a twelve-foot shovel-nose and were caught in a sudden savage storm. The line by which they were towing the shark caught around the propeller, the engine stopped and they were helpless. With a crash the yacht was flung against a point of rock jutting out from the island, but a fresh wave swept her into deep water. Mr. Hedges managed to cut the rope and the engine started again. It was dark as pitch and the wind blew with such incredible fury that a heavy coil of rope was whipped off the deck like a feather and whirled into the air. The rain was like a waterspout and waves broke clean over the little ship. When at last it grew a little lighter, Mr. Hedges found to his dismay that they were being driven right out into the Pacific. But the sturdy little engine was still running, and after a desperate struggle they gained the lee of the island, anchored in safety and fell down exhausted. What roused them was the discovery that the yacht was leaking like a sieve. Pumping hard, they made for Balboa, where ten days were spent in repairs before the *Cara* was again fit for sea.

Back in Panama Bay, Mr. Hedges set to work to beat his own record in size of fish and going out in a panga with a harpooner, struck a sawfish which raced away at a furious pace. It was ninety minutes before they saw it, then it rose and began to thrash the water, making tremendous sideway sweeps with its great saw. Had the boat been within striking distance, one blow would have cut it in two. Mr. Hedges fired twice and as his bullets thudded home the great beast dived. In a few moments it rose again, making a tremendous commotion and a fresh hail of bullets finished it. But it was so big that it was out of the question to tow it, and they had to wait until the *Cara* came to their assistance, when the great beast was towed into shallow water and left until the tide fell. There was no doubt about its being a record, for it proved to be twenty-nine feet long, while its weight was no less than forty-five hundred pounds.

Going out early next morning, the anglers had the luck to see a most amazing battle between a fourteen foot shark and a giant sawfish. The shark rushed at the sawfish and tore a great chunk from its side, but as it turned the wounded monster swung with incredible speed and all aboard the yacht heard the thud as the great saw struck the shark, almost cutting it in two. A second blow killed the shark outright.

A record tiger shark, more than twenty feet long and weighing seventeen hundred and sixty pounds, was the next notable take; then as it was getting near the time when they had to leave for England, the two anglers made up their minds to make one more effort to beat all records and for this purpose went back to their old fishing ground off Taboga.

"I should like to catch a real whale of a fish," Mr. Hedges said to Lady Brown, and smiling she answered, "We are going to. I feel that we are going to."

A few minutes later one line began running out. "Here's the big fish," cried Lady Brown, and sure enough the line tautened with such force as to pull the anchor clean out of the ground, and the yacht started away toward Morro Island, seven miles away. Robbie wanted to start up the engine, but Mr. Hedges would not allow it, for the strain on the line was as great as it would bear. There was nothing for it but patience. At last the fish circled, then dived and began fighting desperately deep down, making the whole yacht quiver with its struggles. It did not seem as if any line could stand the strain. But it held, and up out of the water came a great saw. Once more it forged ahead and with joy they saw it heading for the shore.

Five hours had passed since it was first hooked, and it seemed at last to be tiring. Mr. Hedges had the idea of getting to land in the dinghy, carrying the line, then fastening it to a rock, and so dragging the fish to the beach. Robbie and he dropped the dinghy overboard and were in the act of pulling ashore when the monster suddenly came to life again and dashed away, towing the dinghy stern first. She was whipped past the yacht, then slewed sideways and upset. There was nothing for it but to abandon the dinghy and swim back to the yacht. From the deck they could see the dinghy bobbing in the distance, and cursing his own stupidity, Mr. Hedges got the engine started and went in chase. They caught up, got an iron hook around the line, hauled it up and made it fast to the capstan, then fastened the capsized dinghy astern. The tide was nearly full, and with infinite care they got the yacht into a sandy cove and anchored her. Then after baling out the dinghy, they paddled ashore, and this time succeeded in getting the line holding the fish firmly fastened to a rock.

It was seven hours since they had first hooked the great fish and it now seemed to be dead, but to make sure Mr. Hedges put two bullets into it. They got a fresh line around its tail and rested until the tide fell. This proved to be the largest fish they had ever taken, for it was thirty-one feet long, twenty-one in girth and weighed fifty-seven hundred pounds.

Then at last it was time to return to England, and with the little yacht loaded with specimens, they returned to Balboa, went through the Canal, and at Colon found a steamer to take them home.

CHAPTER XII

WHEN your father was a boy, the youth of this country was thrilled by the story of a pioneer trip across Africa made by H. M. Stanley, the famous explorer who followed in the footsteps of Livingstone, the great African missionary. Stanley was almost the first of many explorers who have braved the varied dangers which await the traveller in unknown Africa.

Many years later two explorers of our own generation thought it would be interesting to make that same trip across Africa, taking with them a moving-picture camera so that they could film Unknown Africa—its beasts, birds, scenery, natives, and wonders—and bring home a record which would interest large numbers of people who could not see Africa for themselves.

The journey across Africa from east to west is the story which you are going to read about in this chapter. It was begun in April, 1913, and ended with the return of the expedition to London fourteen months later. In between those dates the two white men who carried through this great adventure had travelled on foot from Mombasa on the east coast of Africa through what is now Kenya Colony, Uganda, the mighty Congo down to Matadi, on the west coast of the "Dark Continent."

In several respects this journey will become historical in the history of modern exploration. It was one of the first great feats of exploration made, not to discover new lands or to create new records in endurance, although considerable endurance was necessary to ensure success. It was not made for the purpose of shooting wild beasts for their horns, or to photograph them when dead. In point of fact only two animals were shot during the whole journey and these were in self-defence.

This journey across Africa was made for the express purpose of making a film of Africa as it really is so that the students and public of the whole world might be instructed and amused. It was, in fact, the biggest film achievement made up to that date.

And now, before coming to the actual story of the expedition, let me say one or two words about Mr. Cherry Kearton, one of the two men who made this journey and the photographer of the expedition. Mr. Cherry Kearton is a photographer of wild life and a lecturer whose name is now known throughout the world. He spends all his time making fresh journeys or lecturing in Great Britain and the United States on journeys he has made. He has exhibited his animal films and lectured before the Royal Family at Windsor Castle and before the President of the United States at the White House.

All this is well known, for to-day Mr. Kearton is one of the leading authorities on travel photography. But it is not so well known that this remarkable man, so quiet spoken and serious that a stranger might take him for a prosperous city merchant, took his first pictures of animal life when he was still a boy, and with a camera which he had bought from a friend for 4/6d, about a dollar and a dime in American money. He knew hardly anything about photography in those days; so it is not surprising that when he developed his plates in a "dark room" made by simply pulling down the blind, all the plates were blank.

Later he discovered the reason, and his next effort was more successful.

He was working then in a publishing house near Fleet Street, and had he stayed there he would almost certainly have become a famous editor. But the thirst for adventure was in his blood, and he gave more and more of his time to photographing wild life. He would wait for hours hidden in a bush with his camera in order to photograph a bird sitting on a nest, or a stoat passing. And eventually he gave up Fleet Street work and decided to devote his life to his work of photographing life in the wild, of which he can justly claim to be the pioneer. How much the world owes to that decision—what we should have lost if Cherry Kearton had never gone abroad with his film camera—every boy who has seen one of his films must realise.

With him on this journey you are to read about was a single companion, Mr. James Barnes, another well-known traveller and writer. It was arranged that James Barnes should handle the writing part and Cherry Kearton the pictures of the journey.

In one or two respects the trip was partly unsuccessful. It was found that inside the dark forests it was impossible to take pictures without an exposure of at least one second. And you cannot get a fully grown lion to "look pleasant" and keep still for so long just because you happen to want to photograph him. The result was that many opportunities for taking amazingly interesting photographs, especially of elephant herds, had to be missed. But this journey was a success in that it proved that hunting wild beasts in their jungles armed only with a camera was possible; and it was this journey, brilliantly planned and carried out to the letter, which led to all those interesting trips in Asia and Africa which Cherry Kearton and other animal photographers have made since the war, and which are such a popular feature when they are shown in the moving picture houses.

The journey really began with the arrival of the expedition at Nairobi in East Africa. There they secured a band of black porters to carry their equipment, and also the services of Mr. Lydford, a young white hunter who knew the country through which they were to pass, and also had an interest in photographic work.

Three mules completed the expedition, and a start was made in wet, cold weather.

A few days' marching, during which game gradually became more plentiful, took the travellers out of the rich green country into a land where there was every evidence of a drought,—parched-up grass, dried bushes, trickling rivers in a strange contrast to the country on the other side of the mountains they had crossed.

On Monday, June 2, 1913, they made their longest and hardest march of the journey, covering over twenty-two miles without water, and reaching the bank of a river called the Uashu Neru. By this time they were in the heart of real African country, described by Cherry Kearton himself in these words:

"It was like marching into a painting. To the north rose mountain after mountain in fantastic form. In the first mile we descended 900 feet. Buffalo and rhino spoor were plentiful, rock rabbits abounded, but we saw no other living thing until in the afternoon we sighted a troop of giraffe in the distance."

They were in the land of the palm tree now, and the river banks were fringed with graceful fanlike branches. The heat, too, was increasing, making it necessary to rest for some hours at midday. But they pressed on to Archers

Post, where two bush tracts met, and where they found a solitary Englishman living alone, with only a gramophone and a miniature golf course he had laid down for company.

On June 23 the expedition arrived at the "picture ground," a tract of country full of water holes used by big game, and almost rainless. When Cherry Kearton and his companions camped there, they found to their joy that no rain had fallen for twelve months, which greatly increased the chances of the big game they wished to film coming to the holes in search of water.

Investigation showed that there was abundance of wild life in the neighbourhood. Elephant and rhino, giraffe, zebra, gazelle, leopards, and lions had all left traces behind them which could be recognised by the experienced explorer, and hurriedly Cherry Kearton and his companions started to build the "blinds" or concealments behind which they intended to wait and watch in order to photograph the unsuspecting animals when they came down to drink at the water holes. Inside these hiding places they waited day after day, under a grilling sun which sent the temperature up to 120 or 130 degrees, for the opportunity to take the photographs which they had come so far to get. Many days they had no luck at all. Ten hours of torrid heat and cramped limbs did not produce a single picture. But there were other days when the excitement and photographs taken well repaid them for all the waiting.

Hidden away behind the grass shelters, Cherry Kearton and his companions learnt much about the drinking habits of wild animals. Some drank only at daybreak, others at nightfall, the giraffe once every five days as regularly as clockwork. Some of the game were never seen to drink at all, and as these were the only water holes for miles around, they must have crept down after darkness fell.

It needed much hard, patient work to get a series of pictures of the various animals drinking. Such pictures in a film were a source of wonder ten years ago. To-day most of those who read this book have seen these pictures in films of wild life in the jungle. The next time you see one, remember the hours of waiting, the heat, and the agony from insect bites and other causes which the big game photographer must undergo when hunting big game with a camera.

Imagine, for instance, the plight of Cherry Kearton and his one companion when not one or two, but a whole company of fully grown African lions decided to meet only a few yards from their grass shelter. All night the two men crouched in their flimsy hiding place while the roars of the king of beasts resounded through the night. If one of those lions had detected their presence, it would have meant two men and one rifle against an unknown number of lions—and with the darkness on the side of the lions. It is this sort of experience which makes every day in the African jungle an adventure.

Before leaving the water holes Cherry Kearton got a moving picture of no fewer than twelve giraffes drinking together. It was a most interesting strip of film, for the giraffe is the most timid of creatures, with very keen eyesight, and the approach of the giraffe to the water was a signal for large numbers of smaller beasts to come down as well. They knew that the giraffe would not have shown themselves had there been lions or leopards in the vicinity.

On the march southward again, they reached the Uashu Neru to learn of a marauding lion in the vicinity. A search failed to find any trace of Leo, but some weeks later Claydon, the solitary white man mentioned earlier in this story, found it. Or rather the lion found him, with the result that he had to go into hospital for three months to get patched up.

The following day the travellers got some excellent photographs of a contest between a solitary jackal and a horde of vultures for the carcass of a zebra killed by a lion the night before they found it. The jackal kept the vultures at bay for some time, but when some hundreds of these birds of prey had dropped out of the sky they made a concerted attack and drove their solitary antagonist off. The pictures of that episode made an interesting record of greed in wild life.

A few days later Kearton and his companion paid a visit to one of the great and unknown natural wonders of the world. This was the Magadi lake of solid soda—a great glaring sheet of white crystals seven miles long and two miles wide, with a constant miasma rising from it that reminds the traveller of a chemical laboratory. There is soda enough in that one spot to supply the whole world for five hundred years, but no one will envy the workmen who try to get it back to civilisation.

The next time the expedition took pictures it meant going back to Nairobi for the purpose of securing a galvanised iron water tank! This unusual item of their equipment was necessary because Kearton and Barnes had set their heart on securing pictures of a herd of wild buffalo—and it is difficult to photograph a herd of a hundred charging buffalo that will attack anything and any one at sight.

The problem was solved by sinking the iron tank in the middle of a swamp, partly filling it with stones and getting into it before the buffalo spotted them. Once inside the herd could not cross the swamp to reach them and they could turn the handle of the moving-picture camera in safety. This ingenious notion enabled Kearton to get some good "close-ups" of the herd when previous attempts had ended in failure.

The country abounded in man-eating lions, and Fritz, one of the native hunters, was constantly risking his life during these excursions. In the end he did it once too often, for after assisting in the deaths of over sixty lions, he was himself killed by one in January, 1914.

There is a saying in Africa that if you keep after lions long enough, they will get you in the end, and at Nairobi, Cherry Kearton saw a dozen graves of men killed by them.

Altogether Kearton and his companions saw about a dozen lions on this trip across Africa. And they were searching for them. In the case of the hunters who go out for fourteen days and manage to shoot six fully grown lions in that short time, it frequently happens that the explanation, if known, would be found in poisoned bait put down where the lions feed. It is easy to "bag" three or four lions a night by this method.

Generally speaking, the African lion, although he exists in large numbers, will not attack men in daylight. Native villages are attacked at night, and the solitary hunter is always in danger, but if you are not out to kill at any cost, you can travel great distances even in the heart of Africa without actually seeing a lion. Cherry Kearton, for instance, met a man living in an outlying district who in eight years there had not seen one lion, although he had heard them roaring in the distance many times. In order to preserve the African lion from extinction, the Government has now placed a limit on the number that may be shot in any one season.

More weeks of travelling, at first by train and later by more primitive means, brought the expedition to Uganda, and on Christmas day they reached one of the most beauti-

MR KEARTON WITH LEGGING WHICH A LION HAD
BITTEN THROUGH   166

ful sights of the whole journey. This was Lake Llonga-llonga, described in Cherry Kearton's own words as "one of those liquid gems that Nature seems to have placed in exactly the sort of setting to display its beauty. It is a little sheet of light-blue crystal lying in the depths of what must have been once an old volcanic crater. It was comparatively a new discovery. The sight of it held us entranced, for we had been travelling through a broken, hilly country, burnt and parched from the lack of recent rains, and there from the top of a hill we looked down and saw the blue sparkle of the waters surrounded by a fringe of forest trees, palms and hard wood mingled—a perfect sanctuary for bird and beast and man."

After crossing the Semliki River, Kearton managed to get some pictures of what must have been the king of all the crocodiles. From within a hastily constructed shelter the photographer saw the monster rise out of the water, walking on all four legs and so large that there was at least two feet of space between his bulk and the sand. As far as could be judged this remarkable saurian was at least thirty feet in length. After seeing that crocodile, the expedition could believe a story put on record by another African pioneer of a rhinoceros being caught and dragged beneath the surface by these brutes.

Food was short in this region, and in order to avoid eating up the scant supplies available for the native inhabitants, the expedition could not stay long. Without delay they were on the march again, and entering the forest country.

Just inside the forests they came upon the track of elephants and decided to try and get some photographs of these great beasts in their natural state. To do this Cherry Kearton and Barnes climbed up into a tree and made a plat-

M

form of reeds on which they placed the film camera and prepared for action.

The elephants came—including a perfect specimen of male elephant with tusks that would have been worth much in London—and other beings came too. The other beings were swarms of ants who discovered the adventurers hidden up the tree and promptly made a concerted attack upon them.

The ants were all over them; down their backs, in their hair, up their sleeves. And they bit unmercifully until both the white men were frantic. And in the midst of this battle with ants a fine herd of elephants charged right under the tree.

Miraculously, Cherry Kearton forgot the ants and began to turn the handle of his camera. There were ants in his beard, ants all over him, biting as hard as they could, but his hand was perfectly steady as he photographed the elephants dashing past below them.

Hardly had the herd disappeared, when both men slipped down the tree and made for a water hole, where they dropped out of their clothing and cleansed themselves of the malicious ants in the only way possible. Nor did they return to the tree for the rest of their belongings until next day, when they went over from the camp to fetch them armed with bottles of paraffin and other ant-fighting appliances.

A little farther along the road to Irumu the expedition experienced a typical African storm. Clouds piled up overhead, until a single lightning flash heralded the breaking of the storm. In an instant the clouds seemed to burst and the rain came—such rain as few men see twice in a lifetime. Up the hills a solid wall of water advanced toward the spot where the expedition was camped. Everything was blotted out. Objects a hundred yards away could not be seen, so dark did it become. A moment later the wind came too, and before any one could move, tents and stores were blown away, tent poles snapped in two, and the members of the expedition were seeking to protect themselves from hailstones that nearly knocked one senseless.

There was nothing to do but cling to the stores and wait for the storm to pass. The native porters had run for shelter to the huts of the near-by village, where they crouched panic-stricken. And anyway, no man whose body was largely unprotected by clothing could have withstood the blows of the hailstones.

In five minutes the storm was over. It ceased as suddenly as it had begun, and the adventurers began to collect together the wreckage of their camp.

The expedition had to face two more storms after that, but although considerable damage was done to the tents, this did not matter very much, as after reaching Irumu they were able to live in the "rest houses" established by the Belgian Government through the Congo territory for the convenience of travellers.

Just beyond the frontier station of Irumu they reached the edge of the great African forest. It was a wonderful sight. A mighty rampart of timber stretched away north and south for more than eight hundred miles, covering the entire country to the west. In that forest lived people who saw no sunlight under its mighty canopy. Yet a few miles to the eastward trees were scarce and the natives rarely found any shade. It was one of those patterns which Nature weaves on such a grand scale in the mighty continent of Africa.

Within those mighty trees lived pigmy tribes little known to white men, possibly even undiscovered races of savages that still eat human flesh. That forest in the heart of Africa is the last home of witchcraft and sorcery. Paths have been cut through it by pioneers, paths that are reasonably safe to follow. But on either side stretch unknown forests for three hundred and twenty-five thousand square miles that have never been fully explored since the world began.

The expedition now faced the most difficult stage of their journey. For one thing they were racing against time in order to catch the monthly steamer at Basoko. Failure to catch it would mean another month in tropical Africa. And by this time Kearton and Barnes had experienced nine months of constant marching under tropical suns, and both were feeling the effects of the prolonged effort.

But if the forest trail was difficult, it was also a wonderful journey. Their path ran continually through thick dwarf bushes and other growths whose blossoms and berries added a touch of colour to the everlasting riot of greenery. At places the scents given off from buds and blossoms were overpowering. Underfoot mushrooms and other fungi grew from rotting masses of dead and decaying foliage. And at every step one saw countless insects.

It was a land of orchids, great trees and intertwined jungle—a wonderland that captivated the explorers but where also lurked disease and death.

The next stages of the journey were made by canoe along the river ways that take the place of roads through the great forest region. These canoes were simple hollowed-out trunks of trees, but the native paddlers were able to cover thirty miles a day in them, which is surprisingly good progress under the circumstances.

At Benalia, famous as the town to which the great Stanley returned with his search parties after his relief expedition that sought to find Livingstone, Kearton and Barnes met the first doctor they had seen since leaving Uganda, hundreds of miles away to the eastward. He was needed too, for in this town they also saw the first traces of "sleeping sickness," that dread African disease which scientists are trying so hard to find a remedy for. How terrible are its ravages in the Congo country may be realised by the fact that it has swept away a quarter of a million people in the course of the ten years before the war.

All along their route the expedition found deserted villages from which every inhabitant had either fled or died. Sleeping sickness and smallpox are still the twin curses of this forest land.

Small wonder, then, that Kearton and his companion were anxious to catch that steamer and not be faced with the prospect of a whole month of waiting in such an unhealthy spot after the privations they had undergone.

Everything possible was done to urge on the native crews of the canoes. On some days they managed to cover forty miles.

When nearing the end of the canoe journey Barnes got a bad dose of fever, and they decided that they simply must catch that steamer. On the last day, therefore, they pushed off early and rowed until midnight. Long before then the native crews were mutinous and were only prevented from landing at one of the native villages by threats. And at midnight two tired white men saw the lights of the tiny river station where the steamer would call looming out of the darkness. Half an hour later they landed and walked up to the fort, there to learn that the steamer would call the next morning. They had won their race against time by a few hours.

When they got on board the steamer the next day at Barumba, two hours along the river, Cherry Kearton had found that he had lost forty pounds since starting out from

East Africa and Barnes was lighter than he had been when at school. But that is the price which the fittest adventurers must pay for nine months of arduous journeying along the equator.

The fourteen days on the steamer were not pleasant. There were only five cabins for white men on board and all of these were occupied when they embarked. Therefore they had to live and sleep on deck. When it rained they were wet through. When the wind blew, they were half frozen, despite the fact that they were in Africa. And there were cases of sleeping sickness on board among the natives, which did not make for peace of mind among the white passengers.

The steamer carried them back to civilisation. Their adventurous journey across Unknown Africa was completed. They had travelled for fourteen months ever westward and reached the Atlantic Ocean at last. And they had made their precious film which would enable the public to see, comfortably seated in halls up and down the country, the sights which they had seen.

Preserving that film had not been an easy matter, for in that climate films will quickly become spoiled and useless unless in the hands of an expert. Cherry Kearton regarded his films as the most precious part of their stores. They were packed in strong steel water-tight cases, inside which were strong wooden boxes containing the film. In all he took over twelve thousand feet of pictures of jungle and native life. And it says much for the leading film adventurer of our generation that less than five per cent. of all that film was spoiled—a record in tropical photographic work.

And besides the film which these two white men brought back from the heart of Africa were the memories which they still have. These memories cannot be better described than in the words of James Barnes:

"As I looked out of the window of my hotel on the same view of Trafalgar Square on which I had gazed some fourteen months before, it seemed all a dream. The weather was exactly the same as when I had left it—cold and rainy—although it was now springtime. The same old man was selling papers at the corner; the be-medaled porter at the door stood in the same place. Despite the sizzling coals in the grate, I felt chilled to the marrow of my bones. I felt the call. I would have given something for the sight of the wide stretch of the grey-green plains dotted with thorn trees, the warmth of the spreading sunshine, and the gleaming pinnacle of Kenia rising above the belt of white clouds. Then again I thought of the gloom of the forest, of the cold, damp mornings and the prospect of the long trudge through the muddy ooze; of the many painful sights and the sickening villages; and I was glad to be back safe with it all behind me."

CHAPTER XIII

A FEW years before the war a young undergraduate at Oxford, desirous of securing for a paper he had to write for an examination some first-hand knowledge of the military architecture of the Crusades, persuaded his parents to give him two hundred pounds and set out on a visit to the little-known desert country of Syria.

He was only a boy, but a very adventurous boy who was bitten with the determination to do things "thoroughly," so on his arrival in the Near East he did not follow the usual path of the tourist, but straightway adopted native costume and set off barefoot into the Arabian desert to learn all he could about a land and a people that had fascinated him ever since he was old enough to read.

For two years this young British boy "lost himself" in the wilds of the desert. At the end of that time he returned to take his degree—with one hundred pounds still left of his original capital!

The other hundred pounds that his two years' travels had cost him were later on to be revealed as the finest investment of our generation for the British Empire. That first visit to Arabia resulted in far more important and spectacular things than writing a thesis. It marked the beginning of a dream—the dream of a united Arabia, a country whose people would stand together, shoulder to shoulder, back to back, instead of carrying on interminable petty revolts and rebellions among themselves.

That dream was to destroy another rival conception—the German vision of a Middle East under the sway of the Kaiser. And it was to end in the driving of the Turks out of Arabia and Syria, in the throning of a native king, and in the entry of the British boy into Damascus as a "prince of Mecca."

But that is anticipating events in the story.

In those days before the Great War—days which seem so far off and yet are in reality so close—no one knew of Thomas Edward Lawrence except his tutors at Oxford and a few experts who were interested in the fascinating study of antiquity, which together with poetry, was the great interest of young Lawrence's life from quite an early age.

To-day there are many people—the great ones of the earth—who would be proud to have Colonel Lawrence dining with them. But they do not see him. This most amazing adventurer of our age, whose deeds will rank with those of Drake on sea and Gordon on land, prefers solitude and a life of simplicity. He likes books better than battles, and since the war has disappeared from public gaze as completely as he did when he left Cairo at the beginning of it and went out into the desert to realise his dream of uniting the Bedouin Arabs and driving the Turks out of the land they had oppressed for centuries.

Imagine a fair young man, very slight and quite short, with blue eyes, a high forehead, and a disproportionately long jaw. He is dressed in robes of spotless white and carries the short curved sword of a Prince of Mecca, the insignia worn by descendants of the Prophet Mohammed—an honour to which very few are born and hardly any one achieves. On the fastest of camels he travels, from village to village, quite alone, for his attire wins him respect and reverence from all men—except the Turks. *They* know him as their greatest enemy and have put a price of one hundred thousand pounds on his head. But they do not catch him in spite of his solitary wanderings, for he is never where they expect him to be. Instead, he pulls their ears and he twists their tail with an ingenuity which they swear is given to him by "his friend the devil."

That is a picture of Lawrence in the early days of the war—days when he saw the first slight chance of his dream of Arabia united under its hereditary king coming true.

Since the war Colonel Lawrence has written about this great campaign which, with a handful of British officers, was carried out in the deserts of Arabia. Most of the rest that has been written concerns his more amazing personal adventures. There were plenty of these, of course. Lawrence dynamited the Turkish troop trains until it came to be regarded as a little hobby of his. Dozens of times he penetrated for miles behind the enemy lines, disguised as an Arab, and quite regardless of the fact that there was a large price on his head. He gathered information of the greatest value to General Allenby who was conquering Palestine to the west, and himself led a Bedouin army that held and defeated many times its own numbers of Turkish troops.

We could fill this chapter with stories such as these. But before telling any of them we know that Colonel Lawrence himself would wish you to know something about the real reason for the work he did in Arabia—the great plan which he prepared for Prince Feisal and the Arab army and helped to bring to a triumphant conclusion.

When he first visited Arabia, Lawrence found the wandering tribes which inhabited it a true desert people. The majority of them still spent their lives travelling from place

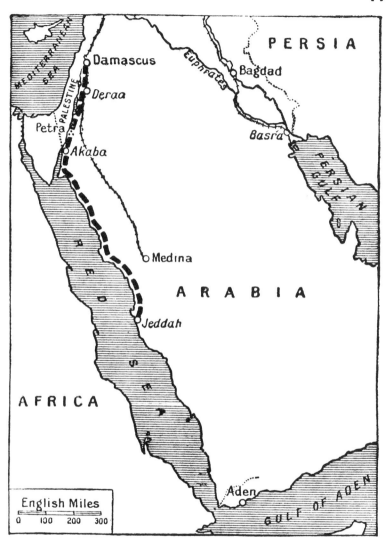

PERSIA

MEDITERRANEAN SEA

Damascus

Euphrates

Bagdad

Deraa

PALESTINE

Petra

Basra

PERSIAN GULF

Akaba

Medina

ARABIA

RED SEA

Jeddah

AFRICA

Aden

GULF OF ADEN

English Miles

0   100   200   300

to place, fighting, trading, living in tents of woven camel hair, good friends but bad enemies—just as you read in the Bible, in fact. There were a few educated Arabs in Damascus, the capital city of Syria, and in a handful of smaller Arabian towns such as Mecca, Medina, and Akaba. But the real Arabs were the people of the desert—good fighters, excellent horsemen—but without any idea of the art of government at all.

It may well be understood why the Turks, who had been their masters—and bad ones at that!—for generations, did nothing to discourage this mode of life. It may equally well be understood what Lawrence had to teach them.

When war broke out Lawrence was in Arabia, working on some excavations. He was promptly invited to serve in the map department of the Army Headquarters at Cairo as a second lieutenant, and before long he became the chief of the department, engaged in collecting secret information about the Turkish forces then menacing the Suez Canal and Egypt, from their military bases in Arabia.

But "when the cat's away, the mice will play." Never was there a more opportune time, thought the Arabs, to strike a blow for freedom than while their oppressors were busy with other schemes.

So they did strike a blow. The Shereef Hussein, most powerful of all the Arabian nobles, and ruler by birth of a land where blood descent is as powerful as it is anywhere else in the world, gathered together the tribes under his sway, and actually captured Mecca, the Holy City of the Moslem world. But alas, after this sensational success, they found their scanty supplies of arms and ammunition giving out, and it seemed as if the rebellion would only result in a defeat made even bitterer by their former hope of victory.

This was the moment that Colonel Lawrence chose to go to help the Arab rebels. He secured two weeks' leave from Headquarters in Cairo and went to Jeddah, one of the towns on the shores of the Red Sea held by the Shereef Hussein and his disorganised army.

The first thing he asked for upon his arrival was the Shereef's permission to travel by camel to the camp of the Prince Feisal, his son, and inspect the Arab army for himself.

It was a distressing sight. They had no supplies and there was hardly any ammunition left. Many of the men were living on what little food they could pick up by the way. Success seemed farther from them than it had ever been.

But Lawrence had faith and determination. Instead of agreeing with Feisal when the Arab commander pointed out that they had not enough ammunition left to defend Mecca when the inevitable Turkish reinforcements were brought up by the railway leading from Damascus, the young man merely asked him: "When will your army reach Damascus?"

Eagerly Lawrence began to work out his great idea. He knew that while the Turkish Army, if it were large enough, could hold the towns, it could not fight in the desert. Trained troops and artillery are no use in shifting sands, where only the camel is swift. And the Arabs had the camels!

The Arab revolt, too, would be of immense assistance to the British Army in diverting Turkish attention from Egypt. Lawrence saw immense possibilities in continued and irritating attack by the Arabs from inland, with a certain amount of assistance from the British naval forces in the Red Sea.

His enthusiasm and energy having won over the Arabs to another attempt, he secured complete freedom of action from Headquarters at Cairo and in October, 1916, became a sort of Adviser-in-Chief to the Arabian Army.

His first task was to win over all the independent tribes to join in a "Holy War" for the freeing of their country. With only two companions he went out into the desert to raise the flag of revolt. At every nomadic encampment he stopped and addressed the fighting men on the call that he brought to them— the call to arms. Speaking their own language like a native, protected by reason of the fact that he came from the camp of the most powerful sheik in Arabia, he kindled their emotions and convinced them that this was the moment for which all true Arabs had been waiting for generations.

The first tribe to join the revolt was the Harbs, the largest tribe in all Arabia. They numbered two hundred thousand. News of this went ahead of him, Lawrence saw to that. He also made sure that sufficient arms and ammunition arrived for this great striking force he was building up.

While he was gathering this new army together in the desert, Feisal was advancing north from Mecca toward two small ports on the Red Sea still held by the Turks. And the great march of the Arabian army under Colonel Lawrence and the Emir Feisal, which was to carry them through a thousand miles of desert and end within the gates of Damascus itself, began!

It was a work of perfect coöperation. As Feisal's men approached, the guns of the British fleet bombarded the Turks out of town after town—into the arms of their enemies! British battleships enabled the Arab army to march across waterless desert for hundreds of miles by landing water and supplies to them from the sea. At one point of their march, ten thousand men crossed one hundred and twenty miles of waterless desert, where there were not even

ONE OF THE "IRREGULARS" WHO FORMED COLONEL LAWRENCE'S
"FLYING SQUAD"   180

thorns on which the camels could subsist, without the loss of a single man from hunger or thirst, and suddenly appeared before a bewildered Turkish Army that imagined they were still encamped somewhere a hundred miles away.

This clearing of the Red Sea coast was the first stage in Colonel Lawrence's carefully planned campaign. And one of his favourite strategic tricks in it was the continued harassing of the Turks by "flying bands" of Arabs.

These "flying bands" belonged to a special camel corps, mounted on the swiftest beasts and commanded by Lawrence himself. With this force at his back he could travel in the desert for six weeks without once returning to his supply base for food or water. Each man carried on his saddle a bag containing forty-five pounds of flour. That was his ration for six weeks, during which time the camel corps would probably travel two thousand miles across the desert. No other people but the Arabs could have lived a strenuous life on such a diet in the burning heat of Arabia.

But Lawrence's corps not only lived—they frightened the Turks to death. Again and again, when the Turks holding the towns and the railway that brought supplies from Turkey to Medina thought that there was not an Arab for miles, Lawrence and his camel corps would dash out of the desert, attack them and dash off again before the Turks realised what had happened. And they could only watch them go, for they had no camels and no knowledge of the desert.

It was at this time that Colonel Lawrence added to his attainments the delicate work of blowing up Turkish supply trains on the railway we have mentioned.

His plan was to put a charge of explosive, which he called a "tulip" because of its shape, under the rails just before a Turkish troop or supply train was due, and then retire a little way into the desert and await its coming.

In due course the train arrived, the engine and many of the carriages were blown up, and Lawrence would reappear from behind the rocks to seize his capture. It might be a supply train, in which case the stores were exceedingly useful for Feisal's army, or it might be a troop train, from which the unfortunate survivors were rounded up and marched away as prisoners.

The laying of the explosives Lawrence always carried out himself. He would not teach the Arabs how to handle explosives and there was no other man there who understood the use of them until the arrival of Colonel Joyce later on in the campaign.

The Turks were always searching for Lawrence and said that he must have a charmed life. But this "charmed life" was due to a brilliant brain and an expert knowledge of both the railway system and the times that the Turks would choose for running their trains—however unexpected.

Lawrence could at any moment have so damaged the railway that it would have been impossible to use it again, but he wanted the trains to keep running. Every load of Turkish troops brought down into Arabia meant so many fewer Turks fighting the British in Palestine and Sinai. And the Turkish stores from supply trains which had been blown up often fed his army for weeks on end. So Lawrence let through a few trains now and again just for a little encouragement to the Turks to send some more!

One of Lawrence's most remarkable exploits was the blowing up of a trainload of Turkish troops rushed down to Medina, one of the towns that the Turks still held.

The Turks had no idea that the mysterious white man they had never been able to set eyes on had heard that the train was starting. Even now no one knows how Colonel Lawrence heard about it. But as he carried a portable wire-

less set on his camel and always listened to the Turkish official orders while eating his breakfast each morning, it is
possible that he learned of the train's departure by wireless.
Or perhaps a spy brought in the news.

Be that as it may, the Turks were taking no risks, so
they had the whole line patrolled every two hours by troops.
Surely now, they said, this train will be safe from that Lawrence man.

But it wasn't. Travelling for two days across country as
bare and scorched as any on earth, Lawrence reached the
hills overlooking the railway with his camel corps just in
time to hide his force away before the first Turkish patrols
appeared.

For eight hours they crouched there, until the leader
was satisfied that the patrols were passing every two hours.
And then, at midday, when the sun was hottest, he slipped
down to the track and buried fifty pounds of powerful explosive beneath the rails. That done, he connected it by a
wire buried in the sand with a position up the hillside,
smoothed away every trace of his work, and walked backward up the hill, wiping his footmarks out with a camel's-
hair brush as he went. He then settled down in the open
and waited for the train.

It came, with guards holding loaded rifles on top of the
carriages and on the engine. They were on the lookout for
that wicked Lawrence! But all they saw was a solitary Bedouin Arab sitting on the hillside, apparently asleep.

But the train went up with a mighty roar all the same,
as Lawrence's mine exploded. In it were four hundred soldiers. Many were killed, but the rest got out hurriedly and
started to rush at the lone Bedouin sitting there in the open.

That day the Turks learned something new about the
mysterious Colonel Lawrence. They learned that he was a

N

crack shot. As the leading men drew near to the Arab he rose, and drawing a heavy revolver from the folds of his cloak, fired so effectively at them that they promptly retreated—to entrench themselves behind the train and to blaze away through the wheels.

But Lawrence had thought of that move too. On the other side of the track some of his camel corps suddenly appeared with two machine guns and opened fire on the now thoroughly demoralised Turks. Most of them were either killed or wounded, and the rest had had enough of the Englishman for one day and fled into the desert, leaving the train to its fate.

While all these daring raids were being carried out, the advance of the main Arab army along the shores of the Red Sea continued unchecked. At last the forces of Hussein, who had by now been made king, arrived within striking distance of the important port of Akaba, the capture of which would not only be a mighty blow to the Turks, but would open the road that led to the invasion of Syria and eventually to the very gates of Damascus.

The Turks did not believe that Akaba could be captured. For one thing the approach to it lay over the precipitous Solomon Mountains, terrible country for a well-equipped traveller let alone a Bedouin army. In addition, Colonel Lawrence had set out with only two months' supply of food, some of which he had used to feed Turkish prisoners.

But he captured Akaba. He marched his half-starved army right across the mountains and appeared suddenly in Akaba on the morning of July 7, 1917. And so amazed were the Turks and the Germans who held the town at his getting through the mountains that they surrendered without fighting.

Lawrence and Feisal had now accomplished the first stage

THE HOLY CITY OF MEDINA, THE FIRST PLACE TO BE CAPTURED BY THE
REVOLTING ARABS

184

COLONEL T. E. LAWRENCE IN THE DRESS OF A
"PRINCE OF MECCA"   185

of the campaign. They held the Red Sea coast. They also had an army of two hundred thousand desert warriors raised either by Colonel Lawrence on his recruiting trips into the desert, or composed of tribes who had volunteered upon hearing the news of his early victories.

The one thing that they had not got was food, and in this respect the situation was so desperate that Lawrence decided to return to Egypt and report to Headquarters upon the progress of the rebellion and the fall of Akaba. Incidentally he intended to ask for food to be rushed to that town for his starving army, which was existing upon unripe grapes and the meat of camels killed during fighting outside the town.

Tired out already by two months of continuous trekking and fighting in one of the most desolate parts of the earth, Colonel Lawrence set out on his fastest camel to cross the Sinai peninsula to civilisation and secure help from the British Army.

The story of that ride alone would make a chapter of this book. For twenty-two consecutive hours he pressed on across the desolate mountains and sands of Sinai until—utterly worn out and dropping with fatigue—he reached Port Tewfik, Suez. There he went to a hotel and enjoyed the first bath he had been able to get for more than a month, the while Arab boys brought him a succession of iced drinks!

It was at the railway station at Ismaîlia, on his way to Cairo, and while General Headquarters were still without any news of the fall of Akaba, that Lawrence first met General Allenby, who had come to Egypt from England to lead the British Army operations against the Turks in the Sinai Peninsula.

Admiral Wemyss, who had commanded the British naval

forces operating along the Red Sea Coast, introduced these two great leaders of the war, and from Lawrence's own lips Allenby heard of the progress of the Arab campaign.

So impressed were both Allenby and Wemyss with the Arab victories that they at once offered to send a vessel to Akaba with supplies. Admiral Wemyss went further, for upon hearing that the Arabs were afraid lest the Turks should return to recapture the town, he sent his flagship through the Suez Canal to anchor in the port. The presence of this great battleship, with its mighty guns, reassured Feisal's army and showed them as nothing else could have done that Colonel Lawrence spoke truly when he told them that Great Britain would help the Arabs to drive the Turks out of Arabia.

From this time onward the Arab armies were no longer cut off from the rest of the world. Between Allenby advancing in Sinai to the west, and Feisal's two armies—the "regulars" led by Colonel Joyce and the Bedouin "irregulars," or the desert fighters, led by Colonel Lawrence—constant touch was maintained, so that each might profit by the other's victories.

Of Feisal's two armies, that composed of Bedouin irregulars was by far the larger, totalling two hundred thousand men—the largest army ever raised in Arabia. We have heard a little of their exploits under Lawrence. The smaller army, led by Colonel Joyce of the Connaught Rangers, was composed mostly of Arabs who had served in the Turkish army. They were used to storm cities, or to round up big Turkish forces in the neighbourhood of towns where men on camels would have been useless.

After the fall of Akaba, the Arab forces advanced to Petra, a deserted city built over two thousand years ago and immortalised as:

"A rose-red city, half as old as Time."

Here, amid the crumbling temples of a far distant age, along roads over which Trajan's hordes had marched and rocky peaks which had defied the might of Alexander the Great long centuries before, the most amazing battle in the history of our times was fought in September, 1917.

Hearing that the Turks were advancing in force, and fearing that his forces would not be strong enough for them, Colonel Lawrence sent one of the Arab commanders to round up all the able-bodied Arab women for miles around and to get them to reinforce his troops.

The women answered the call in hundreds, and when the battle began charged side by side with their menfolk, fighting as fiercely as the best of them.

Imagine the battle. Lawrence had two mountain guns and two machine guns. His "army" consisted of a horde of Bedouin men and women armed with all sorts of ancient weapons, some on camels, some on horses and the rest on foot. This was the force that was pitted against Turkish troops equipped with the latest artillery and arms, and aided by German aeroplanes from above.

After a long struggle the Turks succeeded in capturing the trenches beyond Petra. Believing the whole Arab force was retiring to Akaba at that, they swept down triumphantly into the narrow valley in which Petra was built.

Lawrence, watching from the top of the hills, waited until the whole Turkish force had rushed into the gorge. Then he fired a rocket as a signal for his hidden forces to attack.

Down rushed the Bedouin men and women, with a fury before which the Turks fled demoralised. One thousand of them succeeded in fighting their way out of the valley, but the Arabs captured all the Turkish transport, a complete field hospital and hundreds of prisoners.

After the battle Lawrence, disguised as a Bedouin, penetrated behind the Turkish lines and secured there a copy of the report on the battle. It read:

> We have stormed the fortifications of Petra, losing twelve killed and ninety-four wounded. The Arab losses are one thousand dead and wounded and we counted seventeen British officers among the bodies.

The amusing thing about this communique is not the lies in it, but the fact that Lawrence was the only British officer present at the battle. Not only did the Turks lose the battle of Petra, but Lawrence, by winning it, had opened up for Feisal's army the road for the invasion of Syria.

While preparing to advance into Syria, Colonel Lawrence continued to busy himself with his two "hobbies" of train wrecking and collecting information behind the Turkish lines. The train wrecking I have already described. In all, this amazing young man blew up seventy-nine trains during the campaign. His work collecting information behind the Turkish lines was even more dangerous.

His usual procedure was to travel into Turkish territory disguised as an Arab woman. He knew from experience that the Turkish soldiers thought it beneath their dignity to say "Who goes there?" to a woman, and he thus managed to collect much information of great value to the general campaign without being discovered.

But it was perilous work. At this time the Germans were offering a huge reward for his capture or death, and one false step would have led to a horrible end. But Lawrence did not let this deter him. Again and again he spent whole weeks far inside the enemy lines, gaining information about the defences of the towns which Feisal's army would be storming before long.

He explored the Turkish railway all the way up to Deraa, the main junction. He even penetrated into Damascus itself as an Arab woman and walked through the bazaars of the town without being discovered at the very time that thousands of Turks were rallying there for another effort to smash Lawrence and his crazy army of desert fighters.

Once—and once only—he was actually captured by the Turks. On this occasion he had entered Deraa, dressed as a Circassian Arab, and was strolling along a street, when Turkish soldiers arrested him as a deserter from the Turkish army.

It must have been a terrible moment. If the Turks discovered who he was, or even that he was British, it meant a terrible death from torture.

He was taken to headquarters and cross-examined by the Turks, but his knowledge of Arabia was so perfect that they even then thought he was an Arab deserter from their own army. They were not satisfied, however. Every able-bodied man was supposed to be under arms. What, then, was he doing in the Ottoman Empire when it was at war without being a soldier?

To find out they tortured him—tortured him, but did not break his unconquerable spirit, for when the excruciating agony caused him to cry out—he cried out in Arabic!

And that little fact perhaps is one of the most remarkable achievements of Colonel Lawrence. How many men, half dazed with pain, would remember at that awful moment that their only chance of escape was to forget they were British and continue the deception?

Lawrence did it, and was afterward flung, more dead

than alive, into a hut. When he regained consciousness it was night, and before dawn he had managed to escape.

It might have been thought that one such narrow escape would have satisfied the most adventurous of men for a lifetime. It satisfied Lawrence to the extent that he took care never to be caught again, although he continued his spying.

The rest of this great campaign, which finally resulted in Palestine, Syria, and Arabia being freed from the Turk, was fought out by Feisal's army in close coöperation with General Allenby's victorious army in Palestine.

In September, 1918, Colonel Lawrence captured Deraa, the important railway junction where a few months before he had been captured by the Turks. Had they only known then that the great Lawrence was in their possession, Deraa might have been a Turkish town to-day. But he escaped, as has been told, and brought back to the Arab line with him all the information he wanted for an attack on the town.

It was a picturesque army that advanced on Deraa. There were one thousand baggage camels, four hundred and fifty Arab regular troops mounted on racing camels, four machine-gun units, two aeroplanes, three armoured cars, a company of picked men from the Egyptian Camel Corps, a battalion of Gurkhas from India mounted on camels, and four cannon manned by French-African troops. In addition to this carefully selected striking force, there was Lawrence's own bodyguard of picked Arabs, a force one hundred strong, whose many-coloured robes formed a striking contrast to the pure white worn by their leader.

In all, this army only totalled one thousand men, but with it Lawrence carried out his last great raid. Across miles of parched desert, with water holes often four days apart, he marched his force by a wide detour far behind the Turkish lines around Deraa.

Sometimes he had to shift his camp twice in one night to avoid discovery. Again and again the Turks got on his track, only to find when they reached the reported enemy camp nothing but empty desert. Like the Arab he was, Lawrence had folded his tents and silently crept away.

Once in position, he proceeded to blow up the railway bridges over which the troop trains must run if the Turks were to send reinforcements against Allenby in Palestine, then just beginning his last victorious advance. The whole Turkish railway system was disorganised. Food, ammunition, men—nothing could be sent to the help of the retreating Turks, so well did Lawrence and his little band do their work.

The Turks heard of his coming with consternation. They knew that the main Feisal army was still to the south and had thought Lawrence was with it. But when the advance of Allenby made retreat the only way of escape, Lawrence and his force engaged them by night and day, dashing out of the desert to attack and disappearing as quickly whenever the Turks got together superior forces.

In this last great raid upon the Turks, Lawrence and his Arabs killed over five thousand Turks, captured eight thousand, and took one hundred and fifty machine guns and thirty cannon. At the end of the fighting the remnant of the Turkish army was in full retreat both from Palestine and Syria.

The road to Damascus lay open.

Late that night the first enthusiastic Arabs from Lawrence's force rode right on to Damascus, where the fires from the munition dumps fired by the retreating Turks painted the famous city a lurid red.

But Lawrence was worn out. Now that victory had come —complete victory, both for the British and for his dreams —he went into his tent and slept. He had been fighting almost continuously, with hardly any sleep, for a week!

The following morning, at seven o'clock, on October 31, 1918, saw the glorious end of the great campaign.

Colonel Lawrence, dressed in the robes of a Prince of Mecca, and accompanied by one other officer, drove into Damascus in a Rolls-Royce car, the first Christian ever to enter the city as a conqueror.

The entire population turned out to catch a glimpse of this mighty warrior, the most famous man in all Arabia. They hailed him as a conqueror sent by Allah to deliver them. They had heard dim tales from the Turks of his wonderful exploits in freeing their country, and they shouted his name along the miles of streets like a giant chorus.

Thus did Lawrence of Arabia at twenty-nine bring to an end the most romantic story of our generation. He had seen his dreams come true; he had helped to drive the Turk from Arabia and to give their country back to the Arabs. With his entry into Damascus his great work was complete.

That day Lawrence called the local Arab leaders together and, together with Feisal, appointed a temporary council to rule the city until the election of a proper authority after the war.

But for four days he stayed there, Lawrence himself was the real ruler of Damascus. During that time he kept order among a population bent on looting. He even issued a special postage stamp, which is now very rare.

At the end of the four days he decided that his task was ended. All through the campaign this modest and brilliant man had given the credit for the victories which he had won to Feisal and to the other Arab commanders. Now that Damascus was in their hands, and all Syria freed from the Turks, the Arabs could be left to rule themselves.

There were more big days in Lawrence's life after his return from Arabia. He attended the Peace Conference with Prince Feisal on the Arabian delegation. He was offered great honours and he refused them. If he were asked to define his own success, he would probably put it down to "an infinite capacity for taking pains."

For some years after the war this Prince of Mecca, whose name is still heard in the many-coloured bazaars of the East as the name of the deliverer of Arabia, lived quietly in England, spending his time collecting beautifully printed books, and writing "The Seven Pillars of Wisdom," his classic account of the Arabian campaign. Some day Colonel Lawrence may return to Arabia, but that day is not yet. For in 1927 Thomas Edward Lawrence changed his name by deed-poll to Shaw, and joined the Royal Air Force as aircraftsman.

CHAPTER XIV

I N all the British Empire there is perhaps no wilder or less-known country than that enormous peninsula called Cape York which forms the northeastern corner of the continent of Australia. It lies between the reef-sown Coral Sea and the great Gulf of Carpentaria; its length exceeds that of England and in shape it is roughly a triangle with a base of rather more than three hundred miles. The northern end is separated from New Guinea by the narrow Torres Straits; its southern part merges into more or less settled Queensland; but the peninsula itself is a country of thick, tropical forest, of swift rivers and steep hills, much of it as unknown to white men as it was in the days when the great Captain Cook sailed past its shores in his little *Endeavour*.

Now a curious thing about this country is that, in spite of its rich soil, its tremendous rainfall and its amazing variety of splendid timber, the coconut palm, common all over the Pacific, is not native there. During the present century the coconut palm has become the most valuable of all trees known to man, and land on which it will grow is eagerly sought for. Some years before the Great War it came to Mr. Jack McLaren, a young man who had for some years past been travelling and trading among the islands, that a coconut plantation on the shores of Cape York might prove a very paying speculation. The climate was suitable, the soil was rich, there were no cyclones to destroy the palms. Also there were, he thought, plenty of natives who would surely be glad to exchange their labour for trade goods. So in 1911 behold our adventurer aboard a small, dirty, ill-found sailing craft, by name the *Marie Esebia,* cruising along the eastern shore of the peninsula, hunting for a site for his plantation.

He needed two things, good land and a good harbour, but for many weary days he searched the coast without discovering what he required. "Never," he has written, "had I seen so many fine harbours edged by barren soil, or so many unsheltered beaches edged by land that would grow anything you liked." The captain, the captain's wife, and the crew all thought he was crazy, and the only white man he met on his wanderings observed that "he thought it was a mug's game." The only way to make a living on that coast was, he said, to cut sandalwood.

At last McLaren found an island which looked promising, and got the skipper to put him ashore while the vessel went to a place where a cargo of trepang awaited her. So he was dumped on the beach all alone, feeling very small and helpless. The captain, however, had promised to be back in three days and meantime McLaren explored, only to find that the island was quite unsuitable. The three days passed, they lengthened to a week, but there was no sign of the *Marie Esebia.* The explorer had to cut himself down to one meal a day. On the twelfth day arrived a canoe with three people. They were natives, a man and two women. The man wore no clothes at all, the women little more. They took the presence of a white man quite as a matter of course, and when McLaren told them of his plight, the native at once ordered his women to cook fish and himself volunteered to take the castaway to the mainland to a harbour where he could hail a passing boat. This Stone Age man was far kinder and more considerate than most of his civilised cousins, yet later McLaren discovered that he was wanted by the water police for all sorts of offences from petty theft to murder. Happily for our explorer he had no need to accept the kindly criminal's offer, for on the fourteenth day of his marooning, the schooner turned up. Her crew, the skipper explained, had got drunk and run her on a reef where she had stuck for twelve full days before she could be freed.

By this time McLaren had made certain that his promised land was not to be found upon the eastern shore of the peninsula, so he sailed north, and rounding Cape York, set to searching the western coast facing the great Gulf. He landed on beach after beach, he rowed up narrow creeks, but it was always the same story. Arable land in one place, harbours in another, but never the two together. Then when hope was almost dead, he sailed one morning into a harbour, the mouth of which was almost hidden by islands so placed as to give shelter in every direction, and all along the shore saw jungle—"thick, tall jungle, purple in the early light and subtly tingeing the breeze with the scent of flowers." He landed to find there was no catch about it. Simpson's Bay, as it was called on the chart, was exactly what he had been looking for. He raced back to Thursday Island, and from the land authorities obtained a large document making him owner of the desired section. Then came the purchase of tools and stores, and finally the obtaining of passage in a coasting vessel which would land him and his belongings at Simpson's Bay.

There he found himself entirely alone; he had not even a dog. Bark huts along the beach showed the place to be a favourite camping ground, but the huts were empty and the ashes cold. He slung his hammock, turned in with rifle and revolver beside him, and spent a sleepless night listening to the wail of curlews, the grunting of alligators, the howling of dingoes, and the imagined voices of stealthily approaching natives. The morning broke clear and sunny, his fears fled, and the first thing the wanderer did was to select a site for his future residence. Then on the trunk of a great tree he carved deeply his initials and the date:

J. M.
7/10/'11.

He began clearing the site and building his house. Though far along the beaches wisps of smoke rose, no human being approached him. What was to be done he had to do himself. Up to now he had always had natives to help him, but here he was master and labourer too. He ached all over, his hands became raw, he dripped with perspiration and took twice as long over simple tasks as a labourer would have done. Ants were his chief enemy. If he left a box on the ground for an hour they were at it, riddling it through; they ate the handles of his tools, the piles supporting the house, his clothes, his food. He began to have a horrible fear that, when he planted palm trees, they would eat them too. So fighting ants and bodily unfitness, he struggled on until one afternoon he rose from a task to find himself facing a man. A tall man, black as coal and entirely naked, with oddly expressionless eyes.

McLaren's first instinct was to spring for his rifle, but somehow he could not do it. The man's hands were empty, but McLaren had heard the native trick of dragging a spear between the toes, so he stood and watched. For fully half a minute the pair faced each other, then the native grunted. "To-morrow," he remarked, evidently believing this to be a word of greeting. At the sound the spell was broken, and looking down McLaren saw that a spear was truly between the native's feet. The white man offered trade tobacco, the black man accepted the gift, made a slight sign and a second native stepped soundlessly out of the bush. He too was given tobacco, whereupon he dived into the jungle to reappear with a quantity of clubs and spears which he laid in a heap on the ground. Then the first man offered his hand and managed to convey the fact that he was the white man's friend and that his companion was also his friend. They sat and smoked and told McLaren that their name for the spot was "Utingu," meaning, "the Place of many Big Trees," and asking why the white man was building a house. Was it a trepang station, or was it for storing pearl shell? This gave McLaren his chance and he quickly told them his object and his need for labourers. They shook their heads. They were hunters, not workers. Still there were plenty of people in their tribe. Perhaps some might care to work.

That same evening the tribe turned up, each carrying on his or her back their personal possessions, and accompanied by a large pack of unhappy-looking dogs. Most of the women had clothes of some sort. One, for instance, wore a skirt made of an old flour bag on which was stencilled the words "Lily-White." Of men some had trousers, some shirts, some nothing at all. McLaren thought he had never seen more savage looking savages and that night lay awake, far from happy. But nothing happened and he rose cheerfully, expecting a busy day in engaging labourers and setting them to work. Instead, all was quiet, and going down to the camp at ten o'clock—behold, the black folk were all still sound asleep. Only the dogs were awake and they set up such a racket that presently the humans roused, stretched, yawned, and slowly came to life.

So McLaren set to work to explain to the chief what he wanted. He had, he said, tobacco, cloth, sheath knives, and many other things, all of which he would give in exchange for work. It took a bit of doing, but at last he made them understand, and selecting a dozen men, took them to his camp and gave them each a ration of flour. But all the others joined in, old men, women, and children, each provided with a piece of bark or an old jam tin and each expecting a ration. They took it for granted that he would employ them all, and were decidedly upset when flour was given only to the men engaged. They were pacified with presents of tobacco and straggled back to their camp happily enough.

So real work began at last, but if he had plenty of labourers, McLaren found them dreadfully inefficient. They were Stone Age people, accustomed to the use of flints and shells. They had never used a steel tool in their lives. Saws, chisels, and hammers were a mystery to them, and their unfortunate employer had to spend fully half his time in repairing buckled saws and damaged tools. It was no use punishing them. Indeed, it would have been most unwise to try anything of the kind, for after all it was not their fault, and they were perfectly aware that such was the fact.

Another difficulty was to make them keep any sort of hours. They were accustomed to huge quantities of sleep. What was more, they slept so soundly that they were very difficult to waken, and according to their ideas it was nothing short of crime to wake a person suddenly. When a man slept, so they said, his spirit left him and went roaming. The awaking must be done slowly so as to allow the spirit to return, for otherwise the sleeper might be left without a spirit. Surely it is most strange to find this belief that the spirit is released during sleep, which is held so firmly by

o

modern occultists, prevalent among a race who are at least ten thousand years behind modern civilisation.

It was difficult also to persuade these natives to work on succeeding days. They had worked a whole day, they said, and were tired. It sometimes took hours of argument to bring them up to the scratch. In all ways they showed their utter contempt for time. They dawdled over their meals, chewing each mouthful very carefully, yet when after spending perhaps an hour over his breakfast a man was got to work, he had only to disturb a wallaby when he and the rest would snatch up their spears and rush off in pursuit, chasing it until they killed it. What seemed to their employer the oddest thing of all was that they suffered quite badly from the heat. The climate of Cape York is, of course, very hot, for it is only a few degrees south of the equator, yet that people who had always lived in such a climate should feel the heat quite startled McLaren. Yet they did, and so much so that after the first few weeks it was found necessary to give them three hours' rest at midday instead of the usual one hour.

McLaren had to watch them the whole time. If he left them some would sit down and smoke, others would lie flat on the ground and go sound asleep. They were not a bit ashamed when he caught them like this, and scolding and ridicule were both quite useless.

So, as you may gather, McLaren's task was not an easy one. Yet somehow he kept them at it. By degrees he got his house finished, a big roomy place sixty feet long, with furniture made from packing cases covered with cloth from the store. Behind was a kitchen with fireplace and shelves, the latter made of the flattened bark of trees. Also a bathroom with a homemade shower. Round the house he planted a fence of shrubs, lovely things from the forest with leaves of gold, bronze, and green, and some bearing masses of exquisite flowers. The verandah was hung with orchids, blue, red, yellow, and pink and white. McLaren lighted the whole place with acetylene gas, which he thought would surprise the natives, but he was disappointed to find that they took it quite as a matter of course. It was just white man's magic, and they let it go at that. They themselves lived in huts made of a sheet of bark laid on a framework of sticks. The bark was shifted as the wind changed, so as to keep off the rain.

Yet these savages, so McLaren found, had the most amazing knowledge of nature. They knew every tree, plant, and root, and what each was good for, either as food or medicine. If he plucked a weed haphazard, even the children could tell him when it flowered and seeded, where it would or would not grow, its name and every little detail of its life. They had the same knowledge about animals, birds, and fish, and were amazed at the ignorance of their employer in these matters. In fact, they went so far as to appoint a teacher. This was a man whose name was so hard to pronounce that McLaren named him "Jimmy," a change which he accepted quite happily. Among the many strange things that Jimmy showed his pupil was the Dance of the Birds. These birds, known as Native Companions, are storklike creatures, and hundreds danced together in the centre of a great dry swamp. They formed in groups, each of a score or more; they advanced and retreated, doing a sort of quadrille figure; they pranced and bowed in the most wonderful fashion. It was a wonderful and beautiful sight.

Although these strange people found it difficult to work two days running, yet any one of them could live without food for a week or, even in that great heat, go without a drink for days. They were also tireless travellers and could walk hour after hour through thick bush, over steep hills, at the same time keeping a perfectly straight course through the heaviest forest. It was impossible for any of them to get lost, even in strange country, for all had a sixth sense of direction and locality which they shared with the wild creatures.

Shortly before McLaren's arrival at Utingu one of the tribe named Kaio killed another man in a quarrel. Just then a police boat happened to put in and Kaio was arrested and taken away to be tried and probably hanged. One dark night, when the police boat was four hundred miles away from his home, Kaio managed to slip overboard, and naked as when he was born, swam for the shore. The distance was three miles, the sea a mass of furious tide rips which taxed all Kaio's strength to battle with. He reached the shore exhausted and found himself naked and weaponless with four hundred miles of unknown country between him and his people. It was not only that he had no food, or weapons with which to procure it, but he had to cross rivers swarming with crocodiles, others too swift to swim, and to pass through the country of hostile tribes, any member of which would kill him on sight. The journey took him almost three months, yet he arrived safely, a little thin, but strong and healthy and delighted to get back.

Dancing was a habit of these people which gave McLaren no end of trouble. Any excuse was good enough, even the capture of a kangaroo, and once they started they went on dancing, singing, and screaming until they were exhausted. What was worse, they got so excited that they became half mad. At any ordinary time there was always the risk that they might take it into their heads to spear the white man if only to get hold of his coveted trade goods, but when they got worked up into a frenzy with their dancing, their eyes glaring, their lips covered with foam, then the risk became very serious indeed.

They were the most extraordinary mixture, being so much behind the times that they had no real sense of right or wrong—hardly more, indeed, than monkeys. Yet on the other hand, they were very affectionate toward their own, they tended their sick or injured with the greatest care, and they thought little of risking their lives for each other. On one occasion when a man swimming in a creek was seized by a shark, another, a mere boy, swam to his help and actually fought off the shark with his bare hands. They very rarely lied and still more rarely stole; they respected their elders and were kind to the old people. Strangest trait of all for people so low in the scale, they were extraordinarily kind to their dogs. Not only did they not thrash them, but any man would go hungry rather than that his dog should starve. One man sat up all night poulticing the broken leg of his dog, yet the dog was so old that it was quite useless.

By degrees the ground was cleared, the palms planted. They grew finely, but so did the weeds. When the rains came you could actually watch the weeds shooting a foot or more in twenty-four hours.

Up to this time McLaren had been doing his own cooking and living very roughly, but suddenly there landed at the camp from a Thursday Island lugger, a little old black woman dressed in a blouse and a skirt of printed cotton, who announced that she was a good house servant. Mary Brown, as she called herself, had been stolen as a child by a pearler who wanted a servant for his wife. "A quiet, good man," Mary described him, "and kind like anything." Then she had grown up, missionaries got hold of her and called her "Mary Brown" and made her "wash plates and scrub floors and peel potatoes and do like that always—always," until Mary got "fed up" and went back to the wild. "My body, it come old," explained Mary, but if she was old she was cheerful, a good worker, a capital cook, and her arrival made all the difference in the world to McLaren. And when he got ill with fever she looked after him splendidly. She soon found a husband and she would send him out into the bush to hunt wild turkeys and their eggs, or down the beach to spear fish, or catch turtles. She herself found wild vegetables and fruit. She was very prejudiced against canned food. "You all time eat from tin three times a day —my word—that make your belly come angry feller, and you come sick."

So after Mary's arrival things were very much easier and the work went on well. What was more, the natives began to get really fond of their white master and he heard them singing, "The white man is good and kind, and our hearts are glad he is here." McLaren felt that he had at last become "a settled and respectable person." And then, just when all was going so well, one day the whole tribe turned up ready for travel. "Must go for walk-about," explained the spokesman. McLaren said everything he could think of but it was no use. They stood sullenly silent. It was Mary who explained. Their eyes were tired of looking at the same thing, their feet were tired from walking on the same ground, and their bodies were tired from sleeping in the same camp. In plain English they were bored stiff. So they went. And Mary with them, and left their boss all alone, and alone he remained for fourteen weeks. Yet oddly enough he was not lonely. He had his dog Togo and he had the birds, the laughing jackasses that giggled and chuckled all day, birds of paradise, cuckoos, a most amazing cuckoo as big as fowl that hatched its own eggs instead of foisting them on other birds—and, besides these, certain friendly, cheeky little birds that got so tame that, if not fed, they would go into the kitchen and steal. He had also an adventure, a very terrible adventure.

One intensely hot night he lay awake on his cot when he heard a rustling sound and springing up grabbed his gun. The gas container was empty and the light in the sitting room just flickering out revealed a huge carpet snake twelve feet long, making straight for Togo. Togo sprang up barking, and the snake went straight up the wall. A little bonfire of matches showed the monster clinging to the ridge pole, and McLaren shot it with his gun. Down came its great length, down and down, until it hung like a cable from the ridge-pole. Though its grisly head was shot to bits, it still seemed full of life. Togo sprang on the table and grabbed it, his master beat it with his gun. Blood from the mangled head dripped hissing upon the burning matches, then all of a sudden the whole horrid thing broke loose and fell with a crash on the table, putting out the flame. "I screamed," says McLaren, "I know I screamed." For in falling the serpent had got a coil around his arm and was constricting with all its awful strength. The coil was hard as iron and as cold. The power was so terrible that the whole arm was paralysed. With his other hand McLaren laid hold of the door post, but the snake in its turn got its tail around a leg of the table and so long as it had that purchase its hold could not be broken. It seemed hours that he kicked, fought and struggled in the dark. The whole thing was like a nightmare translated to reality. Togo, too, gripped and pulled. At long last the table overset and once the brute had lost its purchase its grip relaxed. Mangled as it was, the monster wriggled slowly out on to the verandah where McLaren followed it and blew it to pieces. Then he refilled the gasometer and lay shivering and shaking until daylight. For nights afterward he hardly slept, and presently there came upon him a terrible attack of fever which left him in a coma which, as he afterward realised, lasted for thirty-six hours. But he did not know that until later, when a ship came in and he found that he was a whole day out in his reckoning.

It was a wet and windy day when the tribe returned, but in spite of the grey sky and heavy squalls McLaren was happy as ever he had been in his life. Mary Brown was as happy as he. She vowed she had known that he was ill and that she would never again leave him. The natives themselves were thoroughly glad to be home for they had badly missed their rations of tobacco and food. Often they had gone hungry. Also they had suffered losses. One young man had been taken by a shark, another speared by a wandering bush tribe. An old man had been snake-bitten and a child, wading, badly injured by the barbed tail of a great stingaree. They told him of the murder of a white man by natives at a spot three hundred miles from their camp, giving him every detail, even to the number of the club blows, and to McLaren's amazement told him that this killing had happened on the day of their return. They explained that the news had been sent by smoke signals and later, when a ship came in, he found that what they had told him was true in every detail.

Some visitors had accompanied McLaren's own particular tribe and later other strange tribes came. His tribe quarrelled bitterly with the other tribes. Sometimes it came to spear thrusts and club blows, so that for whole hours the camp would be in an uproar. Happily McLaren now had another assistant besides Mary. This was a native named Billy Number Five who, like Mary Brown, had knocked about and seen something of the world. He was a capital fellow

who kept the others at work and proved a most capable overseer. On one occasion the row became so serious that Mc-
Laren and Billy had to go down and take a hand. Armed
with a revolver, McLaren forced the principals in the riot
to the house and tied them to the verandah posts until they
had cooled down a little. Oddly enough, they did not resent
this treatment.

Then came still more serious trouble. The same bush
tribes that had speared their young man was found to be
camped near by, and that night there was strange quiet in
the camp. Mary explained, "Them bush fellers walk about
plenty in the nighttime and might be they hear, if people
belong you and me sing u'ar songs."

Next morning McLaren found the men sharpening
spears. No one answered when he spoke, none took any heed
at all, and presently forty men marched out in single file,
fully armed. For two days nothing was heard of them and
McLaren was desperately anxious. He thought of following them, but knew it was useless.

It was midnight when they returned to celebrate their
victory in a mad dance. But two young men were missing,
and though McLaren was told that they had gone on a
visit to another tribe, the sight of two ominous looking
bundles tightly wrapped in shredded jungle canes told another story.

In January of the fifth year of what McLaren called
"his crowded solitude," the first palm bloomed and bore
fruit. This gave him the greatest delight, for it was real
proof of the success of his lonely venture. And now the
plantation was becoming known, McLaren began to have
visitors. An American professor who was a very great eth-
nologist was among them. He greatly puzzled the natives by
measuring their heads, but they took it cheerfully enough.

The professor never knew that Billy had privately informed his fellows that the visitor was completely mad. A bird man, a prospector, a missionary, and a playwright were other callers.

At last, after eight years of life in the Place of Big Trees, its owner was offered a good price for his plantation and after long hesitation accepted it and set forth on his wanderings once more.

CHAPTER XV

U NDER the title of "The Frontiersman" Mr. Roger Pocock wrote the first part of his life-story thirty or more years ago. The narrative was crammed with breathless adventure, but its author had by no means exhausted the subject, as was shown when "Chorus to Adventure" appeared in 1931. Mr. Pocock is a born adventurer, and he will continue to adventure as long as he lives. He has been a trooper in that wonderful body the Northwest Mounted Police, and fought in the campaign against the rebel Riel; he has been a missionary among the savagest savages on the British Columbian coast; he took part in the South African War, and although long past the age limit, won a commission in the Great War.

He has also been cowboy, prospector, pedlar, photographer, law clerk, telegraph operator, and scout. He has written novels and plays—Miss Lena Ashwell is his sister —also he has a wide experience in film work gained at the home and centre of the moving-picture industry, Hollywood, California.

What was perhaps his biggest adventure was his solitary ride from Fort Macleod at the foot of the Rockies in British Columbia south through the whole of the United States to the City of Mexico, a distance of three thousand six hundred miles. This is the story chosen for this chapter.

It was on June 28, 1899, that Roger Pocock rode out from the gates of Fort Macleod in Canada in order—to use his own words—"to make a record in horsemanship or to get killed." He had before his eyes two great records, that of the Cossack Peskkof who rode a pony from Vladivostok on the Pacific coast of Siberia to St. Petersburg, a distance of five thousand miles, in one hundred and ninety-three days; and that of the great American Scout, Kit Carson, who years ago rode from the Mississippi River to California, two thousand two hundred miles, through wild country among hostile Indians. For actual distance Mr. Pocock could not hope to break Peskkof's record, nor for risk, that of Carson. The standard he hoped to set was in horsemanship and scouting on difficult ground. About the difficulty of the trail there was no possible doubt, for in the course of his ride he had before him the whole breadth of the American desert, a matter of fifteen hundred miles across country much of which is as waterless as the Sahara.

For the first part of the way he rode in company with old friends of the Mounted Police and so passed through the Blood Indian country and down to the Border where, on a ridge which marks the boundary between British and American territory, stands a lonely cairn of stones, many of them scratched and painted with the names of those who have passed by. In Northern Montana he came upon Blackfeet Indians, fourteen hundred of them living in a mile wide ring of cone-shaped, smoke-browned tents. The drums were rumbling, it was the great yearly ceremonial with dances, sham fights and much racing of half-wild ponies. Cowboys, trappers, freighters, all sorts of frontiersmen, were watching, for it was the Fourth of July—Independence Day—the most popular public holiday of the United States.

Afterwards for many days Pocock rode under the shadow of the Rockies through country once full of cattle but now

THE COMB RIDGE

This ridge, bordering the Utah Desert, is 150 feet high and 100 miles long.   Horses belonging to
Roger Pocock's ' outfit ' are seen in the foreground.

A MAIL-COACH OF " BUFFALO BILL'S " DAYS

Photographed by Roger Pocock near the Grand Cañon of Colorado.

given up to sheep. More than once he met herds of wild horses when the leader, a big stallion, would come charging down on the lone rider, mane and tail flying, ears back, teeth bared, neighing an angry challenge. And though it was largely bluff, Pocock's horse would shiver with fear. He passed settlements, mostly small, some of which were almost abandoned. One called "Three Forks" on the headwaters of the Missouri, which is three thousand miles long, was quite a large town, yet had only three families remaining, the rest having left to escape the pests of mosquitoes.

He reached the Yellowstone Park, its valleys twice the height of the top of Snowdon, and its mountains rising a stark mile or more into the blue. He rode by a cool brook threading its way between pools of boiling water, and came upon acres of white rock, where jets of steam blow off with a roar like that of a thousand steam sirens. Pots of boiling mud every colour of the rainbow, geysers spouting boiling water, and lovely little lakes showed up one after another. The Park is a reservation where no one may use a gun, so the bears walk up to the back doors of the tourist hotels and turn over the piles of rubbish in search of food. One big beast raided Pocock's lone camp, and ate everything from bacon to flour, leaving the venturer nothing but some coffee and tobacco. Troopers and guards of all kinds patrol the Park, yet only fifty miles farther on Pocock came into the country of the outlaws who lived by robbing trains, tourists, and banks, and by stealing cattle wholesale.

The outlaws' stronghold was at Jackson's Hole, under the stupendous shadow of a vast mountain called the "Grand Seton." Several times in the day's march Pocock passed log cabins where hard-faced men watched him suspiciously until satisfied that he was neither sheriff nor emissary of the law. There were no women in these cabins. The whole country was overrun with game, grizzlies, cinnamon and brown bears, elk, wolves, foxes, lynx, wolverine, beaver, marten, and polecat. The polecat or skunk is a harmless little creature, common all over the United States, and has no fear of man, for well it knows that no man will molest it, since it has the power of ejecting a fluid, the smell of which is terrible. Also the creature is peculiarly subject to that dread disease hydrophobia, and when infected will bite everything in its way. One night Pocock roused from sleep just in time to save himself from being bitten in the face by a mad skunk.

The skunks were much less friendly than the bandits. "I was welcomed," says Mr. Pocock, "in the homes, camps, even strongholds of the most desperate criminals. In a town I took elaborate precautions to secure my treasure belt, harness, and horses against thieves or cheats. Among outlaws who live by robbery and defend themselves by murder, I travelled seven hundred miles with no misgivings. Twice I ran some risk, but that was through being mistaken for a robber. The bandits among whom I camped and travelled did not pose as such, but by cautious enquiry I found some of them to be notable men with a price on their heads 'dead or alive.' "

Mr. Pocock found that a system of robber bands existed along a curved line two thousand five hundred miles in length. Many had, in 1899, been already destroyed but there still remained the Jackson's Hole and Hole-in-the-Wall gangs in Wyoming, the Brown's Park and Robber's Roost gangs in Utah, a gang near Wilcox, Arizona, certain Border ruffians on the Texas-Mexico line and the Indian Territory gangs—in all some four hundred men living by robbery under arms. The central stronghold was the Robbers' Roost in Utah.

The origin of this gang is an odd story. Years ago an

eccentric Englishman, son of a noble family, founded a
big ranch in Southeastern Utah near the Blue Mountains,
and to run it collected all the "bad hats" he could find. They
robbed him out of business, then took to robbing others, and
in the end became the Robbers' Roost gang, numbering in
all thirty-four men. During his big ride Mr. Pocock attempted to visit the stronghold, but when he innocently enquired the way at a Mormon Settlement, the whole neighbourhood was at once warned against him. They took him
for an outlaw. He could get nothing to eat, and had no end
of trouble. He had to ride miles and nearly starved before
he could find a meal. The actual Roost stands on a high
tableland where the Green and Grand rivers meet to form
the Colorado. This plateau is entirely surrounded by terrific gorges and can only be reached by two very difficult
trails. On the surface the place appears to be just an ordinary ranch, with corrals for horses and cattle, but one of
the residents at the time of Mr. Pocock's call had four mur-
ders to his credit, and two of the men, Danes, had spent
twelve months in a coal pit, hiding there from hot pursuit
after a big bank robbery. Needless to say, the stock at Robbers' Roost is all stolen. The methods of cattle stealing are
amazing. On one occasion a bunch of two hundred head
were taken right across the Grand Canyon, which is a mile
deep and many miles wide. When the trail failed, the robbers rigged a windlass on top of a cliff and making each
animal in turn fast by the horns, hauled it up. They forced
the poor beasts to swim the river. Now the Colorado is very
muddy and runs at a furious pace. The wonder is that only
a third of the poor beasts were drowned.

The robbers do their shopping in Mormon settlements
where they are careful to pay for everything in hard cash.
Consequently they are quite popular. In all his journey Mr.

Pocock met one man only who openly expressed his contempt for the outlaws. One day an outlaw rode up to his ranch. "Shut your mouth up about us," he said curtly, "or clear out of this district." The man cleared out.

When business is slack the outlaws amuse themselves by killing elk. This is against the law and the forest rangers get on the warpath. Just before Mr. Pocock's arrival there had been trouble between a ranger who supplied a lumber camp with venison—at a price—and one of the outlaws. The ranger managed to stop the supply and the lumbermen, as well as the outlaw, went gunning for him. Mr. Pocock spent a night in camp with this ranger—not a very happy one.

Leaving Robbers' Roost, Mr. Pocock found himself faced with the worst problem of his journey—the long ride across the great desert. To the eastward lay the State of Colorado, a mass of high mountains, and beyond that New Mexico, a country where there was little or no forage for horses. If he turned westward he would have to cross Death Valley, that great waterless sink said to be the hottest place in the whole world, and then the horrible Gila Desert. Going straight ahead, he would meet a country cut into dice by a maze of terrific canyons, and beyond it the country of the Navajo and Apache Indians, tribes who at that time were not entirely trustworthy. All three routes led to Mexico and as one seemed as bad as another, the venturer chose the middle one and rode on.

About this time he met a man riding in the same direction as himself—a barber by trade and—though Mr. Pocock is too kind to say so—quite plainly a terrible fool. However, any company is better than none in the desert, so they rode together up Green River Valley to Green River City where the Union Pacific Railway spans the river.

ROGER POCOCK AT THE END OF HIS RECORD RIDE

ROGER POCOCK

From a photograph taken shortly after he had completed his
wonderful ride.

When crossing by the railway bridge they were chased by a train, and Mr. Pocock's horse was forced into a quicksand from which he was rescued with difficulty.

Leaving the river, they climbed gentle hills which went up and up "like rollers on a sea beach thousands of feet high," and at last reached Red Creek Canyon, where they again passed an outlaw stronghold, and had the interesting experience of supping with its chief tenant. Grand Junction, Colorado, was the next stopping place and there Mr. Pocock's barber found a job and left him, and he, after two days' rest, and a good meal on milk, fruit, and chocolates, hit the trail once more, and climbing ten thousand feet found himself in a lovely parklike country with grass, song birds, and frosty nights. But trouble was in store, for he found himself faced by the Unaweep Canyon and then the Canyon Dolores into which he dropped down a terrifically steep four thousand foot bank of grass. Once in this vast trough of the mountains he could find no way out, and it was not until the third day that he saw a cattle trail leading up out of the furnace-hot depths. That trail Mr. Pocock likens to "the ruins of a London set on edge" and "his horses fought desperately rather than face that particular stairway to Paradise." Up on a ledge which hung above space his saddle horse got a rope under its tail and bucked like a fiend. Later the led horse fell over a ten-foot ledge. "All three horses," he writes, "plunged, reared, and fought me in places where there was really no room for argument." When at last, after hours of toil and peril, he gained the heights, he met some cowboys.

"How did you come?" they asked.

"Followed your tracks," was the answer. "Where you drove the cattle."

"We didn't," the cowboys told him. "We headed cattle

P

into the bottom and they worked their way up hunting grass." So Mr. Pocock had ridden with two pack horses where no man ever rode before.

Next day he struck a sheep herder with a big flock of sheep. This was cattle country and sheep ruin the pasturage. Where a horse or cow nibbles, a sheep pulls up the grass by the roots and reduces the country to desert. So Mr. Pocock rode hard that day and at night found cowboys and warned them. What happened he never knew, but the battle between the cattle men and the sheep herders had raged bitterly in the West for many years.

From the high grassy parks Mr. Pocock rode down into the desert, following the trail of the mail riders, and so found his way to the Mormon outposts. The scenery shall be described in his own words:

I came to a part of the Desert where there stood natural rocks which, sculptured by wind-borne sand, stood sheer upon a plain like castles, temples, and embattled palaces of some dream city. They seemed quite near when first I saw them through the quivering heat, but a ride of fifty miles hardly brought me abreast of their walls and spires. . . . No building ever raised by human hands could rival those lone rocks in their awfulness, their haunting beauty. Then I came to a wave of sandstone towering about one hundred and fifty feet above the rock sea. Its known length is more than one hundred miles, and like the crest of a tidal wave its overhanging comb seems poised for the fall—yet frozen as though by enchantment, remains poised for ever. For a day I rode under the wave, seeking a passage, and when at last a passable traverse was reached, I found it led only into a chaos of other such breakers most difficult to thread.

This was the country of the Navajo Indians, and before traversing it Mr. Pocock had engaged as guide a Navajo named Manito. He spoke Spanish and no English; Mr.

Pocock had no Spanish, so they rode in silence. Manito found fuel for camping, grass for the ponies, but his leisurely ways were a sore trial to his employer. One day they met a Navajo chief riding a scarecrow pony yet with silver trappings on his bridle and wearing valuable desert turquoise as necklace.

"Where you from?" he asked.

"England."

"England. Is that a fort?" demanded the lordly Indian.

The Navajos have a right to their pride, for they alone, of all Indian tribes, withstood the flood of the Spanish Conquest and held their lands against the invaders. To-day they number over twenty thousand and are probably among the richest savages in the world. All through the canyon and ravines of this region were relics of an ancient and wonderful civilisation—cave houses, towers of dry stone, and remains of great irrigation ditches.

The heat of the sun was terrible, blistering the rider's hands and face; the wind, like a furnace blast, filled his eyes with sand; the only vegetation was spiny cactus, the only living things rattlesnakes, poisonous Gila monsters, tarantulas, scorpions, and centipedes. Manito had abandoned his white employer and the lone rider was lost. Then to crown his misfortunes, Burley, the pack pony, ran away. On Chub, his plump saddle animal, Mr. Pocock gave chase across naked rock, and just as he was beginning to feel that it was all up, suddenly there rose into sight a row of poplars. It was the Mormon oasis of Tuba for which the cunning Burley had been making his bolt.

Here Mr. Pocock rested a little, then rode forth into the Painted Desert, where he met a prospector who told him that the voices of the dead were leading him to a cave of gold. The man was mad—mad with desert madness, not an uncommon fate in this splendid yet terrible wilderness. At length Mr. Pocock sighted San Francisco Mountains, where there is good grazing, and he gave his tired horses a week's rest. Coaches laden with tourists went through in clouds of dust, and to the rider, after long weeks of utter loneliness, such a sight was very fantastic. The tourists were bound for the Grand Canyon of the Colorado and at dawn Mr. Pocock sat on the rim rock, staring down into blue mist which had no bottom. The northern wall was twelve miles away and in the depths below all London might be lost. As the mist cleared he saw mounds far below. Yet these were mountains bigger than the Grampians. He sat in a pine forest like that of Norway, but in the depths at his feet was a climate like that of Central Africa.

Presently he was riding down a trail blasted out of the face of the cliffs. "It was," he says, "like riding down the outside of St. Paul's Cathedral from cross to pavement, multiplied by fifteen." At last he reached the lost river, the Colorado, which, sunk in the foundations of the world, winds for six hundred miles at a depth of six thousand feet below the surrounding deserts. The walls of this mile-deep cleft blaze with wonderful colours ranging from pale prim-rose and orange to deep crimson and even to violet.

The traveller reached Phoenix, a town of twelve thousand people with trams and electric lights, which was crowded with cowboys, prospectors, farm hands, Negroes, Apache Indians, and low-caste Mexicans. Then he plunged once more into the desert and once more got lost. He saw an old man chasing his pack horse and helped him. The stranger showed him a piece of charred human skull. "Picked this up this morning," he said; "old white man like me. I found the stake. The Apaches got him. Yes, it's a bad country. T'other day I found a boot with a leg in it."

Texas Bob—that was his name—entertained the traveller at his camp and set him once more upon his way.

Speaking of the Arizona people, Mr. Pocock says, "They are the finest men I ever met, but they have paid for their education. I was the guest of one rancher, the best of citizens, who never kills except in self-defence, yet is said to have twenty-seven notches on his gun stock."

Every one bore a gun and Mr. Pocock, though he thinks a revolver a worse nuisance than an umbrella, found himself compelled to follow the fashion rather than be flouted as a lunatic. Of the many stories told him of queer doings in this part of the world one shall be related here, for the trouble took place during Mr. Pocock's crossing of the State.

Johnny Herron kept a saloon on the Mexican side of the Border, and having bought some horses, failed to put the proper number of stamps on the agreement. For this or some equally trivial offence the Mexican police took Herron, and word crossed to his friends on the American side that he was in bad trouble. So a party rode after him, and laid an ambush by night on the trail for his escort. Of the three latter, one got away badly wounded, the other two were shot to bits, and Herron was released. Was he grateful? Not a bit. He was wild, and the way he talked to his rescuers was a caution. The fact was that Herron dared not show his nose in the United States where years before he had been sentenced to twenty years' imprisonment, but had managed to escape from prison. And now his "rescuers," having shot up the Mexican police, had made that country also too hot to hold him. The only thing for the poor fellow to do was to go and live in Naco, a town where the main street forms the boundary line between Mexico and the United States, and there trust to luck that the police of both countries would not come hunting him at one and the same time.

Reaching the Mexican border, Mr. Pocock found a small civil war starting up. It appears that on October 23 the people of the town of Bisbee came down to Naco for a baseball match and the Mexican guards, under the impression that the excursionists were invaders, opened fire, wounding one of the holiday makers. An American went for the guards, but the guard beat him over the head and made him prisoner. The cowboys who tried to rescue him were also captured. So by the time that Mr. Pocock arrived, the borders on both sides were lined with troops and one hundred and fifty American cowboys were making ready to invade Mexico and capture Mexico City.

Mr. Pocock found it best to turn eastward and hired a Mexican as guide. But the Mexican was a loafer and on the third day Mr. Pocock emptied his canteens, hoping that a little thirst would quicken the man's movements. Instead, the guide left him, after putting him on the wrong trail and, but for the fact that the adventurer soon realised that the trail was a wrong one, he would probably have died of thirst. As it was, he used his eyes and found the real trail, and when at the last gasp, luckily fell in with an American cowboy whose canteens were full.

"Last night," said Mr. Pocock to the cowboy, "did you see my fire? I was signalling for help."

"Or to scare away the Apaches?" returned the cowboy with scorn. Never again so long as he was in that country did Mr. Pocock light a fire at night. But the cowboy was a good sort and led the lost Englishman to a little ranch where, being very weak, he was able to rest for a while. Then they passed him on from camp to camp to the edge of the Mexican cattle range.

That saw the end of lonely night camps, and disposing of his pack horse, Mr. Pocock rode from one big fortified house to another, finding them rarely more than a day's march apart. Twenty years earlier the whole of this part of Mexico, a country as large as France, had been swept bare by raiding Apaches who stole the cattle and killed every man, woman, and child. Now this country was under control of the United States Government, and the Indians dared only to catch and torture an occasional traveller.

Mr. Pocock came to the ranch of Don Luis Terrazas and rode across it. It took him a week, for the breadth of that ranch is nearly equal to the distance between London and Plymouth. He met the eldest son of Don Luis travelling in state. First an army of riders ten abreast, then horse wranglers with a herd of horses, bullock carts with stores, a group of men in uniform, and behind all this a coach drawn by six white mules travelling at full gallop. Mr. Pocock still had some hundreds of miles to go and it was lonely work, for he spoke no Spanish. Yet almost every night he was treated to the best that some Mexican family could afford, and usually slept in the one big living room inhabited by the fowls and the family. It was only the poorest who would allow him to pay. At last he came to a ridge of cultivated land and looked south over endless fields of maize. He had conquered and crossed the desert, and was now in civilised Mexico.

The first thing civilization did for him was to infect him with influenza, which left him so ill he could hardly sit in the saddle. Yet he kept on. The people were no longer hospitable; thieves and beggars abounded, and their cruelty to animals made him sick with disgust. At a place called Silao he caught the hotel keeper stealing forage from his horse and there was a row. "I certainly was very rude," says Mr. Pocock. "The man went the colour of a lemon, his legs wobbled. Presently the house was surrounded by police who marched Mr. Pocock and his horse off to prison for "insulting a citizen." Since the hotel proprietor appeared to own the town, things looked ugly for the adventurer. A fellow countryman had at that time been rotting for five years in a Mexican gaol, unable to pay the bribes demanded, and beyond all aid from the British Foreign Office. Another Englishman had died in prison of yellow fever.

Luckily for Mr. Pocock there were Americans in the town who had witnessed his arrest and they started to the rescue. In the evening one came to say that he could be liberated on payment of a certain sum. He flatly refused, demanded that the Governor should come in person and apologize on penalty of a cable to the British Minister. The Governor came, and it was as Mr. Pocock had demanded.

The gaol cured the influenza, but gave Mr. Pocock dysentery and the rest of his ride was "one long nightmare of pain." Yet on the last day he rode forty miles and then saw electric lights starring the darkness. He rode through five miles of suburbs and was at last in Mexico City.

Here are some figures of this wonderful ride. The distance was three thousand six hundred miles, or about that from London to Chicago. The time taken was from June 20, 1899, to January 21, 1900, that is, two hundred days. But of that time Mr. Pocock was actually travelling only one hundred and forty-seven days, so the average works out at roughly twenty-five miles a day. Three good horses covered practically the whole journey, but including pack animals, nine in all were used, and the cost of these horses

—incredible as it may seem—was only a little over two hundred and twenty-five dollars.

Speaking of this ride that great frontiersman W. F. Cody—"Buffalo Bill"—said, "I envied him the trip."

CHAPTER XVI

NO other explorer of our generation, not even Nansen or Amundsen, can claim to have spent so much of his life north of the Arctic Circle as has Vilhjalmur Stefansson. He is a Canadian by birth, but was educated in the United States. He was employed on various American newspapers and made his first journey north, to Iceland, in 1904, when he was twenty-five years of age. In 1906 he visited the Eskimos at the mouth of the Great Mackenzie River and since then has been almost continuously in the Arctic. His best known books are "My Life with the Eskimos" and "The Friendly Arctic." He has proved that it is perfectly possible for white men to travel through the Arctic regions for years on end, living, and living well, on the seals, bears, caribou, and other animals which are found there. He has had the rare and extraordinary experience of discovering a race of men previously unknown, and it is this adventure which is the subject of this chapter.

Exactly north of the Great Bear Lake lies Langton Bay, an inlet from the Arctic Ocean, and it was from this bay, on April 21, 1910, that Stefansson and his little party started eastward on their way to Coronation Gulf, and the great unknown lands to the northeast. He expected to be a year away from any sources of supply, other than those which the Arctic lands can furnish, but was poorly equipped for so long an absence. He had no good dogs, no white man with him, but only three Eskimos. These were Natkusiak, an Alaskan Eskimo, Tannaumirk, a boy from the Mackenzie River country, and a woman, Pannigabluk. He had no silk tent for summer use; only an old canvas one, heavy and full of holes, and—worst of all—only two hundred cartridges for his own high-power rifle. In all, the party had four rifles with nine hundred and sixty rounds of ammunition, but these were of different calibres so that cartridges which would fit one would not fit another.

His people were not happy at the prospect before them. Eskimos are superstitious, and queer stories were rife of the tribes their leader proposed to visit. "Nagyuktogmiut" was the name they went by; it means, "People of the Caribou Antler," and its origin, it was said, was as follows: When a girl was to be married she was led out into the open and all her suitors stood in a ring around, each armed with the antler of a bull caribou. At a given signal all rushed at her, each trying to hook her toward him with an antler. Often, so the tale went, the girl was killed in the struggle, but if she survived the man who hooked her took her for his wife. It was also believed that the Nagyuktogmiut killed all strangers. Stefansson's Eskimos did not want him to think them cowards, so they pretended that the reason why they were afraid of the journey was that they would starve. They declared that the country to the east had no game.

Start, however, they did, and six days later reached Cape Lyon, which is the farthest point east on which American whalers have ever landed. Although Coronation Gulf is not really so very far north it is usually choked with ice, and was at that time far less known than many parts lying farther north, while it was believed that the land beyond Cape Lyon was quite uninhabited for at least two hundred miles.

When he started, Stefansson's party had provisions for two weeks only, so it was necessary to shoot as they travelled. The plan of campaign was that the three Eskimos took care of the sledge, the woman walking ahead to pick a trail through the rough sea ice, the men steadying the sledge or helping to pull it. If they saw a seal or a bear one of the men would go after the animal while the others stayed by the sledge. When it came to camping time, if no game had been seen, the woman stayed in camp to cook supper and the two men went off in opposite directions to hunt. This plan doubled the chance of getting game, but was sometimes wasteful. The very first day, for instance, Natkusiak killed with one shot two huge bearded seals, each weighing at least seven hundred pounds, while Tannaumirk slew a fat grizzly bear. Most of the meat had to be left behind as it was impossible to load more than a hundred pounds on the sledge.

Stefansson himself obtained most of the food. He always started earlier than the Eskimos, and while they worked along the sea ice parallel with the coast, he would strike four or five miles inland. Using snowshoes, he was able to travel faster than the Eskimos who, however, managed to average fifteen miles a day. He went inland in order to find caribou, but had not got any by the time they had reached Point Pierce, five days from Langton Bay, where further progress was stopped by an easterly blizzard. The Eskimos argued that since this country was evidently gameless it would be best to turn back before they got weak from hunger. Yet while they talked they were gorging themselves with boiled seal's flesh and blubber. Of course Stefansson knew that it was not hunger they were afraid of, but these mysterious people who "killed all strangers."

However, just to show them that they were wrong, Stefansson went out *in the blizzard* to hunt. To us who have read of the howling horrors of an Arctic blizzard, such a performance seems sheer lunacy, but that surprising man, Stefansson, calmly tells us that nine tenths of Arctic blizzards are not bad enough to keep a healthy man indoors, while if you do find caribou in a blizzard the chances of approaching them are much better than in finer weather. "I wanted," he says, "to kill a few for the moral effect it would have on my party." Five miles inland he had the luck to run into a band of seven and shot three of them. Of course he did not want three, for one was as much as they could eat between them. It was done just for the effect on the Eskimos, and it was the only time during the whole of the journey that Stefansson killed more meat than was actually needed.

The abundance of meat had its effect, and for a time all went well. It was not until May 2 that anything exciting happened. On that day the Eskimos were having a hard pull among rough sea ice and Stefansson, as usual, was hunting along the coast. He saw ptarmigan, but could not afford to waste cartridges on such small game. Indeed, the smallest game he would shoot at was wolf, and a wolf, he tells us, when fat, makes excellent eating. Early in the afternoon he noticed a yellow spot on the sea ice about three miles from shore. He watched it a while and at last saw it move, so feeling sure that it was a polar bear, he took his bearings and started running toward it. When travelling over sea ice you must be very careful about your bearings, for the high ridges called *pressure* ridges cut off the view. Every quarter mile or so he climbed a ridge and had a look round, but the bear was not visible. That was just as it should be, for it meant that the great beast was lying down. When at last Stefansson thought that he was near the bear he climbed a high ridge, but still could see nothing. He made up his mind that he had not gone far enough and decided to walk a little farther before circling in search of the bear's tracks. With his rifle still buckled in its case on his back, he was climbing down a steep ice slope when he heard behind him a sound like a hiss of an angry goose. There, only twenty feet above him, was the bear. That hiss was a fatal mistake on the part of Master Bear. Stefansson sagely observes: "No animal on earth can afford to give warning to a man with a rifle." If the bear had had sense to remain silent as he charged, the story would have had a very different ending.

On May 9, after nineteen days' steady travelling, they reached Point Wise near the entrance to Dolphin and Union straits. Here driftwood was scattered on the beach and suddenly they came upon piles of chips. Some one had been chopping a log with an adze. Their hearts beat faster, for it seemed as though they were actually approaching the home of the unknown race. That night they were too excited to sleep much and the three Eskimos chattered eagerly about the meaning of the signs. All three were scared, but now they no longer wanted to turn back, for the spirit of adventure was stronger than their fears and they were so eager that they got up sooner than usual next morning in order to start at once. All that day they kept on finding chips and shavings on the beach, but it was not until next morning, when east of Point Young, that they saw footprints and sledge tracks on the snow. These they thought had been made about three months earlier. The next thing they found was a deserted village of over fifty snow houses. "Its size," says Stefansson, "took our breath away." None of the Eskimos with him had ever seen villages of more than twelve or fifteen houses.

A trail led from the village and Stefansson made up his mind to try to find the people who had built the village. So leaving Pannigabluk in charge of the camp and most of the gear, he and the two men took the trail across the ice. The reason for leaving the woman behind was Eskimo etiquette. When approaching strange people only the able-bodied men advance.

Tannaumirk got scared and begged to remain with Pannigabluk, but at the last minute he decided to go with the others. As for the woman herself, she was quite cheerful and they left her mending stockings.

The going was good and travelling at six miles an hour in about two hours they arrived at another deserted village. The village was on sea ice and Stefansson knew that on the ice each village is about ten miles from the next. The reason is that the seal hunters find it best to work a radius of about five miles, then when all the seals within that radius have been killed the community moves just far enough so that the new circle shall not overlap the old one.

Climbing to the roof of one of the houses in this second village, Stefansson saw little dark figures in the distance. They were seal hunters, each sitting on a block of snow by a seal hole, waiting for a seal to rise. Since they were about half a mile apart one from another, Stefansson thought it would be unwise to approach one at full speed, so going on quietly, he stopped the sledge about a hundred yards from the nearest. Tannaumirk, seeing that the seal hunter did not seem very formidable, actually offered to go forward and speak to him. As he said, his own dialect was probably nearer to the stranger's tongue than that of Natkusiak. He walked on and when he was within about five paces of the sealer, the latter jumped up, picked up a long-bladed knife which lay beside him, and made ready to receive an attack.

Tannaumirk stopped short and cried out that he was friendly.

Instead of answering, the other began a sort of chant. It was plain that he thought the stranger to be a spirit and the Eskimo's belief is that when in the presence of a spirit, a man must make some sound each time he draws breath for otherwise he will be stricken dumb. As this man afterward told Stefansson, he could not believe that the strangers were anything but spirits, for their dogs, harness, sledge, and clothes were all quite different from any that he had ever seen before. Besides, Tannaumirk had not made the peace sign, which consists in holding out the hands to show that one has not a knife. For some minutes Tannaumirk went on talking and at last lifted his coat to show that he had no knife.

Then at last the sealer got confidence enough to search him to see that he had no knife hidden about him. When he found that he was really unarmed, he invited him to come to the village, but first he was to tell his two companions to keep well behind, and that when they got to the village they were to stay outside until the people could be informed that the strangers were friendly.

The other seal hunters came up, each armed with a spear and a knife, so the visitors were under strong escort as they walked to the village. Here every man, woman, and child —forty in all—were out of doors and waiting eagerly. The man whom Tannaumirk had first approached explained the state of things and all came up running to be introduced. Or rather they introduced themselves, for each as he came up would say, "I am so-and-so. I am your friend. I have no knife. Who are you?" The women were in the greatest hurry, for all wanted to go back to their houses and cook something for the visitors to eat.

STEFANSSON BRINGING A SEAL TO CAMP

They were charming people, simple, well-bred, and hospitable, and to Stefansson's delight he found that their dialect differed so little from the Eskimo language which he knew that he could talk to them quite easily. At once boys were sent flying for snow knives and house builders' mittens. Then the best builders set to work to erect a house for the visitors. The latter were not allowed to lift a hand, and when the house was finished, it was furnished with skins, a lamp, and all other necessaries. "We hope," said these kindly folk, "that you will stay with us until the last piece of meat is eaten, and now we will hold holiday, for it is the first time we have ever been visited by strangers from so great a distance."

But the odd thing was that even then they did not know that Stefansson was one of the *Kablunat* (white men) of whom they had heard vague reports. It was not till next day that they realised this fact. "Could you not tell it from my grey eyes and the colour of my beard?" asked Stefansson.

"But we did not know what complexions the *kablunat* had," they answered. "Besides our neighbours to the north (in Prince Albert Sound) have eyes and beards like yours." "That," says Stefansson, "was how they first told us of the people who have since been dubbed the 'Blond Eskimos,' but whom I have preferred to call 'Copper Eskimos,' since they differ from other branches of their race in their extensive use of copper."

It was May 12 when Stefansson discovered the Union Straits Eskimos. Three days later, after being entertained in the kindest fashion, he set out with Natkusiak and one local man for Victoria Island, which is a great stretch of country far larger than England. After a sixteen-mile march they found the first village on the sea ice close to the shore of the island. Every one was asleep, so the guide

Q

went forward to warn them of the coming of strangers. All poured out, yet in spite of their excitement the men stopped to tie their dogs, so that they should not fight with the strange dogs. Then nine men came forward with their hands raised. "We are friendly," they said. "Your coming has made us glad." It should be mentioned that the Eskimos have nothing like our custom of shaking hands, nor any words of salutation or of farewell. Each guest was then taken to a separate house to be fed and entertained, and the people were kindness itself. Even the dogs were fed with boiled meat, "for dogs like to be treated well just like men do," they said.

But it was the appearance of these people that amazed Stefansson. As for Natkusiak, the way he put it was this, "These people are not Eskimos. They merely talk and act and dress like Eskimos." Later Natkusiak said, "Three of them look like white foremast hands on a whaler. And aren't they huge? And one looks like a Portugee."

Some of these men had strong beards of a light brown colour. They reminded the explorer of "stocky, sunburned, but naturally fair Scandinavians." A young woman had the delicate features one sees in some Scandinavian girls. Among the men the hair of the head was often brown or even reddish, a thing utterly unknown among the ordinary Eskimos, who have brown eyes and hair as black as that of a Chinaman. In other words, these people who talked and acted like Eskimos looked like white folk.

What is the explanation? Some have suggested that the blond race may be due to mixture with Hudson Bay free traders, but this is absurd. None of the traders so much as knew of the existence of these people or came anywhere near their remote country. Far the more probable explanation is that Blond Eskimos are descended from the Scandinavian colonists of Greenland. Owing to the Black Death and the defeat of Norway by the ships of the Hanseatic League communication was cut off between the Greenland colonists and their homeland and when the sailors of England rediscovered Greenland the colonists had disappeared. What more likely than that the remnants of the Europeans intermarried with the Eskimos, for after all, Greenland is not so very far from Victoria Island.

Travelling still eastward Stefansson fell in with other parties of the Blond Eskimos, most of whom were fishing on the inland lakes through holes picked through seven-foot ice. Their hooks were of copper, like their knives and spearheads. Many caribou were seen and Stefansson was able to kill enough not only to feed himself, but also his kindly hosts. Speaking of rifles it is noteworthy that these Eskimos, whose bows would kill a caribou at perhaps fifty yards, were not all amazed at the performance of Stefansson's weapon. If, as Stefansson says, he had shewn them a bow which would shoot fifty yards farther than any other bow, they would never have ceased marvelling. The rifle, however, was quite beyond their understanding. It was therefore a miracle, something supernatural and beyond wonder. Their thought is made plain by this instance. With his field glasses Stefansson showed them that he could see caribou at distances beyond their unaided sight. All they said was, "Now that you have found the caribou that are here to-day, will you not also look for the caribou that are coming to-morrow and tell us where to lie in wait for them."

The more Stefansson saw of these primitive folk the better he liked them. They were the kindest and most hospitable folk imaginable, kind not only to visitors, but also to one another. Whatever their origin they remain the finest type of their race still existing.

CHAPTER XVII

IT will probably come as a surprise to many of the readers of this book to find a chapter devoted to an adventurous journey across "unknown" Australia. We are so accustomed, when speaking of the Commonwealth, to think of the large towns that we forget that there remain great tracts of land in the interior about which comparatively little or nothing is known. The southern half of this mighty land of bush and desert was thoroughly explored years ago, but in the Northern Territory there are still places where the appearance of a white man is a most unusual event.

We must remember, then, that the total population of the Australian continent is less than that of Greater London, while the country is nearly as big as the United States of America.

The northern part of the country is a land of vast empty spaces populated mainly by natives. In this great "No Man's Land" under the British flag there are but two thousand white people, most of whom live in or near the only town there, Port Darwin, and a few minor settlements. In the interior of that region which is four and one half times the size of the United Kingdom, one finds a few isolated homesteads, or cattle stations, of enormous proportions where white men live in twos and threes. There are no fences, no roads—even tracks are rare—and no telegraphs. To the stranger on a journey it seems that he is in a virgin land. One may travel for weeks without seeing a sign of a human habitation or meeting a soul. The pioneer may die of thirst or fatigue out in that limitless bush and his body never be found.

A wild, romantic country, crossed by very few men. Certainly not the sort of country most people would choose for a motor journey. That, however, did not prevent Michael Terry, a young Englishman, from deciding to cross those empty lands in a motor car. He was a modest young man who planned this adventurous journey. In the book which he wrote about it afterward he did not claim to be an explorer. Indeed, he pointed out that it is believed that the first white men to cross Northern Australia were gold miners who completed the journey on horseback as long ago as 1886. But his own journey made in 1923 was unique in one respect at least, it was the first time that the empty northern part of Australia had been conquered by a motor car, or indeed, by any wheeled vehicle.

Exploration does not consist only of going where no man has been before—it also includes going in a different manner from that of any of the earlier travellers in the region. And therefore it is only just and true to say that, even irrespective of a second journey across Australia which he has made, Michael Terry is entitled to rank among the most daring explorers of to-day, much as he himself would disagree with such a statement. For Michael Terry, like most men who do things worth while, is a very modest person.

It was on February 6, 1923, that Michael Terry, accompanied by Richard Yockney, set out from Winton, in Queensland, upon their adventurous journey.

They had managed to buy an old Ford car, and upon this had loaded their equipment. Money was short and surely so ambitious an expedition never started out with smaller supplies. When Michael Terry took the wheel and drove the Ford over the first mile of their long journey they had only forty gallons of gasoline (petrol), sixteen gallons of oil, twelve gallons of water carried in a special tank, and the equipment of guns, ammunition, spare parts, road-making tools, axes, cameras, spare clothes, blankets, food and medical supplies. Of course, one cannot carry enough petrol or food in one small car with a homemade trailer behind, to last for a journey which will probably take at least a year, but they hoped to be able to replenish their supplies from time to time along the route. That was, providing their small stock of capital held out. If it didn't —but like true explorers, neither Terry nor Yockney thought about what would happen if they were stranded in the middle of the empty land that lay ahead.

As to exactly what did await them out in the wilds they had very little information. The latest map was secured from Melbourne, but it was of little use, for the empty north of Australia has never been systematically surveyed.

They did know, however, that they would have to cross the Murranji Track, a three hundred mile stretch of empty country linking the eastern and western portions of the "Never, Never Land"—a popular name for this region. In all that three hundred miles water is scarce, the compass is the travellers' only guide, and no motor car had ever crossed it.

Between the last point where motor cars were used on the eastern side of the Continent and the first point where motors were to be found four hundred miles from Broome, at the other end of the journey, was eight hundred miles of roadless, trackless, sun-scorched country. A land of mountains, rivers, plains, and bush—where if anything went

THE FORD CAR AND HOME-MADE TRAILER IN WHICH MICHAEL TERRY CROSSED NORTHERN
AUSTRALIA WITH ONE COMPANION

wrong with the car it would be impossible to find a garage or a mechanic to help repair it. Michael Terry did not quite know how he was going to get the gasoline to carry them over this part of unknown Australia. He did not know what would happen if they met a bush fire with petrol on board. Or if they missed the water hole when their small drinking tank was empty.

If they were lucky they would be able to penetrate to the great cattle stations of the interior. And from there it would be possible to get pack horses and travel to the coast for more gasoline. It would take time, but they did not mind that so long as in the end they could drive their "tin Lizzie" into Broome, on the other side of the Continent.

No wonder that before they drove out of Winton on that February day in 1923 one of their friends chalked on front wheel of the car the inscription "Left for an Unknown Destination 6/2/23." That night the two adventurers camped in the open bush for the first time, and before sleeping counted their money. They had with them supplies for less than one fifth of their journey. And they had just £8. 2. 3. in English money left. It was certainly going to be a real adventure!

The first forty miles of the journey—from Winton to Ayrshire Downs Station—was slow progress. Sixteen miles out a piston gave way, which necessitated a wait at a small holding close by while another was secured from Brisbane.

At last another start was made, but five miles out in open country the long drought was broken by a violent thunderstorm. There was nothing to do but to pitch a camp which would be as dry as possible and wait until the next morning.

There was a long tarpaulin among the kit, sufficient to cover the car and the trailer. These were placed side by side, with the sheet stretched between them and over the loads, leaving enough space for the blankets on the ground. Trenches were dug round the camp to carry off the water. Hardly had they prepared before the storm broke. Down came the torrential rain, while the violent lightning made one think of home and warm beds.

No meal could be cooked that night, and while the storm raged the tent flapped perilously, as though it might collapse at any minute.

The next day the sun was shining and once more they pushed on. Eight miles had been covered when once more the rain came down again. They were now crossing peaty ground, which made travelling by motor easy enough in dry weather, but which rain turned into a gigantic bog. There was nothing to do, therefore, but camp again in the open. That night Michael Terry learnt what real rain is in the north of Australia. In all they had two inches in one night, or about as much as falls during a wet fortnight in an English winter!

Terry and his companion had decided, after adding up their funds at the beginning of their journey, that they would lose no opportunity of selling their services as mechanics to any car owners they met during the early stages of the journey, and thus increase their capital. Fortunately for the expedition, the first two cars they came across had broken down—and they made them both go again. By this means they completed the first fifty miles with more money in their pockets than they had possessed when leaving Winton, and their spirits rose accordingly. But there were ominous signs of trouble ahead. The rainy season had now begun in earnest, and just as horse-travelling is impossible during the dry season because of the absence of water, so motor travel is difficult when it is wet because of the absence of roads and the flooded state of the rivers.

The fact that MacKinlay, a fair-sized town, where more repair work might be found, lay only sixty miles ahead, however, caused them to decide to push on despite the risks of getting stuck. The first river was forded after great exertions, and with the car skidding and slipping in all directions over the wet ground they made slow progress. To climb the smallest slope it was necessary for one to get out and push. At times the car slipped backward instead of going forward. But at last, when Terry had almost decided to abandon the car and push on to MacKinlay on foot, they climbed a small rise, and saw the town four hundred yards away.

An hour later the "tin Lizzie" and its two adventurous passengers drove down into the main street, there to be welcomed by the entire population of about a dozen men.

As they had hoped, there were broken-down motor cars in plenty at and around MacKinlay that needed attention, and also on their route from that town to Cloncurry, eighty miles farther on, which marked the end of the first and most civilised stage of the journey.

This stage Michael Terry had expected to cover in a few days. Actually, owing to wet weather and "good business" in the motor-repairing line, it was on June 28, nearly five months later, when they set out from Cloncurry for the wilds. The following day the expedition passed Duchess, a tiny mining township where they said good-bye to the railway. For the rest of the journey their route lay through country where the "iron horse" is still unknown.

At Lagon Creek, a little farther on through the hilly country, the two adventurers came upon a camp of silver miners, who proved friendly and offered to allow the strangers to watch them at work.

The car was given a rest while the whole party walked over the "mine," an outcrop or surface vein of silver on a bare patch of hillside which had then just been discovered.

Up to the time of this visit, the outside world had not realised the importance of this "find." Nor did Michael Terry and his companion, for when the miners very kindly suggested that they should abandon their perilous journey and stake a claim next to the one they were working, Terry declined with thanks, thereby losing the only easy fortune he found on his trip. That piece of bare ground which the miners offered to Terry and Yockney proved to be the richest in the district and was shortly after taken over by a syndicate for a purchase price which was about fifty thousand dollars.

Good progress was being made now, sometimes as much as one hundred miles a day being covered. And what was equally important, in view of the fact that doctors had been left behind, both travellers were keeping perfectly fit on a plain diet which consisted principally of corned beef, bread, tea, and jam—the almost universal food of the bushman in these parts of the world.

On July 3, the explorers reached a great plain stretching to the far horizon and bare of all vegetation except sunburnt grass.

Across the plain ran a wire fence—the longest fence in the world. That fence runs right down the western edge of Queensland for six hundred unbroken miles. A wire gate enabled the car to cross it, and as the wheels of "tin Lizzie" drove through both men felt the thrill of excitement. For that fence marked the boundary of the Northern Territory. They were at the beginning of the "Never, Never Country" and real adventure!

Roads had now disappeared, and there were only the most primitive tracks or the open bush to choose from. Generally the rough tracks made the best substitute, but occasionally awkward patches were found where cattle had passed during the wet season and churned up the mud with their feet. It remained as they had left it, hard baked by the sun and anything but pleasant to motor over.

The car jolted and shook over the rough patches far worse than over the most neglected English lane until damaged springs seemed a certainty. At first travelling dead slow was tried to ease the awful bumping, but this only made matters worse.

The steering wheel tore at Michael Terry's fingers as if anxious to break something, the trailer bounced and bounded about like a thing possessed. Speed was increased and things seemed to be a little better, if only because when the bumps sent the wheels bounding in the air, the car bounded forward and missed several bumps before they touched earth again.

It was here that Terry saw his first mirages. Water in the desert is a well-known mirage which every schoolboy has heard about, but in the Northern Territory the adventurers found a new sort of trick which the sun and the atmosphere played on the traveller.

This was in revealing to him objects which in reality are hidden below the horizon. Trees might be seen at breakfast to disappear later in the morning, only to come in sight again just before nightfall—this time in reality and not as the result of any deception.

The "deserts" of Australia, by the way, are not all sand like those in Africa or Arabia. They are flat tracts of country in which are trees, scrub, grasses, and other vegetation, but no water. In some ways they are more dangerous to the stranger than would be a real desert, for unless you know the country there is nothing about them to suggest that you may be thirty or forty miles from the nearest water hole.

Despite the difficulties of travel, good progress was made during the first days in the Northern Territory, and Alexandra Station was reached without mishap.

"Station" is the word used in Australia for "ranch" or "farm." The Alexandra Station, where Michael Terry and his companion rested for a day, is the second largest cattle ranch in Australia, having an area of 10,620 square miles, which is equal to seven million acres. On this giant farm are about forty-five thousand cattle and fifteen hundred horses, but the station is unfenced and the animals roam across the Territory at will, except when a great "round-up" is in progress.

Here Michael Terry saw camel convoys for the first time. The camel is largely used in this remote part of Northern Australia on account of the fact that poisonous weeds grow there which a horse would eat and a camel does not. Each beast can carry a load of a quarter of a ton for about fifteen miles daily.

The camels are owned by Afghans from Northern India, and the camel trains are used to carry goods from the nearest port or railway station, often about three hundred miles away. Some day proper roads will be constructed and then the work will be done by motor cars. Or perhaps before that time the aeroplane, already used for carrying the mails in outlying parts of Australia, will be used for goods traffic as well. At present, however, there are neither roads nor aeroplanes to do the work, and so the

twelve thousand camels in Northern Australia are necessary if settlers are to live in the far interior at all.

The next stop was at Alroy Station, forty-two miles
farther on. This ranch was referred to by other settlers as
"a small place," yet it was three thousand square miles
in size and had twenty-five thousand head of cattle.

Here Michael Terry and his companion repaired two
motor cars for the owner before pushing on. They were
asked by the overseer to build him a trailer for his Ford
car similar to the one they had for themselves. But instead of doing this, they sold him their trailer, for their
load had been considerably lightened during the journey
out, and the rough country ahead was no place for a
trailer if one was not essential.

Having sold the trailer they bought enough benzine to
enable them to reach Newcastle Waters, three hundred
miles farther along the trail, and once more set out westward. Incidentally, you will realise how far they now were
from civilisation by the fact that the cheque given them
for the repair work they had done could not be cashed until they reached the end of their journey. It was posted all
round Australia to Cloncurry, and the cash for it was received the following December! In this remote part money
is seldom seen. The few white men buy and sell entirely
by cheque, which can be easily carried in the pocket. These
cheques drawn by responsible white settlers can always
be given in exchange for goods at the cattle stations and
the few stores in the Northern Territory.

After leaving Alroy, the country became wilder and
the weather hotter. Nowhere was there a particle of shade.
The only track was a "cattle pad," made by beasts walking
in single file. One wheel of the car could follow this narrow
track, about a foot wide, while the other had to bump over

tufts of grass, stones, holes, and every kind of obstacle just off the track. Speed was forgotten, and the Ford could only creep forward across the plains at about four miles per hour.

That sort of travelling is exciting at first. There is the fun of trying to keep your equipment in the car instead of having it flung out on the track as she bumps about. But after about a hundred miles of it, the novelty wears off and you begin to sigh for just ten miles of a real English road.

Of water there is hardly a sign, and during the first fifty miles of the journey beyond Alroy, Michael Terry passed the grave of a traveller who had been found shortly before by a monthly postman, dead from thirst. A hole in his water can, the pitiless sun, and the "Never, Never Lands" had claimed another pioneer out there where no help could be found.

The postmen mentioned are among the most wonderful men in all Australia. Every month the mailman starts out from Camooweal on his thousand-mile journey with letters for the far scattered cattle stations. His horses are changed at each station, and so splendidly do these men keep to their time-table that you can set your watches by them. If your watch shows that the postman is late in arriving, then your watch is wrong. Rains may come, horses go lame, the mailman may feel sick, but still the letters arrive to the minute. No postmen in the world have a finer record, or are so little known.

Michael Terry had now entered upon the most difficult stage of his long journey—the six hundred miles of virgin country across which no motor car had ever travelled. And he had petrol enough for only half that distance. At Newcastle Waters, however, if the pot holes in the track had not smashed any axles before then, he hoped to arrange for pack horses which would bring additional supplies from the coast and thus enable the rest of the journey to be completed.

It was rough going all the way, and it seemed doubtful whether the decrepit Ford car would stand it long enough to enable them to reach Broome in safety. But it was useless to think about that. The only thing to do was to push on, rising before sun-up in order to take advantage of every minute of daylight.

They were lucky in one respect. Their route lay through a hundred miles of country which had contained but one safe water hole before 1922. In that year the Government had dug a series of new wells every twenty miles in order to open a new route by which cattle might reach the coast. Michael Terry, therefore, knew that his water supply was assured.

They had other adventures, however, including a meeting with a wild buffalo who gave them a very bad few minutes by charging the Ford, only to pull up in the nick of time and when they had imagined escape to be impossible. Apparently the beast was merely curious over this funny thing he had never seen before.

At times the track was so bad that it took an hour to do one hundred yards. One had to drive while the other pushed! Less determined men would have abandoned the attempt while there was yet time to return to Queensland, for ahead lay a range of steep hills they had to descend, and once down those, nothing on earth would have ever got the car up again. But Michael Terry and Richard Yockney had set out to cross Australia by motor car, and to cross it they intended, whatever the difficulties.

Outside Newcastle Waters Station, when the stiffest part of the journey lay just ahead and the gasoline supply was nearly exhausted, Michael Terry was lucky enough to find a contractor working on the erection of a new windmill for raising water, who had a supply of gasoline.

The contractor was persuaded to trade eight gallons of the precious fuel in return for two days' work, which both the travellers set about with light hearts. This unexpected piece of good fortune meant that they would not have to wait for weeks while one of them travelled by pack horse to the coast for a supply.

Thanks to this lucky meeting, on August 14, they were able to set out again, with the bonnet of the "tin Lizzie" turned toward the uncharted Murranji country. There the plains stopped. Three hundred miles of virgin empty Australia lay ahead of them before they would see another sign of civilisation. If their ten-year-old motor car gave out before that three hundred miles lay behind them, they would very probably never see a white man again. But that is the risk which every pioneer takes.

Just before reaching the "Jump up," as the range of hills on the edge of the plain is called, they passed the last known water hole. They had completed half their journey and henceforth must rely upon luck and bushcraft to find the vital supply of water for their motor and their own needs in a country never mapped and almost unknown.

When the end of the plain was reached, a good spot was found for descending the hills into the broken country below. The descent was only a matter of about two hundred feet, but driving a motor car even that distance over a trackless hill is a ticklish business.

It meant a whole day's work with pick and shovel, clearing some sort of a path. Then a small tree was cut down and tied behind the car, for the gradient was too steep for brakes to be relied upon. The presence of sharp stones on the descent made it necessary to put on new tires, with the old ones on top of them if punctures were to be avoided.

When all this had been done, the last night was spent on the plateau, and the next morning, at sun-up, the perilous descent began.

The passage down was accomplished in safety, but it marked a definite stage in the journey, for once down that slope there was no going back. Either they must reach Broome now, or perish.

Now began the toughest part of the whole journey. There were no maps to guide them. Sometimes they covered only four miles after a hard day's work. Rivers had to be forded. Dingoes, the wild dogs of Australia, made the night hideous with their howling.

In the heart of this wonderful Murranji country Terry found the homestead of a lone white man, where they rested. In the garden of this remarkable farm, hundreds of miles from the nearest town, was an amazing display of vegetables. Tropical fruits such as bananas grew side by side with radishes the size of turnips, while cauliflowers measured two feet six inches across.

After bidding farewell to the lonely white man at Montijinnie, the country became worse than before. It became an unusual thing to do more than ten yards without a stop. Twice the tires were wrenched right off the wheels, and dozens of times one or both front wheels would drop between two stones and remain there, jammed immovably until the stones were levered apart. Meanwhile, in the heat the engine boiled all day long and to keep it working at all meant using up water which might be needed if a water hole was not found by nightfall. Luckily for the travellers, however, this proved to be one of the best watered parts of Northern Australia.

R

This sort of progress meant the engine running on bottom gear all the time, with a correspondingly heavy consumption of gasoline, and Michael Terry knew that his small stock must last a little longer before more would be available.

That morning they passed through a corner of Victoria River Station, the largest cattle ranch in Australia, where they got on to a regular horse-team track and made for Wave Hill Station, sixty-four miles up the river.

To travel at twenty miles an hour after the sort of progress they had been making was luxury indeed, and Wave Hill was reached the next day after a pleasant run. Here Michael Terry delivered a letter which he had brought from Anthony's Lagoon, on the other side of the unknown Murranji country, the first letter ever to be carried from east to west across Australia by motor-car mail.

At Wave Hill Terry was able to secure a further supply of gasoline, thus again avoiding the delay of sending two hundred miles up to the coast for a supply. It was all the gasoline the station had, but upon hearing the expedition was trying to ride across Australia, the overseer parted with it generously in order that they should not be delayed. The car was examined before starting out again, and found to be in good order. The Murranji country had been crossed without maps or roads in sixteen days for the two hundred and seventy odd miles. What that meant may be realised from the fact that eighty of those miles took twelve days to complete.

The distance to the next cattle station was one hundred and thirty miles, and after securing directions from the hands at Victoria River it should have been easy going.

But shortly after starting off again, Michael Terry

sighted his first bush fire, and knew that he was face to face with the greatest peril of all.

The fire was some distance away, but bush fires travel rapidly, and change their direction with every shifting of the wind. There was, therefore, very little sleep that night.

Shortly after starting out next morning thick black smoke clouds gathered right ahead. As they approached nearer, flames were seen mounting fifteen feet above the ground. And the fire stretched from side to side as far as the eye could see.

There was no chance of driving round it. One could only turn and bolt or ride through it.

To turn and retreat until bare country or water was reached meant wasting valuable petrol. And they had none to spare. So they decided on the desperate course of attempting to ride through it.

With wet rags over their mouths, they drove for the fire as hard as the car would go. The ground was bumpy and it meant hanging on for dear life, while the gasoline which must have been spilling out of the carburettor added to the risk of the car catching fire.

Fortunately they found a gap on stony ground amid the grass and across this the car charged. The scorching breath of the fire licked their faces, the smoke made their eyes smart. It was an agonising moment. For what seemed like hours they were enveloped in flame-laden smoke. In reality it was but a moment or two before they reached ground already burnt clear—and therefore safe.

It had been a near thing. By great good fortune they had escaped with nothing worse than a slight damage to their provisions—sugar was mixed up with tea and their flour sprinkled over everything during that dash for life!

That afternoon the travellers reached Invernay Station safely.

The season was now getting on. The weather was very cold at night, and the rains were nearly due. To be caught in open country by the wet would mean a delay of perhaps weeks. Therefore in spite of a serious doubt whether the remaining gasoline would last more than a hundred miles, the adventurers set out again for the next station, which was one hundred and twenty-four miles away.

Michael Terry's intention was to run the car as long as a single drop of gasoline remained, and then walk the rest of the distance to the homestead in the hope that fresh supplies could be obtained there with which to complete the journey.

From the white men at Invernay Station he secured rough plans of his route and once more set out.

Fifty-six miles out they stopped at a water hole and re-filled their tank, noticing as they did so that the water was becoming blackish and unpleasant to drink. This was a sign that they were nearing the western boundary of the Northern Territory. Sure enough, that afternoon they crossed the boundary into Western Australia.

That night the gasoline gave out, and they turned in with the unpleasant knowledge that they were still many miles from their destination and would have to set out on foot the next morning.

At daybreak they set out. Only the lightest gear was carried. No blankets—just a small quantity of bread, meat, tea, sugar, and quart pots—enough for a light meal at mid-day. A revolver and brandy and a gallon oil-can which had been thoroughly boiled out and filled with fresh water completed their load. Thus they set out due south, expecting to make the homestead before nightfall.

It turned out to be a hot day and the walking was tiring. But they pressed on. Both knew Australia too well to feel quite happy about their plight until they saw the haven they sought looming up over the skyline.

At midday the broken country gave way to scrub. On the edge of this they sat down for a midday meal. It was then that they made the tragic discovery that their fresh water had become contaminated by oil. Somewhere in a corner of the tin oil must have been left and it had made the water unfit for drinking.

They tried straining it through a shirt several times. Then they boiled it in one pot and poured it into another, leaving the oily scum behind. But it still held that horrible taint of burnt oil.

There was nothing to do but to go without the water their parched dusty throats craved and once more, considerably discouraged and tired, they set out. But night came without any sign of either fresh water or the homestead. After a meal of the remainder of the food and a half quart of oily tea, they tried to sleep. It was bitterly cold out there in open country with no blankets and only a cotton shirt and trousers for covering, and sound sleep was impossible. At the first sign of dawn they were up again and pressing on.

All that morning the two stumbled along the track. By now they should have reached the homestead. Something was wrong with their instructions. Or else their memory had played tricks. Whatever the cause, by the time another night found them still in the trackless scrub, they both realised that they were now too weak to walk back to the spot where they had left the car, even if they could have found it, and that they stood an excellent chance of perishing out there in the waterless bush.

In the afternoon everything possible was discarded in a last endeavour to struggle on until water was found. Even private papers were torn up. It was an effort now to rise, a greater effort to walk. Every hundred yards meant taking a long rest to gather strength for the next.

And then, when weakness was gathering its final hold upon them, they found water. Only a tiny spring—no larger than a domestic house pail, but enough to save their lives. Disregarding all instructions about drinking after a long spell of thirst, they gulped it down in great draughts, like cattle. They were saved for the moment—but the desert still surrounded them. They were still without food. Still lost!

The next night spent in the open was worse than the last. Hunger, weakness and cold made sleep impossible. Every hour was a long-drawn-out torment.

The next day was the same—a weary struggle through the scrub with always more pitiless bush before them. And with the coming of the evening, realising that both would not win through to safety, Michael Terry insisted on his companion taking the morsel of food left and trying to find the homestead alone.

Michael Terry spent a solitary night by the tiny spring. He was now so weak that it was an effort to crawl a yard or two to gather wood with which to make a fire. The cold numbed his bones and prevented even the sleep of exhaustion.

He crawled to a tree and lay there, propped up against it, waiting for the end and wondering whether his companion, who had been so staunch all through, would find safety.

There we must leave him until the afternoon of the fifth day after leaving the car, when a search party from the

MICHAEL TERRY   252
Photographed at the end of his adventurous journey.

homestead found him in a state of collapse. It was a near thing, but food, warmth and a feeling of security pulled him through and made this story possible.

Yockney, his companion, had managed to reach the fence of the homestead before he collapsed. There he was found by natives, who ran to the homestead to summon help. Regaining consciousness, he had told them of his mate out in the bush and with all speed horses were mustered, a trap loaded, and the rescuers were away in the nick of time.

Another night was spent under the stars, but with warm blankets, food, and the comfortable knowledge that the worst was over. And a day or two later, gasoline being available, Michael Terry borrowed pack horses and black boys and went out to find the car and bring it in.

The last lap of the trackless country had been completed. But how close they had come to failure. By the skin of their teeth they had battled their way across eight hundred miles of trackless country. Now the road through Western Australia to Broome lay open before them. They had fought the wilds and won.

Of the rest of that journey there is no need to write. Once clear of the worst, better speeds were possible. They had still to pass the most isolated township in Australia. This is Halls Creek, with a population of four white women, eight men, and a post-office.

Here more gasoline was obtained and arrangements made for a supply to be sent back to Soakage Creek to replace the supply borrowed there.

And so back to civilisation.

It was at 3.30 on the afternoon of October 4, 1923, that two very bronzed, travel-scarred men drove a dilapidated Ford car up to the Roebuck Hotel at Broome, Western

Australia. The hotel looked out on to the sea. From the seafront people came to look at these two strange travellers and find out where they had come from. Soon the news spread that the arrival of that battered car meant that a new chapter had been written in the history of Australian exploration—the empty North of Australia had been crossed by car.

That night Michael Terry and Richard Yockney slept in soft beds for the first time for nearly eighteen months. And they found them so uncomfortable that they rolled themselves in blankets and slept on the bare verandah boards!

But they slept the sleep of the satisfied. For they had the comfortable feeling of "something attempted something done." They had reached the "unknown destination" prophesied by the joker at Winton on the other side of Australia.

Since 1923 Michael Terry has organised and led six further expeditions into the Northern Territories, carrying out valuable survey work and adding to our knowledge of the mineral and pastoral resources of that region. The last of these expeditions left Horseshoe Bend in July, 1930, and penetrated to the Tomkinson Ranges on the West Australian border. There Terry and his companions investigated the stock-raising possibilities of the country south of Lake Amadeus, securing information which may result in new pastures being settled in the near future, before this latest expedition returned to civilisation early in 1931.

CHAPTER XVIII

THE distance from Cape Town to Cairo is seven thousand miles, or about as far as from London to San Francisco. But that is as the crow or, shall we say, as Sir Alan Cobham flies. When Major Court Treatt and his party recently travelled by motor car from one end of the African continent to the other, the distance they were forced to drive was thirteen thousand miles, or as far as from London to New Zealand.

So long as you have any sort of road to drive upon distance does not matter much to a good motor car; but there is no road from the Cape to Cairo. True there are roads of some sort as far as Rhodesia, but after that the only roads are bush tracks. A bush track is a native road, a footpath winding endlessly through forests and swamps and over bare hills. It has never occurred to the black man to metal it, so in dry weather it is a twisty line of bare sun-baked clay and in wet a sort of human fly paper. Most of us would think twice about trying to drive our pet two-seater across a ploughed field. Imagine, then, driving two large, heavy cars over thousands of miles of ploughed fields covered with trees and interspersed with swamps, mountains, and deserts, to say nothing of scores of large and deep rivers which had somehow to be crossed.

That is what Major Court Treatt and the hardy adventurers who accompanied him succeeded in doing, and the marvel is not that they took sixteen months over it, but that they ever came through at all. The party consisted of Major and Mrs. Court Treatt, Mr. F. C. Law, journalist, Mr. T. A. Glover, photographer and cinematograph expert, and Mr. Errol Hinds, Mrs. Court Treatt's brother. Last, but not least was Julius, a Swahili, son of a chief of that tribe, a black man who speaks, or can make himself understood, in no fewer than thirty-two different dialects. Julius is also a good mechanic, a first-class cook, and full of all sorts of strange knowledge of the African peoples and African bush. There will be more to tell of Julius later on.

When you make up your mind to drive across Africa you do not just buy a car and start. You have first to do a whole lot of thinking and planning. For one thing there are no gas-filling stations on the way, and every gallon of gasoline and oil, to say nothing of food and spare parts needed in this expedition, had to be arranged for beforehand and dumped in various spots along the route. These supplies were carried to the various spots by porters, ox-wagons, camels, or donkeys, and it speaks well for the organisation that never once did the system of dumps break down.

The cars used were two Crossleys. There was nothing special about the chassis or engines, but the bodies were unusual. Each was fitted with a removable aluminum top and these two tops, when taken off and bolted together, made a large flat-bottomed punt which could carry a car and six men. This was the device for crossing rivers. It seemed a splendid idea, but in point of fact it did not work. Those beautiful tops proved too heavy to drag through the mud of the muddiest rainy season on record and they, like a lot of other expensive fitments, were soon scrapped, and with all sorts of other belongings were jettisoned in the swampy forests of northern Rhodesia. "Our route from Cape Town," says Major Court Treatt, "might almost be traced by the things we were forced to discard. By the time we reached Central Africa we were sleeping on the ground and had no clothes save those we stood in. It is astonishing with what little gear five people can manage."

The expedition set out from Cape Town on September 24, 1924. It was lovely spring weather and the veldt was full of wild flowers. At first it was all plain sailing, or rather driving. They crossed the Limpopo River at a place called Messina, finding the river bed dry sand—so deep and dry that donkeys had to be used to help the cars across. They spent three days camped under the great ruins of that ancient and mysterious city Zimbabwe, where perhaps King Solomon obtained his treasures of gold, and reached Buluwayo without trouble. Then it began to rain and it rained for six months. The rainfall of that winter in Rhodesia was the greatest ever known, the fall being eighty inches against the usual forty. Leaving Buluwayo on Christmas Day the cars did forty miles, then stuck in the mud. The party camped that night and ate their Christmas dinner in a tent where the mud of the floor was ankle deep.

After that it rained every day; some days it rained all day, others only part of the day, but there was no day without rain. And the mud grew deeper and deeper. Over and over again the cars stuck in the mud. When this happened every one jumped out, took shovels and picks, and dug. Sometimes digging was no good, and they had to cut brushwood or grass to make some sort of track for the tires to grip on. It was dreadful work and often the average for a day's journey was not a mile an hour. They came to the

Gwaai River to find it in full flood, and crossed it by driving along the top of a dam. There were only two or three inches to spare on either side of the wheels, and it seemed very likely that the cars would roll over into the flood. But they got across in safety, the first, as they found out later, to drive cars across this dam. They tried to follow the river northward toward Victoria Falls, but the floods defeated them and they had to strike off on to higher ground. Here was no road at all or any sign of road, and it rained as hard as ever. Ten miles a day was the average journey; the record was fifteen. Another flooded river barred their way, one that was impossible to cross.

Here they stuck for more than three weeks and nearly starved. At night they could hear the distant whistle of the big mail trains carrying passengers from Buluwayo to the Falls and the thought of the tourists sitting down in the warm, well-lighted dining cars to a five course dinner nearly drove them frantic. But nothing could be done, for rivers were up behind them as well as in front, so that going back was as impossible as going forward.

At last the river in front fell enough to let them cross, and ploughing through mud at the rate of two miles an hour they reached the Victoria Falls and crossed the Zambesi by the railway bridge. The Victoria Falls are fine at any time, but in rains like these the volume of water was stupendous and the sight magnificent beyond words.

The cars now followed the railway as far as Broken Hill, the great mining centre in Central Northern Rhodesia; here at last they struck a real road and for the first time since leaving the Transvaal were able to drive straight ahead, doing a hundred or even a hundred and fifty miles in the day. It was a strange experience to drive along a road where there were no houses and no people. In two weeks the

ONE OF THE CARS ABOUT TO BE HAULED THROUGH A RIVER

MRS COURT TREATT WITH THE MAJOR ON HER LEFT AND HER BROTHER ERROL
ON HER RIGHT

party saw only one white man, an ivory hunter who had made his camp close by the road.

At last they ran out of the everlasting rain, but the dry water courses which they now met with proved almost as difficult to cross as the flooded rivers. The first they reached had a bridge across it made of poles covered with earth. It looked strong enough, but when they drove a car across it the whole thing went to smash and it took the rest of the day to rebuild the bridge so that the second car might cross. Another bridge laid on great tree trunks seemed strong enough to bear the weight of a train, but the first car had hardly started across when down went everything with a fearful crash. The great logs had been eaten out by white ants, which are the curse of this part of the country, and were simply hollow. The fallen car lay in the bottom of the ravine with the front wheels in the air, one back wheel jammed against a huge boulder and the full weight of the car resting on the back axle. "We may just as well write her off the strength," said one of the party, but Major Court Treatt looked her over and said she could be salvaged. Luckily there was a native village at hand, and collecting the whole population, they rigged block and tackle and by main force hauled the car out. The axle was broken, the steering rod bent, but nothing else appeared to be seriously wrong. They replaced the broken axle with a spare, put the steering rod between two trees and bent it back into line, and the next morning drove off quite happily.

The party were now in lion country and one night the Major had a curious experience. Camp had been made beside a dry river and after supper he was strolling down the river bed when he saw the heads of two lions looking over the far bank. The heads disappeared and he went on very quietly, and creeping up the far bank peeped over.

In the low scrub beyond five young lions were playing by starlight, scampering round and round like so many kittens, enjoying themselves immensely. Another night, when travelling late, the Major saw something moving in the glare of the headlights, took a snap shot and found that he had bagged a fine leopard.

Elephants were seen and since one of the chief objects of the expedition was to get photographs of the wild animals of Africa, camp was pitched and a party went out carrying the cinematograph camera. They followed a herd of elephants for three days, but the tracking was difficult and without Julius' help they would never have found the animals. Julius had the oddest methods of finding his way in the bush. He depended largely on a bird called the ngulugulu which is a black hornbill. He would make a call imitating the cry of this bird to perfection, then if the answer came, all was right and he would push on. But if there was no reply, then they were on the wrong track and had to go back and start afresh. It seems a strange method of pathfinding, and at first the white men of the party were inclined to laugh at the performances of their native guide. But since Julius invariably proved to be in the right, they came at last to believe in his curious methods of divination.

Once, when making films in waterless bush, the party got completely lost and could not find their way back to camp. Though they had with them local natives who professed to know the country, these were quite at a loss. Night came on and they were forced to camp without water. It was high country and the night was bitterly cold. Next morning Julius said that he would watch the vultures and by them find the way back. He went out alone and when he came back pointed out a certain direction that was to be followed, and within four hours led the party safely back to their camp.

The vulture is held in great esteem among the natives as a pathfinder. The natives' story is that the vulture goes to sleep and dreams of meat. If when he wakes up he finds he has changed his position on his perch, then he knows he is right, and flies straight off in that direction. The dried head of one of these vultures is greatly prized by the natives of Central Africa, and they will pay a good price for it. When a man is lost in the bush he ties the vulture's head on his own forehead, and when he wakes finds himself facing in the direction in which he should go. That, at least, is his belief.

The one thing that Julius would not put up with was any change of mind on the part of his employers. On one occasion when after a herd of buffalo, the photographer, unable to find them, declared that he would give up. But next morning he changed his mind and said that he would try again. Julius was horrified. "You will be killed if you do," he assured Mr. Glover, and the latter, realizing that Julius was bitterly in earnest and remembering how often he had proved himself right, decided to stay in camp.

On one occasion camp was pitched near a river in what seemed to be a cleared space in the forest. It was not until late in the evening the party discovered that this was the drinking place of a herd of elephants. The elephants were distinctly annoyed at finding human intruders on their ground and showed their annoyance by trying to walk over the tents. The travellers were forced to get out and build a thorn hedge, but the elephants showed a lordly disregard for such a trifle and three times that night came stamping and crashing up to the camp. At last Major Court Treatt had to get a can of gasoline, pour it on the grass and set fire to it. It was the only way in which to get the great beasts off their usual stamping ground.

Speaking of scaring off beasts by fire, at one camp the travellers made the unpleasant discovery that a big old ant heap near the camp was the home of a huge black mamba. The mamba is a very big snake which is not only extremely poisonous, but also has a shocking temper. It will attack any intruder and it can travel almost as fast as a galloping horse. The question of how to get rid of this dangerous neighbour was solved by Julius, who set fire to the brush on the ant heap, and burnt the brute out.

The most dangerous of African wild animals is not the lion or the elephant or even the huge half-blind, evil-tempered rhinoceros. It is the wood buffalo. Near one camp the party found a herd of buffalo which they particularly wanted to photograph. But these were bad buffalo. The natives of the nearest village told them that they had charged and killed an old woman who was passing them, carrying a calabash. However, the party made a "hide" from which to film the herd, but the buffalo caught their scent and came up snuffling, bellowing, stamping, so the photographic party, thinking discretion the better part of valour, climbed a tree. Major Court Treatt left an old hat in the hide and the buffalo, when they reached this and smelt it, suddenly panicked and went off at a thundering gallop. They galloped straight in the direction of the camp and the Major, watching from his tree, which was a high one, suddenly saw a tree near the camp dotted with little black figures which climbed frantically into the branches. Luckily no damage was done, except to Mr. Glover's feelings. He was very sad at missing his chance of a very fine set of photographs.

Of course the party lived largely on what they could kill and now and then when they reached a river they varied their diet of meat by catching fish. The most sporting of African fish is the Kass or tiger fish. He is a fierce fighter and has such tremendous teeth that he will bite through any ordinary line. The only way in which to hold him is to use a snood of piano wire. Another fine fish is the Nile perch, a monster which grows to over a hundred pounds in weight. You have to be careful when fishing in African waters for crocodiles abound and most of them are man-eaters. When the expedition had with great difficulty crossed a river an old native,who had been watching them with much interest, burst out laughing. When asked what was amusing him he said that he had tried to drive six cattle across the ford a week earlier and every one of them had been taken by crocodiles.

After leaving Northern Rhodesia the party entered Tanganyika Territory where, in place of rivers, they found mountains. Some of the tracks ran up hills that were almost precipices and the only way to get the cars up was to round up all the natives in the nearest village, get them on the ropes and haul the vehicles up by sheer man power. Sometimes it took a whole day to get the two cars up one hill. But there were fairly good roads most of the way through the Territory. They crossed the equator by way of the Eldama Ravine in the Barringo country. This is a great tableland no less than ten thousand feet above sea level, and in spite of the latitude the temperature was quite cool, being about the same as that of a fine spring day.

When they got into Uganda they found the best road they had driven over since leaving Cape Town, and for a time got on famously, but farther north they came to the border of the Soudan Territory and struck into country where the road was a mere track. What was worse, now that they had crossed the equator, they were running into the tail end of the northern rainy season, with the result

s

that they were once more in a country of flooded rivers. True, there were bridges over most of these rivers, but they were built of bamboo and were hardly suited for heavy cars. It was a chancy business, crossing them, for they bounced like spring mattresses. At a place called Mongalla they came to a swamp which they were told would take three weeks to cross. It was out of the question to drive the cars through, so they got a large force of natives and hauled them through. They did this in one day, starting at dawn and ending at midnight. These swamps were a great trial, not only because of their natural difficulties but because of the mosquitoes and other poisonous insects which rose in clouds like smoke and bit savagely.

They entered the Dinka country, the Bahr El Arab, which is populated by one of the finest races on earth—at least from a physical point of view. Most of the men are over six feet high, some being six feet four or even more. Many are able to make a standing jump of five feet, and in a high-jumping competition they would defeat any team of Western athletes. The party was still three thousand miles from Cairo and had before them two hundred miles of the worst country in all Africa. They had expected to find this the worst part of their journey and so it undoubtedly was. It was heavy forest, deep swamp cut up with large rivers over which there were no bridges and very few fords. The natives had rarely seen any white folk, and had never seen a white woman. They were enormously interested in the motor cars, the head lights, and the gramophone, but the greatest attraction of all was Mrs. Court Treatt. Mrs. Court Treatt wore man's dress and this at first puzzled the Dinkas, but the women soon penetrated the disguise and came in numbers to see her. One chief begged the party to camp for a few days so that he might call in all his people to see the white lady. The request, however, had to be refused and the party pushed on. Three hundred Dinkas were enlisted to help and with their aid a way was cut through the forest at the rate of eight miles a day. The swamps were very bad and often it was necessary to make every yard of the road before the cars could be moved. This was done by cutting quantities of brushwood and reeds and laying them down in front of the wheels.

Worst of all was the task of crossing the rivers, some of which were quite wide and sixteen or eighteen feet deep. There were, of course, no boats to carry the cars; there were no trees large enough to build rafts, and there were no fords. The only way in which to get the cars across was to take down the carburettors and magnetos, to empty the tanks and remove all kit, then to attach ropes and haul them across the bed of the river on their own wheels. This meant taking chances, of course, for often the current was so strong that there was great risk of the cars being upset. Once one of the cars stuck in the mud at the bottom of a river and remained there for four hours before it could be extricated. It was quite out of sight below the muddy surface of the stream. Yet when at last it was hauled out and its essential parts put back into place, it started up almost at the first turn of the handle, and ran as well as ever, a fact which speaks volumes for good workmanship. No fewer than five big rivers were crossed in this way, but the work was killingly hard and the Dinkas soon got tired of it. They began to desert and presently all were gone, leaving the travellers to flounder about for another two weeks before they got clear of the swamps. The country beyond the swamps was full of elephants and equally full of holes caused by their immense footprints. The springs of the cars were severely tried in ten days' bumping among these elephant holes.

At last this awful stretch was passed and the tired adventurers reached Arab country where they found roads once more, and so pushed on more rapidly toward Khartoum, the capital of the Soudan.

Once in this civilised country and within sight of the Nile, it might be supposed that their troubles were over, but this was not the case for there was still the Nubian desert to cross. You cannot drive along the Nile because big mountains come right down to the river and there is no road. A way had to be found behind the mountains, and here there is sheer desert without any road. At Halfa the Governor found the party a guide, an elderly Arab with delightful manners, but when about eighty miles out in the desert the old fellow paralysed them all by calmly announcing that he was lost. When the Major pointed to the north as being the way to Cairo, the guide declared he was wrong and pointed out a line which the others felt sure would take them right down into Abyssinia. They drove on for two days, hemmed in on every side by mountains. Food was running short and there was no water. For six long and very unpleasant days they hunted for a way out, and at last found camel tracks, and knew that they were near the Nile. A search party sent out by the Governor of Halfa overtook them, but by this time Julius had discovered a way to the river and they had the pleasure of giving the leader of the search party a lift back in one of the cars.

After that the rest of the journey was plain sailing and at last, on January 24, 1926, they reached the great city of Cairo, where they met with a welcome that made up for some of their hardships. The cars were taken back with the party to England and when unloaded at Dover were found fit to travel at fifty miles an hour. Pretty good for engines which had been through sixteen months of travelling over country which no car had ever before managed to cross!

CHAPTER XIX

THE EXPLOIT OF CAPTAIN LINDBERGH

T HE greatest individual feat in all history " is what the famous Polar flyer Commander Byrd called Charles Lindbergh's lone flight across the Atlantic from New York to Paris, and he is right. As a mere feat of endurance, one that proves how fit a man can be, it is amazing.

The distance flown was thirty-six hundred miles and the time taken thirty-three and one-half hours. Merely to keep awake for so long a period would try most of us severely, but an airman has much more to do than merely to keep awake. He has to be continually watching his compass, altimeter, and other instruments, besides being in constant control of his steering. His trained ear must be always alive to the slightest change in the sound of his thundering engine, and all his senses must be constantly alert. The strain is heavy even when all conditions are favourable; it is terrific when flying through fog and rain and sleet, as was the case for fully a thousand miles of Lindbergh's long journey. In mind, brain, and body a man must be well-nigh perfect before he can hope to succeed in such a tremendous trial.

Some foolish people have called Charles Lindbergh "the Flying Fool." How unjust it is to use such a phrase will be realised when we say that the young pilot was partly responsible for the designing of his plane, which he calls "The Spirit of St. Louis." "They call me *lucky,*" says

Lindbergh, "but luck is not enough. As a matter of fact, I had what I regarded as the best existing plane for the purpose of my flight, and I was equipped with what were, in the circumstances, the best possible instruments for making the flight. I hope I made good use of what I had."

Lindbergh's machine was a Ryan monoplane with a comparatively small engine, a 220-horse power, nine-cylindered Wright "Whirlwind." The weight of the plane, with its full load of petrol and oil, was two and a half tons. The machine was built by the Ryan Company at their works at San Diego, California. The story is that one day Lindbergh telegraphed, asking the firm whether they could build a plane capable of crossing the Atlantic, and they answered "Yes."

A few hours later came a second telegram from Lindbergh telling them to get on with it. The company's chief engineer immediately went to work and devoted all his time to drawing the plans; the workmen were equally enthusiastic, and sixty days later, after a few trial flights, Lindbergh said, "Well, good-bye, boys, I'm going to New York," and off he went in the new plane. The machine itself cost only about seven thousand dollars, but the instruments installed are said to have been worth seven thousand more. No one else but Lindbergh himself flew the machine before his great flight, and it is interesting to note that he crossed the American Continent without the slightest trouble in about twenty-two and one-half hours actual flying.

Thursday, the day before his flight, Charles Lindbergh spent sight-seeing in New York. In the evening he went to a theatre, and did not get to bed till midnight. At a quarter past two he woke up and got out of bed to look at the weather. "It looks good," he said, "I guess I'll go." Next morning the report was that the weather was likely to be good all the way across, so he made up his mind to start as soon as possible. His tanks were filled with four hundred and fifty gallons of petrol and twenty of oil, but apart from that his preparations were of the simplest. He had a packet of sandwiches, a couple of bottles of water, a tiny rubber raft and—in his pocket, for luck—the wishbone of a turkey. That was all. He did not even take a change of clothes or a suit of pyjamas.

And so this fair-haired youngster of twenty-five started upon as desperate an enterprise as man has ever dared to undertake. His original intention had been to take with him his black cat which had ridden with him in the cockpit for many a hundred miles, but at the last moment he decided to leave his mascot behind. "A bit too tough for kitty," he said. He laughed as he climbed into the cockpit. "I am entering my death chamber," he remarked. "If I arrive in Paris, it will be just like receiving a pardon from the Governor."

The ground was rather soft and "The Spirit of St. Louis" had difficulty in arising with her big load, but once aloft, she was followed for some distance by five press aeroplanes as she shot northward along the coast. It was ten minutes before one on the afternoon of Friday, May 20, 1927, when Lindbergh left New York and he was soon out over salt water. The distance from Cape Cod, where Lindbergh left the land, over the sea to Nova Scotia is three hundred miles, and this was the pleasantest part of the flight. The motor acted perfectly and the weather was fine and clear. Lindbergh went a little north of his shortest route in order to sight St. John's, Newfoundland, and make quite certain of his position. He flew low so that people could see him, and send word where he was at that hour.

It was ten minutes before nine on Friday night that

he left St. John's and turned eastward over the ocean. The weather had changed and he found himself driving through the cold grey fog that so often covers the Grand Banks of Newfoundland, and soon this changed to an even colder drizzle of rain. The rain became heavier, and the flier rose and fell alternately, in the hope of finding better weather. He went as high as ten thousand feet and once he came down so low that he was skimming barely a hundred feet above the grey Atlantic combers. It was no use, for high and low alike the chill rain drove upon him.

There was worse to come, for the rain turned to sleet. Now sleet or snow are among the worst dangers that can threaten an aeroplane, for the frozen stuff clings to the planes and other parts of the machine, increasing its weight and decreasing its speed. There are many cases on record of planes being driven down by sheer weight of ice so formed.

The young pilot confesses that at one time conditions were so bad that he actually had it in his mind to turn back. But he said to himself, "Things are probably just as bad behind as in front. I may as well stick it and keep on." So he kept on. Luckily the night was short and with dawn the sleet had gone, but it still rained and there was a nasty, gusty wind. About seven in the morning the plane was sighted by a Canadian Pacific liner more than five hundred miles east of Newfoundland. There was a lot of fog and Lindbergh says that he hardly ever caught sight of the sea and that he saw no ships during the most critical hours of his journey. He had to depend entirely upon his compass for direction.

At midday on Saturday he had his first sight of a ship, the steamship *Hilversun*. It was then still raining. "I was horribly bored," says Lindbergh, "but my engine gave me no sort of trouble, and I had no difficulty with any of the rest of my gear." He did not suffer personally from the weather for his cockpit was entirely enclosed. But this had the disadvantage that he could not look out directly ahead except through a sort of periscopic arrangement. His only uninterrupted view was through windows right and left. He carried no lights but the dials of his various instruments were luminous. His steering was done entirely by one small compass and he had his chronometer just behind him. He wore flying breeches, a moleskin waistcoat under his coat, and an overcoat, so he kept quite warm. His bag of provisions was on one side of him, his water bottles on the other; he had no wireless apparatus and no parachute.

So he drove on, hour after hour. After midday on Saturday the weather improved and Lindbergh flew lower. A little before five in the afternoon he sighted the Irish coast, part of County Kerry, and shortly afterward was seen passing Baltimore, County Cork. At ten to six the machine was observed leaving the Irish coast at Goleen for Cornwall. An hour and a half later many people saw the slim grey plane passing over Cornwall, and at seven forty-nine it was watched as it crossed the sky swiftly, a mile or two south of Plymouth breakwater, heading away across the Channel toward the French coast.

All the way across the ocean Lindbergh had kept his engine throttled down to only three-quarters of its full power, but at this late stage of his journey he seems to have been travelling at a very high rate of speed, for only forty minutes after leaving Plymouth he was sighted over Cherbourg. Indeed during the last part of his journey, he was flashing through the air at very nearly one hundred and sixty miles an hour. Lindbergh first saw the lights of Le Bourget, the great Parisian aerodrome, when he was still thirty miles away, and thanks to the lights and his very excellent maps he had no difficulty in finding his way across the country. When he sighted the Eiffel Tower, he knew he was right. "My heart," he says, "gave just one bound."

At a quarter past ten on that historic Saturday night two thousand people, admitted by ticket to the flying field, heard the hum of an aeroplane flying low. Rockets were fired to give the aviator his direction, and the great beacon lights blazed upward. The plane became visible, circling overhead, and a shout came from the people within the aerodrome, echoed by a perfect thunder of sound from the enormous crowds collected outside the barriers. The vague silvergrey outline became clearer; it came gliding downward, and the plane made a perfect landing on the far side of the aerodrome opposite the sheds. As "The Spirit of St. Louis" taxied smoothly across the ground, a tremendous roar rose from the multitude outside, and instantly they surged forward. There was a series of crackling crashes as the fences gave way and thousands of men and women raced across the field, uttering wild cries. People were flung to the ground and trampled upon; a number were hurt, two very severely. The police did their best but what can two hundred police do against a host numbering more than ten thousand?

Lindbergh stopped his machine and stood up. He seemed by far the calmest and most collected of any one present. "I have made it," he said. "Are there any mechanics about?" Then the crowd reached the plane. *"Portez le! Portez le!"* they thundered. "Shoulder him!" The first to reach the spot was an American, Mr. Harold Wheeler, and to him Lindbergh handed his helmet and scarf. The crowd thought he was Lindbergh, seized him and swung him shoulder high. They were too crazy with excitement to notice that Mr. Wheeler was dressed in mufti and showed no signs of fatigue.

The police formed a ring and struggled desperately to keep the crowd back. Lindbergh himself was lifted out by French airmen and swiftly smuggled away while the mob ran shouting after poor Mr. Wheeler, who had his collar wrenched off and his clothes almost torn to pieces before he could finally make his too enthusiastic bearers understand that he was not Lindbergh.

Others of the people crowded round the plane itself. One might have supposed that the wonderful machine would have been sacred in their eyes, but that was not so. Crazy curio collectors tore great pieces of the covering from the wings and would have stripped the entire plane, but for the combined efforts of police and mechanics who finally wheeled it away and locked it safely in a hangar.

Lindbergh himself was spirited away to the Air Company's offices, where he was given hot coffee and toast. He did not look nearly so tired as might have been supposed. True, he was rather pale and his eyes were bloodshot, yet he vowed he was not very sleepy, and told his new friends that he had not needed to take the caffeine tablets which he had brought with him in case he was overwhelmed with drowsiness. All the same his hands were so stiff he could hardly hold his cup and his face and lips were also curiously numb.

The United States Ambassador, Mr. Myron Herrick, came in and greeted the hero of the great flight and asked him to spend the night at the Embassy, and while the crowd was still shouting for him, Lindbergh was smuggled into the Ambassador's car and driven away. The road to Paris was absolutely blocked with cars and the journey was a terribly slow one, but Lindbergh slept all the way. It was nearly three in the morning before the flying man, arrayed in a suit of Mr. Herrick's own pyjamas, was at last at liberty to have his bath and get to bed. Then he slept soundly for twelve hours and rose as fit as possible ready to go and look after his beloved plane.

Within six minutes of Lindbergh's alighting at Le Bourget, practically every town in his own country was aware of the successful conclusion of his amazing flight, and the excitement was extraordinary. In New York, theatre crowds danced and sang along Broadway and the rivers echoed with the roar of steamer whistles and sirens. Flags fluttered from thousands of windows and every one was delighted.

Joy was particularly great in Little Falls, Minnesota, the small town where Lindbergh was brought up. There were parades, bonfires, bell-ringing, and fireworks. An old Ford car, which the boy aviator had driven, was dragged out and headed the procession. Detroit, where Charles' mother lived and taught chemistry in the High School, also held high fête in his honour.

Mrs. Lindbergh is a Spartan mother, who, while her boy was risking his life above the Atlantic surges, had calmly continued her work with her classes and had refused to say a word to any of the newspaper reporters. "It is far better," she said, "to have my mind occupied than to be thinking all the time of Charles." But when the news did come of his great success, even she broke down in tears of happiness.

A third place where great joy was shown was the city of St. Louis, where young Lindbergh held the rank of Captain in the State Militia. The people of St. Louis had backed him financially and otherwise in the flight and were naturally delighted at his brilliant success. But the thrill that stirred the entire nation had not been matched since the rejoicings which heralded Armistice Day nearly nine years before.

Lindbergh, of course, profited financially by his amazing achievement. His first reward was the prize of twenty-five thousand dollars offered by Mr. Raymond Orteig for the first flight between New York and Paris. He was also inundated with offers from film companies, theatrical managers, and others. He was decorated by the President of France, the King of Belgium, the King of England and by the President of his own country, while some of the most famous societies and the greatest airmen of the world paid him distinguished tribute.

His flight was not the first across the Atlantic. Indeed, that ocean had previously been crossed by airmen on no fewer than six occasions. The first was in May, 1919, when the United States Navy Seaplane N. C. 4 flew by stages from Newfoundland to the Azores, the Azores to Lisbon and Lisbon to Plymouth. In the same year the first non-stop flight was accomplished when on June 15 Captain J. Alcock, D.S.O., and Lieutenant Whitten Brown flew a Vicker's Vimy machine from the coast of Newfoundland to Clifden, on the west coast of Ireland. The distance covered was eighteen hundred miles, just about half that covered by Lindbergh. In 1922 two Portuguese airmen flew to Brazil by way of the Canary and Cape Verde Islands. But they had to make a forced landing on St. Paul's Island, five hundred miles from the Brazilian coast, and from there flew on in another machine.

In January 1926, a Spanish airman, Commandante Franco, flew from the Canary Islands to Brazil, and a similar journey was made by the Marchese de Pinedo in February, 1927. About a month later the Portuguese airman, Sarmento Beires, flew from Portuguese West Africa to the island of Fernando Noronha, a trip of fourteen hundred and fifty miles, and thence across to the mainland of South America.

But Captain Lindbergh's exploit, perhaps because of his youth and his own charming personality, and also because it followed so closely the tragic loss of the French airmen Nungesser and Coli, stirred the imaginations and emotions of the people of Europe and the United States as nothing since the Armistice has done, and brought them into closer friendship.